D1194129

*Creating a Nation of Joiners*

## HARVARD HISTORICAL STUDIES   163

Published under the auspices
of the Department of History
from the income of the
Paul Revere Frothingham Bequest
Robert Louis Stroock Fund
Henry Warren Torrey Fund

# Creating a Nation of Joiners

DEMOCRACY AND CIVIL SOCIETY
IN EARLY NATIONAL MASSACHUSETTS

JOHANN N. NEEM

HARVARD UNIVERSITY PRESS

*Cambridge, Massachusetts*
*London, England   2008*

*Library of Congress Cataloging-in-Publication Data*
Neem, Johann N.
   Creating a nation of joiners : democracy and civil society in early national
Massachusetts / Johann N. Neem.
       p. cm.
   Includes bibliographical references and index.
   ISBN 978-0-674-03079-4 (cloth : alk. paper)
   1. Civil society—Massachusetts—History.   2. Civil society—United
States—History.   3. Citizens' associations—Massachusetts—History.
4. Democracy—Massachusetts—History.   5. Massachusetts—Politics
and government—1775–1865.   I. Title.
   JK3189.N44 2008
   306.209744'09033—dc22                                          2008005243

*Dedicated to*
*Professor Theodore R. Sizer*
*&*
*Don Ernst*

# Contents

*Creating a Nation of Joiners*

# Introduction

WILLIAM LLOYD GARRISON was born in 1805 in Newburyport, Massachusetts, in a small frame house. His father was a skilled mariner, his mother a devoted Baptist. The Garrisons were part of Newburyport's middling ranks, certainly not among the rich merchants and their families who made up the town's elite. After his father abandoned the family, however, Garrison's mother had to struggle to give her children food and shelter. She took work as a domestic servant, low on the status and economic ladder. Garrison grew up poor, reduced as a boy to collecting scraps of food from more privileged families to feed his own. In 1812 his mother placed him in the home of a woodcutter and Baptist deacon in Lynn, where Garrison received a rudimentary education in religion. In 1815 Garrison became an apprentice to a shoemaker, but he had hardly been there when his family was compelled to move again, this time to Baltimore to work in a shoe factory. The factory soon collapsed, and the Garrison family looked elsewhere for work. In 1816 Garrison returned to Newburyport to attend grammar school, his only formal education. In October 1818 Garrison found an apprenticeship at the *Newburyport Herald,* and joined America's newspaper trade. The paper's editor guided Garrison's literary and political education, and Garrison became an adamant Federalist. Garrison later took over the *National Philanthropist,* a temperance journal. Committed to orthodox religion, Garrison embraced the moral reform movement.

In the 1820s, Garrison determined that there was no cause more worth fighting for than liberating America's enslaved African Americans. Despite his obscure beginnings and poor upbringing, Garrison would transform America as one of the leaders of the abolitionist crusade against slavery. He was convinced that slavery was so sinful that there was no moderate position: all Americans must support the immediate abolition of slavery throughout the Union. He publicized his cause through a new newspaper, the *Liberator*, established in 1831. With others, he founded the New England Anti-Slavery Society in 1832. Throughout America, like-minded citizens also formed new associations committed to the immediate abolition of slavery. Garrison's success and the institutional context in which he acted—voluntary associations—were something new. Had Garrison been born a generation earlier, he would have lacked the right and the skills to establish the voluntary associations that generated an influential social movement. By the time Garrison came of age, he and other, many unknown, Americans could participate in politics by organizing at the grass roots.[1]

AMERICANS ARE, in Arthur M. Schlesinger Sr.'s words, "a nation of joiners."[2] Americans form voluntary associations, including nonprofit corporations, to pursue myriad collective goals, both private and public. Americans' tendency to form associations astonished French traveler Alexis de Tocqueville when he visited the United States in the early 1830s. "Americans of all ages, all conditions, and all minds are constantly joining together in groups," he marveled in *Democracy in America*. In a democracy, Tocqueville believed, voluntary associations balance individual freedom with the necessity of working together. They encourage social solidarity by bringing citizens together without having to rely on the state. For these reasons Tocqueville concluded that "the science of association is the fundamental science" in a democracy.[3]

Too often, discussions of American civil society begin with Tocqueville, taking as gospel Tocqueville's claim that voluntary associations express the spirit of American democracy. Tocqueville helped naturalize associations to later generations of Americans. We tend to assume that our Founding Fathers must have felt the same way about voluntary associations as we do. But things appeared quite differently to Americans in 1776. By starting instead with the years immediately following the Revolution, this book tells a different story. It questions the assumption that America's voluntary tradition emerged naturally out of the democratic ideals of the American Revolution. Americans were uneasy about becoming a nation of joiners and accepted it only when other options had failed. Even as Tocqueville traveled across America, the legitimacy of the nation of joiners was being contested by Jacksonians, who condemned the corrupting influence of private organizations that interfered, or what we might today say mediated, between the people and the state. Other Americans, however, were reaching another conclusion, that civil society enhances democratic politics. This book helps us understand both Americans' resistance to and their accommodation of civil society.[4]

Tocqueville's fascination with American voluntarism remained in the background of American thought until the Cold War. In the wake of Nazi Germany and the growing threat of the Soviet Union, scholars turned their attention away from the state and toward civil society. They agreed with Tocqueville that voluntarism helps sustain freedom in a democracy. Associations, they argued, both act as a bulwark against expanding state authority and allow Americans to carry out their civic lives independent of the state. These assumptions guided social scientists who took a "society-centered" approach to American political culture. Robert Nisbet wrote in 1953 that "it is the continued existence of this array of intermediate powers in society, of this plurality of 'private sovereignties,' that constitutes, above anything else, the greatest single barrier to the conversion of democracy from its liberal form to its totalitarian form."[5] Gabriel Almond and Sidney Verba, in their famous study *The Civic Culture* (1965), invoked Tocqueville to argue that "if the citizen is a member of some voluntary organization, he is involved in the broader social world but is less dependent upon and less controlled by his political system."[6] Historians reached similar conclusions. Arthur M. Schlesinger, in his 1944 article from which this book takes its name, observed the "paradox" that individualistic Americans are "the world's greatest example of joiners." Like others of his era, Schlesinger believed that Americans' resistance to state power "created the necessity of voluntary associations to do things beyond the capacity of a single person." Similarly, Oscar and Mary Handlin argued that voluntarism is one of the vital "dimensions of American liberty" that insulate Americans from an overly powerful state.[7]

Far from being an alternative to state power, more recent studies claim, America's civil society depends on the state. Sociologists Theda Skocpol and Michael Schudson, stressing the need for "bringing the state back in," credit the structure of governmental institutions for encouraging and shaping civil society and the public sphere's development. Richard R. John looks to the federal postal service's role in creating a national democratic public sphere. In his examination of the state's role in regulating voluntary associations and nonprofit corporations, William J. Novak concludes that the state is constitutive of civil society. Keith Whittington reminds us of the importance of the rule of law in checking the excesses of civil society and protecting the civil rights of minorities.[8] The state's role in shaping civil society and the public sphere must now be taken seriously. Through its chartering power, the state determines the legal privileges available to corporations and voluntary associations, including the freedom of association and the ability to hold property and capital, to enter into courts, and to outlive its individual members. More important, a charter grants an association public legitimacy. The opposite is equally true. By denying an association a charter, the state refuses to recognize an association's legitimacy and denies it legal privileges available to other groups. Finally, the state determines the legal relationship between itself and civil society. In legislation and in court decisions, leaders decide how "autonomous" civil society should be from the state and when and how the state should interfere in civil society.

Yet even if the state aided civil society in myriad ways, it still would be wrong to conclude that America's post-Revolutionary state governments supported the development of an independent civil society. Political leaders were actively hostile to it. To understand their hostility we must take seriously Americans' ideas, try to understand their concerns. But even here we run into a problem. We believe, and historians have recently argued, that America's voluntary tradition grew out of the egalitarian ideas of the American Revolution as expressed by Thomas Jefferson in the Declaration of Independence.[9] If American ideas promoted the emergence of a civil society from the outset, how do we explain the state's resistance? It turns out that the Jeffersonian ideal of egalitarian democracy did not lead to a celebration of civil society. The Jeffersonian tradition was, and remains, hostile in many ways to a nation of joiners. Jefferson's home state was among the least conducive to the emergence of an independent civil society. Jefferson himself remained fearful of private associations and corporations until his death. In 1824, when the number of associations and nonprofit corporations in America was growing rapidly, Jefferson worried that they "may rivalise and jeapordize the march of regular government." Jefferson, like other Americans of his generation, believed that permitting the spread of voluntary associations and corporations would threaten civic equality by allowing a small minority, a cabal, to exercise disproportionate influence over public life. In time associations would "take the government out of its constitutional hands" by wresting power from the people and their elected leaders. This had happened once before, during the Revolution. To Jefferson, those "were days which no man would wish to see a second time." Facing British tyranny, Americans had no recourse but to organize in civil society "a collateral power, which, with their support, might rescue and secure their violated rights." But America's new governments were republican, deriving their just powers from the consent of the governed. The last thing Jefferson wanted to see was voluntary associations using their organized power to trump the people's will.[10]

Jefferson helps us understand elite Americans' fears. The American Revolution had been fought in the name of the people and, America's leaders believed, republican citizens ought to put aside their own selfish interests to serve the people's welfare. Leaders worried constantly that private groups would fragment the people into special interests, undermining America's republican experiment. Throughout the new nation debates raged over who should form associations and corporations, what purposes those organizations should serve, and what their relationship to the state should be. From political parties to labor unions to colleges and churches, leaders often sought to limit the spread of what they called "self-created" associations in order to protect the common good.[11] In an 1809 Virginia case, Republican jurist Spencer Roane argued that no corporation should exist if its purpose was "merely private or selfish, if it is detrimental to, or not promotive of the public good."[12]

Massachusetts, in this sense, was no different from the rest of the United States. Massachusetts's 1780 constitution prohibited the

chartering of any "corporation or association of men" that promoted
interests "distinct from those of the community."[13] One Massachusetts
leader described self-created associations as a "poison" in the body
politic.[14] The state supreme court declared in 1810 that the state need
not grant legal recognition to private voluntary churches.[15] Massachusetts's post-Revolutionary leadership believed that all associations
and corporations should be subordinate to the state. Forming an association or a corporation was not a right but a legal privilege granted
to particular institutions that serve the public interest. Legislators
used their power over incorporation to determine who should form
an association and for what ends. In essence, the post-Revolutionary
Massachusetts government acted as a gatekeeper to civil society.
What made Massachusetts distinctive, and thus particularly worthy
of study, was the strength of its communitarian tradition, illustrated
by the longevity of the Federalist party. Civil society's main archi-
tects, it turns out, were not egalitarian Jeffersonians and Jacksonians
but Federalists, Whigs, and their middle-class evangelical supporters
who, following the demise of Federalism after the War of 1812, turned
to voluntary associations and nonprofit corporations to implement
their long-standing communitarian principles.[16] Before they could do
so, however, they had to reinterpret the Revolution's legacy to justify
a role for private groups in public life.

The emergence of an independent civil society enabled citizens
to form private organizations to promote their interests and to
shape public opinion. To understand this process, I draw on Jürgen
Habermas's now classic exploration of the "bourgeois public sphere"
of civil society. According to Habermas, during the seventeenth and
eighteenth centuries middle-class Englishmen started to gather in
the public places of civil society, including coffeehouses, salons, and
voluntary associations, where they would read newspapers, learn
about political events, and discuss them with each other. Such discussions in the aggregate formed an educated public opinion that,
Habermas argues, ought to define how citizens engage in democratic
self-government. A philosopher, Habermas is more interested in the
ideal type than the specific nuances of history, but he provides a useful analytical framework to think about how public opinion is generated. He reminds us that in a democracy, public opinion should be
formed by the active involvement of ordinary citizens, and he asks us

to locate specific institutional contexts through which civic deliberation takes place.[17] Many historians have followed Habermas closely,
using his analytic framework to examine print culture or the activities of both elite and ordinary people in public places.[18] Rather than
begin with Habermas's conclusions, however, this study returns to
his original questions: why and how did citizens become involved in
shaping public opinion; what authority was granted to public opinion
in a democracy; what role did organizations play; and how did the
state and civil society relate to each other? To answer these questions
we must start with how Americans themselves conceptualized civil
society and the public sphere and then explore how the contours of
civil society and the public sphere changed in response to new ideas
and circumstances.[19]

The story of the rise of the public sphere looks quite different in post-
Revolutionary America than it does for eighteenth-century Europe
because all Americans accepted the legitimacy of popular sovereignty,
or republicanism, and thus the right of the people to deliberate and give
their consent to laws.[20] In this sense, the post-Revolutionary American
public did not have to justify its own authority, as did the various pub-
lics emerging in the private realm of civil society on the European
continent. For Americans, 1776 marked the beginning of a new regime
that took the people's authority for granted. But American consensus
over republicanism did not lead to agreement over how to connect
public opinion to public policy.[21] Americans disagreed intensely, sometimes violently, as they struggled to implement the people's consent.
At stake was nothing less than what kind of democracy Americans
should create. Federalists and Republicans were divided over whether
public opinion should emerge from the top down or the bottom up,
whether the state or "the people" should be the primary agent in civil
society. In the decades following independence, both parties found it
difficult to separate the people's government, or the state, from the
people themselves in civil society.

This book is organized thematically and chronologically. Chapter 1 explores the efforts of Massachusetts's Federalist leaders to
establish a republican commonwealth during the last two decades of
the eighteenth century, looking closely at Federalist ideas and their
implementation in both law and institutions. Chapter 2 covers the
same two decades from the perspective of those who opposed the

Federalists' vision, especially religious dissenters and Jeffersonian Republicans. Each group discovered that Federalist, and at times Republican, leaders were willing to use state power to limit their ability to form associations. In response, the Federalists' opponents were forced to defend the freedom of association. The result was two conflicting conceptions of the legitimate role of citizens in civil society. This impasse was overcome during the first three decades of the nineteenth century in response to pressures from above and below. At the top, Chapter 3 argues, organized partisan conflict convinced both Federalist and Republican leaders to separate civil society from the state. As parties struggled to control the state, political leaders recognized the value of separating corporate institutions from direct public oversight in order to protect their own interests when the state fell into the hands of the opposing party. Chapter 4 turns our lens to the grass roots, where evangelical ministers helped create a civic movement to promote Protestant values and public policies. In time they lost control of this movement as citizens turned the associational form to more radical goals, most notably the abolition of slavery. Just as elites were coming to terms with the separation of civil society and state, the nature of civil society was changing as ordinary people claimed a role in it.

These two simultaneous transformations of civil society led to three competing conceptions of civil society and its public sphere. Chapter 4 concludes with an examination of how evangelical reformers defended their grassroots organizational activities during the Antimasonic controversy. Chapter 5 turns to Federalist and Whig efforts to articulate a rationale for elite private institutions in a democracy and the institutional outcomes of their efforts. Chapter 6 examines how Jacksonian Democrats, building on Jeffersonian ideas, condemned both the grassroots and elite conceptions of civil society and public sphere, arguing instead for a populist direct democracy.

Despite the effort of Revolutionary-era political leaders to prevent it, by the 1830s America had become a nation of joiners. The proliferation of voluntary associations and nonprofit corporations fundamentally affected American democracy. Private associations and corporations structured how citizens became involved in public life, enabling people from all backgrounds to organize to pressure neighbors and leaders on issues as diverse as whether to prohibit the sale of liquor, limit the number of hours in a working day, abolish slavery, or promote education and the arts. Understanding the rise of civil society is therefore as important to making sense of the development of American democracy as studying constitutional theory and electoral politics. Voluntary associations and nonprofit corporations provide a way for citizens to participate in their shared democracy beyond voting and holding elected office. One might say that it was in civil society that Americans completed the long transition from British subjects to democratic citizens.

# ∼ 1

# The Revolutionary
# Commonwealth

WHO ARE THE PEOPLE? This question was on almost everyone's mind following the breakdown of British authority in the 1770s. Massachusetts citizens agreed that the people existed. It was in the people's name, after all, that both elite and ordinary citizens were risking their lives and livelihoods during the Revolution. But how should Massachusetts put itself back together following the Declaration of Independence? This question divided Massachusetts citizens, as it did all Americans.

From the beginning there were two broad and contradictory answers, answers that ultimately found their place in the Federalist and Republican parties. At both the state and the national level, Federalists argued that the people's will is embodied by the state. In a republic all political authority derives from the people. Once the people consent to a new government, however, the people's elected leaders could speak for them. Moreover, the higher the level of government the "more perfect" the representation.[1] At the national level, President George Washington and his Federalist allies argued that the new federal government represented Americans' highest good because it alone encompassed all Americans. Washington and his trusted treasury secretary Alexander Hamilton, both of whom remembered the divisions that hampered the Revolutionary War effort, believed that the federal government must create unity among citizens. They were convinced that the new government would remain weak until Americans were vested in its survival and strength. Hamilton urged the creation of a national market aided by a national debt and currency and, most important of all, a national bank. Washington and Hamilton believed these new institutions would serve as the "cement of interest" that would bind Americans across space. At the same time, they feared any institutions that threatened unity. They criticized local assemblies and voluntary associations that dissented from the new government's policies. During the Whiskey Rebellion, Washington condemned voluntary associations for destabilizing the new regime. A few years later, as Republicans organized again during the late 1790s, Federalists would pass the Sedition Act to silence them. Even as they encouraged new institutions to link Americans together, Federalists actively used state power to silence rivals.[2]

Massachusetts Federalists followed similar strategies. Only the state government could speak for the entire community, they argued. The Revolution provided an opportunity to undertake a grand experiment in communitarian republicanism. Having broken free from Great Britain, many Massachusetts leaders jumped at the chance to establish a new government that actively served the people's welfare. When delegates gathered in Cambridge in the winter of 1779 to draft a new state constitution, they hoped to establish a "commonwealth" that promoted the interests of all the state's citizens. Massachusetts Federalists encouraged new economic institutions, including banks and turnpikes, to serve the people's interests. But they understood that political communities were about more than just common interests; they were, in anthropologist Benedict Anderson's words, "imagined communities" composed of citizens who share affectionate ties to each other.[3] For the new Commonwealth to take hold in citizens' hearts and minds, residents must feel and act as members of the same community. Aware that many residents did not consider themselves part of a single unit, Massachusetts's post-Revolutionary leadership undertook a conscious plan to use the institutions of civil society to help transform Massachusetts from a fragmented into a united community. To them, civil society was to be created and managed by the state in the service of the people.

THE AMERICAN REVOLUTION was a revolution of "the people" against a government that, patriotic citizens claimed, no longer represented their will nor served their interests. In the famous words of the Declaration of Independence, Americans believed that "the course of human events" proved that it was time for the colonists to govern themselves and "assume among the powers of the Earth, the separate and equal station to which the Laws of Nature and of Nature's God entitle them."[4] Massachusetts colonial leaders had long argued that the British government did not represent them and that the royal governor, whose ties ran to the King rather than to the people of Massachusetts, promoted interests distinct from the community's. Massachusetts had originally been settled in the seventeenth century as a Bible Commonwealth, a corporate community responsible to its people and its godly mission. Following the Glorious Revolution in 1688–1689, however, England's new monarchs William and Mary imposed a new charter on Massachusetts and, as a result, greater royal control. Although Massachusetts had come to terms with royal authority, many colonial leaders argued that only the provincial legislature, not the royal governor and his appointed inferiors, could speak for the people. Drawing from the Country Whig rhetoric of the English Parliament's oppositional leaders, they accused the governor, and during the Imperial Crisis Parliament, of using Britain's authority to promote British interests at Massachusetts's expense.[5] The American Revolution rid Massachusetts of the King. Lacking a noble class and a bishopric, this meant that of Britain's three great estates—the King, Lords, and Commons—only the Commons remained. Any new government would therefore have to serve the common good.

The Revolution strengthened Massachusetts leaders' faith that all citizens share common interests. Starting in 1765, but especially following the passage of the Intolerable Acts in 1774, in which the British government shut down the Boston harbor and revoked Massachusetts's charter in response to the Boston Tea Party, citizens united in a common cause. In statewide extralegal congresses, county conventions, town meetings, or in voluntary committees of correspondence and safety, local and state leaders worked together to overthrow British rule. Ordinary citizens shared the burden. In mobs, in the state militia, and in the Continental Army, they volunteered for the glorious cause. By the time independence was declared, Revolutionary elites had come to think of themselves as leaders of a single united community.[6] They hoped that unity would last following the end of the war, but the possibility remained that the people would divide among themselves without an enemy to unite them. Even in the midst of revolution, Massachusetts citizens were often split by region, religion, and economic interest.[7] To ensure that "the people" ruled, and not any particular interest, Massachusetts leaders were determined to establish a government that privileged the whole—the people of Massachusetts—over the parts.

The first step was to design the new government. When delegates met in a constitutional convention in Cambridge in 1779, they were hopeful that they would be able to set up a commonwealth. Unlike a modern liberal democracy, a commonwealth is premised on the theory that the whole is prior to the parts. Advocates of a commonwealth favored communal over individual liberty because they assumed that in a republic the people share the same interests. A well-constructed government would embody the people's will and thus promote their true interests. The delegates published their proposed constitution and asked citizens to meet in local assemblies to ratify it. The constitution's preamble declared that the Commonwealth of Massachusetts was established by "a social compact, by which the whole people covenants with each citizen, and each citizen with the whole people, that all shall be governed for the common good."[8] To the majority of the delegates, the "whole people" had an existence independent and superior to that of "each citizen." As the Rev. Henry Cumings would put it in his 1783 election sermon to the General Court (Massachusetts's legislature), a person "was born, not for himself alone, but for others, for society, for his country."[9] In their public address urging ratification, the delegates affirmed that "the interest of the Society is common to all its members."[10]

Political theorists today debate whether liberal states ought to be allowed to impose a substantive vision of the good upon citizens.[11] When Massachusetts leaders spoke of the common good they invoked a substantive conception. Comments emphasizing the primacy of the common good over individual interests abound in the statements made by political and religious leaders during the 1770s and 1780s. The Rev. Nathaniel Niles proclaimed in 1774 that "every one must be required to do all he can that tends to the highest good of the state: For the whole is due to the state, from the individuals of which it is composed. Every thing, however trifling, that tends, even in the lowest degree,

to disserve the interest of the state must also be forbidden."[12] John
Adams, the primary draftsman of the 1780 constitution, wrote in 1776
that there must be "a positive Passion for the public good, the public
Interest, Honour, Power, and Glory, established in the Minds of the
People," a passion "Superiour to all private Passions," concluding, "all
Things must give Way to the public."[13] Perhaps few men were as adamant as John Adams's cousin, Samuel Adams. In a 1770 article, Adams
asked, "Where did you learn that in a state or society you had a right
to do as you please? . . . This is a refinement which I dare say, the true
sons of liberty despise. Be pleased to be informed that you are bound
to conduct yourselves as the Society with which you are joined, are
pleased to have you conduct, or if you will please, you may leave it."[14]
Adams went so far as to claim that "a citizen . . . owes everything to
the Commonwealth."[15]

~ DESPITE THE RHETORIC about the common good, not
everyone agreed that Massachusetts was what Federalist leader
Theophilus Parsons called "one moral whole."[16] The most serious
threat to the Federalist vision came from the west, where local leaders
preferred a weaker central government and greater local autonomy.
To western leaders, the Revolution was—to borrow a formulation
from Carl Becker—a revolution at home. In Hampshire, Berkshire,
and Worcester counties, local town leaders had long competed with
county elites tied by patronage to the royal governor, who appointed
his allies to positions on the courts or other offices. The Revolution
allowed town leaders to discredit and to topple county elites. Having
secured local control they did not embrace the proposed constitution's founding premise—that Massachusetts was a single community. They argued instead that Massachusetts was a federation of
autonomous towns. They relied on an older colonial understanding
of Massachusetts in which each town was a unified corporate community, a commonwealth unto itself.[17] As the citizens of Sandisfield
proclaimed, it is "the several Bodies Corporate of which the great
whole is formed."[18] Voters in Sunderland emphasized "that each town
has rights, Liberties, and Privilidges [sic] peculiar to the same, and as
dear to them as any others."[19]

The Commonwealth's advocates knew that not all Massachusetts
citizens supported them. In their public address, the convention's

delegates admitted that some citizens seemed to doubt whether all citizens shared a common interest. They tried to blame the confusion on disloyal residents responding to British machinations.[20] In fact, the divisions represented regional disagreements over the nature of the political community. Western residents understood that the new constitution would speak for "the people" of the entire state and hoped to check its power in order to protect their own.

Regional tensions over the proposed constitution were manifested in debates over legislative representation. Western residents wished that "representation might be weighed by Towns rather than by the Number of polls," or voters, in order to protect local rights.[21] To the Commonwealth's supporters, this idea contradicted the very essence of good republican government. A true representative assembly, John Adams wrote, would be "in miniature an exact portrait of the people at large."[22] Theophilus Parsons agreed that "the rights of representation should be so equally and impartially distributed, that the representatives would have the same views, and interests with the people at large . . . They should be (if we may use the expression) the whole body politic, with all its property, rights, and privilidges [*sic*], reduced to a smaller scale."[23] Both Adams and Parsons shared an assumption that westerners did not, that Massachusetts was a single unified community. In practice, their commitment to representation favored eastern interests, or the interests of the majority, as westerners recognized.

Adams's and Parsons's views were shared by the majority of the constitutional convention's delegates, who, rather than apologizing for trumping local rights, argued that localists' resistance prevented them from even more fully basing representation on "the Principle of equality."[24] Yet pragmatic considerations obliged the Commonwealth's supporters to compromise on representation, an early example of how leaders' communitarian rhetoric did not always reflect the aspirations of those they claimed to represent. Although the majority of delegates believed that towns had no *a priori* right to representation—that right being reserved to "the people"—they needed western support. They therefore agreed to permit all existing towns to send representatives to the legislature. New towns, however, would need at least 150 residents before gaining a representative. The number of representatives per town would then increase on a graduated scale.

Regionalism was not the only threat facing the new Common-wealth. Despite their commitment to an active central government, Massachusetts leaders, coming out of the Revolution, also feared the corrupting effect of power. They therefore sought to protect the rights of the people by drafting a Declaration of Rights delineating those individual and communal rights that no government should violate. An earlier proposed constitution was rejected largely because it lacked such safeguards, and the delegates in 1779 had learned from past mistakes. Article Seven of the Declaration of Rights specifically sought to protect the state's citizens from leaders who might promote their interests instead of the common good: "Government is instituted for the common good; for the protection, safety, prosperity, and happiness of the people; and not for the profit, honor, or private interest of any one man, family, or class of men; therefore, the people alone have an incontestable, unalienable, and indefeasible right to institute government; and to reform, alter, or totally change the same, when their protection, safety, prosperity, and happiness require it."[25] To the constitution's supporters, threats to the common good could come from below, as in the case of western resistance, or from above if leaders were not virtuous. Government must always serve the interests of the people and not those of any "man, family, or class of men." To further protect the common good from corrupt leaders, John Adams insisted on a bicameral legislature. Remembering the power-hungry Rump Parliament during the English Civil War, and James Harrington's critique of it, Adams argued that whenever one body of people is permitted to rule without check from another, that body might serve itself. By having two houses, each would check the other.[26]

The constitution went out to voters in the spring of 1780. Many aspects of the proposed constitution were controversial, especially clauses continuing tax support for the parochial church and the creation of a strong executive. Westerners opposed it in large numbers. Nonetheless, in June 1780 the convention met again, counted the returns, and declared the constitution ratified. There has been much speculation about whether the constitution truly garnered a two-thirds majority. An earlier constitution had been rejected, and the delegates were legitimately concerned that this one would be as well. In their returns, towns often imposed conditions to their assent to particular articles, especially Article Three authorizing tax support for churches.

The result was an extremely messy and complicated set of returns. As Samuel Eliot Morison remarked in the 1950s, "Not even an I.B.M. machine could have coped with them." It is not clear whether the constitution had the necessary support. What is clear is that the committee assigned to count the returns was creative, especially concerning Article Three and another clause prohibiting constitutional amendments before 1795, suggesting that the votes were not there. Nonetheless the delegates proclaimed a two-thirds majority for the entire constitution. They then called for fall elections for a new governor, lieutenant governor, and legislature.[27]

From the very beginning, Massachusetts's leaders faced resistance to the new government. Many western citizens argued that the Commonwealth did not really exist and that Massachusetts was nothing more than a confederation of towns. Despite these objections, Federalist leaders acted as if they had a popular mandate to implement their experiment in communitarian republicanism. Fundamental to this experiment was a civil society carefully managed by the state. Federalists believed that the state should encourage voluntary associations and corporations that serve the public's interests while actively discouraging and at times even prohibiting those associations that threaten them. The institutions of civil society should be dependent on the state, gaining their legitimacy through the higher authority of the people. Rather than consider civil society a realm of free association, Federalists used state power to ensure that only the right associations and corporations received public support.

The 1780 constitution had been designed to aid the Federalists' program by granting the government broad authority over civil society. Like all the new state constitutions, it offered no protection to the freedom of association. The Revolutionary generation did not consider the freedom of association a right. The constitution protected the freedom of assembly, but to eighteenth-century American leaders there was a difference between the freedoms of assembly and association. In republican theory, the people always have a right to assemble to protest unjust government policies. This freedom was not to be used for ordinary circumstances, when voting should suffice, but only when the body of the people concluded that their rights were threatened by the government. For this reason, the myriad assemblies, conventions, and congresses that met to resist British policies during the Imperial

Crisis were justified. The freedom of assembly was a communal right; it allowed an oppressed community to express its collective will. Unlike the modern freedom of association, the freedom of assembly did not protect the rights of minorities or dissidents to associate to oppose the majority's will.[28]

The 1780 constitution did not outlaw the freedom of association but it limited legal authorization of associations to those that served the public welfare. Under Article Six of the Declaration of Rights, the community had the right to ensure that "no man, nor corporation or association of men, have any other title to obtain advantages, or particular and exclusive privileges, distinct from those of the community, than what arises from the consideration of services rendered to the public."[29] Article Six's prohibition structured civil society-state relations in the early national era. It prohibited the state from establishing, or even recognizing, any associations that did not serve what leaders took to be the common good. Debates over who could receive corporate privileges therefore became one of the key moments when questions over the freedom of association arose. Legal recognition of associations is not a trivial thing. Corporate privileges grant associations an existence independent of their members, allow them to hold property and capital, and enable them to sue or be sued.[30]

Article Six reflected a long-standing fear that associations and corporations threaten the people's liberties. British subjects on both sides of the Atlantic had worried that corporations permitted selfish individuals to place their interests ahead of the common good. As early as the mid-seventeenth century, the very un-Whiggish Thomas Hobbes described corporations as "worms in the entrails of a natural man" that undermined the sovereign's ability to represent the interests of the whole people.[31] In the 1720s, radical Whig writers John Trenchard and Thomas Gordon condemned the South Sea Company for improperly using its corporate privileges to benefit itself. Corporations, they stated, are not only "pernicious to trade," but "are equally dangerous . . . in Politicks and Religion."[32] These ideas were echoed by Adam Smith in his 1776 *Wealth of Nations*. To Smith, corporations posed two political dangers. First, they created powerful, wealthy interests that might corrupt governors. Second, they often held monopolistic privileges not held by the people, thus giving a small and selfish minority great power. In reference to the South Sea Company and the East

India Company, whose influence American colonists blamed for the Tea Act, Smith argued that all corporations displayed the "spirit of faction" by placing their own good ahead of the common good. Smith also condemned guilds for their "corporation spirit" by which they substituted "the private interest of a part, and of a subordinate part of society" for the "general interest of the whole."[33]

Associations were made more dangerous when granted the legal privileges of incorporation because the legal status of corporations in English and European law was ambiguous. On the one hand, corporations were grants of privilege to certain persons in return for their performing specific services. On the other hand, the members of corporations often assumed that their charters granted them rights that the sovereign could not legitimately violate. Flip sides of the coin, they led to a similar conclusion: corporations divided society into subcommunities and, once these special interests were created, they would be hard to eliminate.[34] To Americans this lesson was affirmed during the Imperial Crisis. Colonists relied on their corporate charters to protect their autonomy from Parliament. Colonial charters derived their authority from the King, but colonists considered them to be inviolable. In the wake of the Boston Tea Party, Parliament's revocation of Massachusetts's charter in the Massachusetts Government Act struck fear throughout the North American Atlantic seaboard. Although Parliament ignored the colonists' pleas, the colonists themselves had emphasized the rights embedded in corporate charters.[35]

Massachusetts's leadership ensured in Article Six that charters be given only when an institution served the people's welfare. In 1780, other than towns, Massachusetts's only major corporation was Harvard College. In Chapter 5 of the Frame of Government, Harvard's corporate privileges were confirmed but the college was placed under the state's supervision. Harvard's Board of Overseers would now include the governor, the council, and the entire senate, granting the people oversight of the corporation. Even this assurance was insufficient for some concerned delegates to the constitutional convention. One delegate proposed an amendment stating that Harvard's corporate privileges should be respected only "provided that the same be not inconsistent with the fundamental rights of the People of the Commonwealth."[36]

Massachusetts leaders took Article Six very seriously. They encouraged those associations and corporations that served the public good by fostering a community of affection or providing the "cement of interest." On the other hand, they censured associations and institutions that threatened their goals. Surprisingly, Article Six did not limit the aggregate number of corporations in Massachusetts, as anticorporate ideas did in such states as Virginia and New York. Instead, Massachusetts leaders' communitarian republicanism inspired them to establish hundreds of new for-profit and nonprofit corporations that, they believed, promoted the common good. Many of these new corporations served economic goals by encouraging economic growth or the infrastructure necessary to create a unified market, including turnpikes, bridges, canals, and banks. Despite, or because of, Article Six, Massachusetts in the early 1800s led the nation in the number of corporations.[37]

The new Commonwealth had a constitutional mandate to establish and to support new institutions in civil society. Chapter 5 of the Frame of Government first outlined the privileges of Harvard and then expressed the Commonwealth's ambitious civic agenda:

> Wisdom, and knowledge . . . being necessary for the preservation of their rights and liberties . . . it shall be the duty of legislators and magistrates . . . to cherish the interests of literature and the sciences, and all seminaries of them; especially the university at Cambridge, public schools, and grammar schools in the towns; to encourage private societies and public institutions, rewards and immunities, for the promotion of agriculture, arts, sciences, commerce, trades, manufactures, and a natural history of the country; to countenance and inculcate the principles of humanity and general benevolence, public and private charity, industry and frugality, honesty and punctuality in their dealings; sincerity, good humour, and all social affections, and generous sentiments among the people.[38]

In the two decades following independence, Federalist leaders would try to make good on the constitution's promise by increasing public patronage of the church, schools, colleges, learned academies, and fraternal organizations. They believed that the state should play an active role in developing post-Revolutionary civil society.

〜 THE DELEGATES' decision to maintain, in fact to strengthen, the public religious system proved to be the most controversial provision of the new constitution. Prior to the Revolution every colony except Rhode Island, New Jersey, and Pennsylvania had some form of tax-supported religion. In New England, the church had formed the heart of the polity. Puritan settlers had crossed the Atlantic to gather their own churches and to form godly covenanted communities. In covenantal theology, civil government ought to protect the church's interests. The Revolution reversed this relationship. To many New Englanders, the public church remained vital to society, but now should serve the republic's goals.

Article Three of the Declaration of Rights authorized state support for religion. According to its framers, "the good order and preservation of civil government" depended on citizens' "piety, religion and morality." These principles "cannot be generally diffused" without "the public worship of GOD." The state thus had "a right" to mandate localities to support a church.[39] Article Three had been hotly debated in the constitutional convention, as the delegates admitted.[40] To the Article's defenders, only a tax-supported church would prevent "that immorality, and dissipation of manner, which we have great reason to fear would take place, if there should be no provision be made by law for the support and maintenance of public worship and the teachers of religion."[41]

Many citizens, particularly those who belonged to minority churches, worried that Article Three would endanger religious liberty. The freedom of conscience was protected by Article Two of the Declaration of Rights, and the constitution's defenders promised that the freedom of conscience would not be threatened by a public religious system. They noted that Article Three guaranteed each taxpayer the right to determine which church received his support. No persons would have to support a church they could not accept.[42] To worried citizens, this was not enough protection. They remembered that religious toleration had been forced on Massachusetts by William and Mary. To many Bay Colony Congregationalists at that time, religious diversity threatened the Puritan ideal of a single covenanted community. During the Imperial Crisis, religious minorities were not convinced that patriot leaders would protect their religious freedom. In 1774 Baptist leader Isaac Backus led a delegation to Philadelphia to seek Continental Congress's support for the separation of church and state.[43] Congress refused to interfere with Massachusetts's domestic institutions but, in 1778, Massachusetts voters rejected an earlier constitution because, among other things, it lacked a bill of rights.

Historians have divided into two major camps on the question of Article Three, camps that replicate the debate that took place over ratification. Some historians consider Article Three an oppressive throwback to the Puritan past. They see it as a handout to Congregational ministers who supported the Revolutionary cause. Besieged since the Great Awakening with competition from other sects, ministers sought the state's aid to reassert their declining authority.[44] Other historians argue that the primary goal of Article Three was civic not religious. The purpose of public religion was to teach citizens the moral virtues required of republican citizens, not to establish religious doctrine.[45] Debates in the press generally support the second interpretation but the issue remains unresolved. If the public church was simply a utilitarian moral institution, why was its support included in the Declaration of Rights instead of in the constitution's Frame of Government, where the state's obligation to other educational institutions is spelled out? The reason is that Article Three served both purposes. Religion, unlike other civic goods, concerns metaphysical questions the answers to which are derived from revealed or natural law. By publicly supporting religion, the state acknowledged its commitment to transcendent ideals.[46]

Many Massachusetts citizens continued to see themselves as a covenanted people committed to living according to their god's laws. The Revolution reinforced this commitment. Speaking in their pulpits, to militias, and before public assemblies, New England ministers argued that the revolution against Britain must be accompanied by a renewed covenant with God, who sanctioned the rebellion in order to protect his flock from the British crown and the Anglican church.[47] In Massachusetts's first election sermon, held the day the new Commonwealth government opened for business, the Rev. Samuel Cooper reminded elected leaders that Massachusetts was settled "as a refuge from tyranny." Like the people of ancient Israel, the Puritans had been "led into a wilderness" and "pursued through the sea, by the armed hand of power." In the New World, they engaged in "a covenant, a compact a mutual stipulation" to live under God's laws. Cooper admitted that "we want not, indeed, a special revelation from heaven to teach us that men are born equal and free." This idea could be gained through the use of reason, itself a gift from God. But it was also revealed in Scripture. Like Joshua, the rulers of Massachusetts now entered into "a solemn renewal of this covenant."[48]

Opponents of Article Three argued that it violated religious freedom precisely because it made the state a party in religion. As Isaac Backus stated, "The rights of conscience are the greatest rights of any in the world."[49] One writer suggested that Article Three blurred the distinction between *"protestantism* and *popery."*[50] Article Three's most ardent critic, "Philanthropos," worried that "the church and State are not barely to be brought together, but are to be really *united."*[51] Article Three's supporters responded that the freedom of conscience was guaranteed and, more important, the state had a compelling interest in promoting morality. As one writer put it, "Obedience to the moral law is required in both church and state, though for different reasons."[52] Most of Article Three's supporters downplayed the connection between covenantal theology and the public church and emphasized the utilitarian benefits of religion in a republic.

◠ DESPITE ALL the hostility expressed against Article Three, Massachusetts Federalists remained confident that the public religious system would serve the long-term interests of the Commonwealth in two ways. First, it would ensure that all citizens learned the moral values necessary for republican citizenship. Second, it would serve as a common institution in which an imagined community could take shape. By bringing all the citizens of the state together, public churches would provide institutional ties cementing the fragmented polity into a larger whole.

The public church's primary function was moral education. To John Adams, believing in a "future state of rewards and punishments" would encourage citizens' moral behavior.[53] In 1778 the Rev. Phillips Payson argued that "the fear of God, and the terrors of eternity are the most powerful restraints of men; and hence it is of special importance in a free government."[54] Without the public influence of religion, worried the Rev. Aaron Bancroft following the deist Thomas Jefferson's election to the presidency, the United States would follow France into social chaos.[55] Avoiding eternal damnation was evidently a strong incentive for moral behavior.

There was also a softer side to the church's moral educative role. Many hoped that the church would encourage what the 1780 constitution called "social affections." Eighteenth-century thinkers believed that only affection, or love for one's fellow citizens, could transform isolated individuals into a community. Love was more powerful than duty. Ideas about the social role of affection grew out of transatlantic Enlightenment thought. In the early eighteenth century, Anthony Ashley Cooper, the third earl of Shaftesbury, argued contra Hobbes and Locke that human nature has "a thousand other springs" than self-interest. Of these springs, only the affections could promote "public spirit."[56] Building on Shaftesbury's arguments, the Scottish moral philosopher Francis Hutcheson argued that human nature is made for society. Each person, Hutcheson wrote, is endowed with a moral sense that involuntary recognizes the moral worth of their own or another's actions. The moral sense encouraged benevolence, the disinterested desire to seek others' good. Virtuous or "beneficient actions," Hutcheson argued, "tend to the public good." Virtuous citizens would serve the common good by following his or her moral sense, not the demanding and self-sacrificing ideals of Rome and Sparta.[57] As historian Knud Haakonssen argues, the Scottish moral sense philosophers internalized natural law by making its dictates part of human nature.[58]

The ability of all persons to feel compassion or sympathy was considered proof that human nature has an innate capacity for benevolence. Hutcheson called sympathy "fellow feeling," and its social role was delineated by his student Adam Smith.[59] By feeling the pain or joy of another, sympathy acts as a social bonding agent, compelling each citizen to account for the welfare of the other. "Sympathy," a 1793 Massachusetts writer observed, "is that principle in the breast of man, which disposes him to take an interest in the joys and sorrows of others, and to heighten the former, and alleviate the latter, by all means in his power." Thus, "sympathy is the great bond of society, the secret charm, which unites man to man."[60]

Massachusetts religious and political leaders were confident that Protestant Christianity was uniquely capable of promoting the social affections because Protestantism obliged people to love their neighbors and to act with compassion toward humanity. "Religion," the Rev. Jonas Clark argued in his 1781 election sermon, "inflames the heart with the purest affections, and forms the man for every virtue,—for every service, which GOD or his country might require." "Its benevolent precepts," he continued, "are all contained in *love to* GOD and *love to man.*"[61] In a 1786 sermon, the Rev. Samuel West suggested that only Christianity "inspires the hearts of men with the warmest affections towards each other," leading Christians to make "the warmest exertions for the public good."[62]

The Rev. Jonathan French agreed that Christianity promotes republican virtues. "Civil government," he stated, "is a kind of machine" established "for the restraint of such desires and passions as, if let alone, would be ruinous to the public peace and happiness of society." Neither penal laws nor human reason were sufficient to discourage selfishness. Fortunately "the very design of christianity is to reform mankind, to meliorate their tempers, to bring them to discharge their duty to God, and one another." Upon conversion, a Christian's soul and "tempers" are transformed, leading him or her to promote benevolence. "No man can in heart be a true republican," French concluded, "who is not a person of piety and good morals."[63] It is no wonder that in 1799 Governor Moses Gill proclaimed, "Public worship may, with propriety, be considered an important part of education." Public religion would "meliorate the heart, and urge the performance of social and private duties."[64] By promoting social order through the dual axes of fear of damnation and love of all humanity, the public religious system would ensure that citizens put the common good ahead of their own.

IN ADDITION TO religion, leaders believed that all citizens should have access to education. Throughout the new United States, plans were put forth to educate citizens. Among the more famous are Thomas Jefferson's 1779 "Bill for the More General Diffusion of Knowledge" in Virginia and Pennsylvanian Benjamin Rush's call for schools to turn children into "republican machines."[65] New Englanders had supported public education since well before the Revolution. All Puritans needed to read their Bible, so children had to be literate. As early as the 1650s, Massachusetts called upon towns to support schoolmasters.[66] The 1780 constitution renewed this commitment to "cherish the interests" of education.

Since the Renaissance, political writers had argued that rulers must be educated. With the revival of classical values, citizenship emerged as one of life's highest callings. In *Some Thoughts Concerning Education*, John Locke wrote that the English gentry should have a humanist education to prepare them for leadership. Building on his own psychological theory, Locke thought that a proper education would teach future leaders to reason correctly. Since Locke believed that all people were born without innate ideas, education could teach people to take pleasure in the right things, namely those things that reason dictates to be in the interest of the common good.[67] In a republic, citizens elect their own leaders and can themselves become leaders. Education therefore could not be limited to the gentry. "In a republican government," claimed one Worcester writer, "every citizen has an equal right of election to the chief offices of the state." Thus, each citizen, "whether in office or not, ought to become acquainted with the principles of civil liberty, the constitution of his country, and the rights of mankind in general."[68] As the 1780 constitution stated, "Wisdom, and knowledge . . . [are] necessary for the preservation of their rights and liberties."[69]

Educated citizens protected the common good from corrupt leaders. History proves, John Adams wrote, "that whenever, a general knowledge and Sensibility have prevailed among the People, Arbitrary Government and every kind of oppression have lessened and disappeared in Proportion." Uneducated citizens lacked both the skills—such as literacy—and the moral virtues necessary to sustain a republic.[70] Like other Enlightenment thinkers, Adams believed that popular ignorance had allowed kings and popes to rule since time immemorial. The recovery of humanist knowledge during the Renaissance and the destruction of Catholicism's monopoly over Christendom during the Reformation had freed people's minds from the "wicked confederacy" between kings and priests.[71] Ignorance had produced political and religious oppression; education would prevent tyranny from taking root in the new United States.

Public schools, like the public religious system, would also cultivate the social affections. Historians usually emphasize the classical republican goals of education in the early republic and miss the important social function leaders assigned it.[72] While American leaders certainly idealized Sparta, "that boast of ancient republics," they also worried that the classical model had serious shortcomings. Spartan education, one writer pointed out, "being entirely public, stifled those principles of natural affection, of family, and private attachments, on which a great proportion of the pleasures of life depend."[73] Spartan education, another wrote, was "too contracted and selfish." Spartans might sacrifice for the common good but they "paid little attention or no regard to, and had little or no affection or tenderness for, any of their fellow men, who did not belong to, or in some way serve the interest of, their own nation."[74] As Governor Samuel Adams told the legislature, in school, a child's heart should be "deeply impressed . . . with the moral feelings," which, Adams hoped, would "have their due weight through the whole of their future lives."[75]

Schooling in colonial Massachusetts had been inconsistent. Despite the law, many towns neither supported teachers nor even boasted a schoolhouse. In 1789 the legislature sought to rectify the situation by requiring all towns and districts to hire schoolmasters. They mandated that all teachers, from grammar school instructors to Harvard professors, teach their students the knowledge and values necessary "to preserve and perfect a republican Constitution and to secure the blessings of liberty, as well as to promote their future happiness."[76]

In addition to renewing its commitment to public schooling, the General Court also incorporated more than twenty academies between 1780 and 1800. Since corporations had to serve the common good, each charter emphasized that "academies within this Commonwealth for the education of youth, are of common benefit."[77] Despite this assurance, the proliferation of incorporated academies concerned the state's most adamant republicans. Samuel Adams was especially hostile to academies and, as governor, blocked their acts of incorporation.[78] Adams told the legislature that while the founding of new academies reflects a "zeal highly to be commended," he worried that "multiplying them, may have a tendency to injure the ancient and beneficial mode of Education in Town Grammar Schools." Public schools united the community but, Adams worried, if wealthy children attended incorporated academies, "the useful learning, instruction and social feelings in the early parts of life, may cease to be so equally and universally disseminated, as it has heretofore been."[79] Others echoed Adams's concerns. One writer noted that parents who "educate their children in a private way" are unwilling to perform their civic responsibilities.[80] Despite these oppositional voices, most politicians considered academies to be legitimate corporations that served a compelling public interest. Preparing boys for college was expensive and towns were

already hard pressed to support primary schools. Incorporated academies, in tandem with public schools, "are the only means, by which a
general diffusion of knowledge can be effected."[81]

Education began in the home, where mothers were responsible for
their children's moral and intellectual development. Women thus had
to be prepared to fulfill their civic responsibilities. Although Massachusetts's 1789 law on schooling recognized the civic role played by
schoolmistresses, much female education remained outside of formal
institutions. The General Court did not incorporate a single specifically female academy between 1780 and 1800, but there were probably
unincorporated ones, and many academies accepted girls. There were
some positive developments, however. In 1778, the town of Groton
decided to include girls in their census of school-age children. Boston's
citizens also developed a comprehensive plan for public schooling that
included girls in the lower grades.[82]

Higher education should also serve the common good, and colleges
in the early republic were considered public institutions. The 1780
constitution placed Harvard under state control and, since no state
had more than one college, Harvard anticipated retaining a monopoly.
Representatives from western Massachusetts and from the Maine district (which was still a part of Massachusetts) hoped that the General
Court would incorporate new colleges to make higher education more
accessible in the more remote regions of the Commonwealth. Aware
of these pressures as well as the general distrust of corporations, Harvard's trustees defended Harvard's role as the state's most important
public corporation. In a published letter to Massachusetts's first governor, John Hancock, the trustees promised to always serve the interests
of the public, "its Patrons and Benefactors."[83]

Despite Harvard's efforts to protect its monopoly, the legislature
incorporated two new colleges, Williams in 1793 and Bowdoin in 1794.
Each college was produced by both local demands and the Commonwealth's commitment to increasing access to education. Conservative
Congregationalists in western Massachusetts had sought their own college as early as 1762, when they petitioned royal governor Francis Bernard for a charter. Harvard's trustees had resisted vehemently, claiming
that Harvard alone was "the College of the Government." Harvard
succeeded and Bernard refused to issue a charter.[84] In 1793, however,
Massachusetts leaders sought to build stronger ties with westerners.

They thus incorporated a college that challenged Harvard's position. Williams was dominated by Yale-educated Congregationalists, whose orthodox theology differed dramatically from what Harvard was teaching young ministers. This alone suggests the tension between the idealized goals of Article Six and the realities of politics in a pluralistic society composed of multiple interests.[85]

Bowdoin's advocates also lobbied hard for their charter. Invoking the same language that justified academies, Bowdoin's Maine supporters argued that since the 1780 constitution required the state "to cherish and encourage the liberal arts and sciences and all good literature in the *various parts* of the Commonwealth," it could not deny Maine's residents access to higher education.[86] By challenging Harvard's monopoly, the two new colleges raised the specter of competition. Academies served local populations, but Harvard was supposed to educate the Commonwealth's next generation of ministers and statesmen. Yet neither Williams's nor Bowdoin's advocates sought to create a private college. They considered their new institutions also to be public. They sought and received legislative aid, admittedly never to the same extent as Harvard.[87] All three colleges would receive revenues from bank taxes in 1814. Although the legislature did not have direct oversight of Williams and Bowdoin, they reserved the right to alter their charters if the colleges ever placed their interests ahead of the public good.

Massachusetts leaders also intended their Commonwealth to rival Europe in learning and culture. During the Enlightenment, knowledge was considered a source of national pride and the key to social and political progress. Research replaced myth with fact. England boasted several respected learned societies, most important the Royal Society. France had the Académie Royale des Sciences. Pennsylvania claimed the oldest learned society in North America, Philadelphia's American Philosophical Society. John Adams saw no reason that Massachusetts should not have an equally prestigious institution and made sure that Chapter 5 of the 1780 constitution encouraged public support of the arts and sciences. In May 1780, even before the new government went into effect, legislators incorporated the American Academy of Arts and Sciences, followed in 1793 by a charter for the Massachusetts Historical Society. According to the Academy's charter, promoting research in science and American history would "advance the interest, honor,

dignity, and happiness of a free, independent, and virtuous people."
James Bowdoin was the Academy's first president and, following his
death in 1790, was succeeded by John Adams. Other members included
John Hancock, Caleb Strong, and James Sullivan. With such public
men in charge, the Academy and state leaders emphasized the close
links desired between the state and civil society.[88]

The one arena where the legislature sanctioned the formation of
corporations without a special charter from the state was libraries.
Massachusetts followed Pennsylvania by enacting a general incorporation law for "social libraries" in 1798, which allowed any seven or more
persons to "form themselves into a Society or Body Politic." It would
be wrong to attribute too much to this act; its primary purpose was to
encourage wealthy persons to support learning in their communities.
In time, the freedom of association would be extended to other associations. For now, libraries were the exception that proved the rule.[89]

THE ONE VOLUNTARY association that seemed to meet universal approbation among American leaders was the Masonic lodge.
Following American independence Freemasonry expanded throughout the nation, growing from roughly two hundred lodges in 1793 to
more than five hundred by 1800. In 1770, there were thirteen lodges
in Massachusetts, three of them in Boston. At its post-Revolutionary
peak during the first decade of the 1800s, there were at least fifty-
four lodges, again with three in Boston, demonstrating the fraternity's
expanded geographic reach.[90]

Freemasonry's expansion owed much to its rhetorical compatibil-
ity with American leaders' goals. Lodges emphasized their republican
virtues, from providing moral education to encouraging the arts and
sciences. Most important of all, the lodges promoted members' social
affections and strengthened the ties binding citizens together. For
these very reasons lodges were considered subversive in Europe, where
they might create unsupervised sites for public discussion that threatened absolutism.[91] In the new republican United States, however, Freemasons proudly extolled their contributions to the common good. As
Steven C. Bullock argues, Freemasons claimed a place in early national
civic culture second only to schools.[92]

Freemasonry, one of its boosters wrote, "has an absolute tendency to
inculcate every thing laudable and useful to society." It "was instituted

to form men into good citizens and good subjects" by displacing the "warlike" virtues of ancient republics in favor of "the God of Friendship." By fostering the social affections, friendship "renders men more amiable, by the attraction of innocent pleasures, pure joys and rational gestures." In lodges, members come to love each other as brothers.[93] The ideal of friendship resolved the tension between the lodges' exclusivity and secrecy and the Commonwealth's commitment to a single community. Masons echoed Shaftesbury that humans were "*social* beings."[94] Shaftesbury had argued that "universal good, or the interest of the world in general, is a kind of remote philosophical object," and that the social affections were better encouraged in a "more contracted public" where a person could "better taste society and enjoy the common good."[95] The Rev. Thaddeus Mason Harris, in a 1797 address, agreed that men are born with "companiable propensities and affectionate dispositions." But no man could befriend everyone; "some *medium*" was necessary "where our affections may be exercised without being partial and without being indiscriminate." Freemasonry's fraternal lodges provided a "desirable mean between the diffusedness of general regard and the contractedness of individual attachment."[96]

Masons also argued that the friendships made in their lodges helped members put aside their political and religious differences, differences that might otherwise threaten the polity. Some Masons suggested that they did a better job promoting shared values than did churches. "Were . . . the unanimity, love, equality, generosity, and distinterestedness" of the ancient church present "among professing Christians *now*," Harris suggested, "Free Masonry would be less necessary among them."[97] Masons portrayed themselves as an antidote to the problems that vexed the new Commonwealth because they transcended existing political and social divisions.

Despite their commitment to a harmonious affectionate community, white Masons did not embrace their black brothers in Boston. African Americans had established a lodge during the Revolutionary War with the help of British commander Thomas Gage. The African Lodge was chartered by the Grand Lodge of England in 1784. White Masons refused to recognize the legitimacy of the African Lodge's charter, arguing that it violated the Massachusetts Grand Lodge's jurisdiction. At some level, white resistance was probably directed toward the African Lodge's close ties to England. Nonetheless, white Masons did not

attempt to bridge the gap between the races, illustrating the marginal-
ized status of African Americans in the Commonwealth.[98]

Masonic claims to universality, like those of the public church, did
not go unchallenged. Baptists worried that Masons offered a cosmo-
politan and secular alternative to the religious community and some
New England Baptist churches prohibited their members from joining the fraternity.[99] The most vocal critique came from Charlestown's
orthodox Congregational minister Jedidiah Morse. In sermons he
delivered in 1798 and 1799, Morse argued that Masons were part of
a global conspiracy to undermine Christianity. Morse likened Freemasonry to the "Bavarian Illuminati" in Europe and to the atheistic
French revolutionaries.[100] Other critics pointed out that despite their
"pompous professions of philanthropy," Masons did not cultivate
"universal brotherhood," but provided *"benefits to a select party."* Their
secrecy only furthered the threat they posed to the common good.[101]
Masons thus walked a fine line between particularity and universality.
Baptists, orthodox ministers like Morse, and avid civic communitar-
ians questioned the accuracy of their rhetoric. During the 1780s and
1790s, Masons overcame these objections in part because many of the
Revolutionary elite were themselves members but also because their
stated goals comported with those of the Commonwealth.

⌒ IN THE TWO decades after 1780, Massachusetts leaders
greatly expanded the state's role in civil society. They strengthened
the public religious and education systems and incorporated new institutions to promote learning and the social affections. They hoped
that these institutions would together foster an imagined community
with shared interests and values held together by the ties of affection.
Despite their efforts, however, the 1780s and 1790s were not decades
of social and political harmony. Political and religious divisions continued to threaten the Commonwealth. While Federalists supported
those associations and institutions that served what they took to be
the common good, they proved actively hostile to any association that
weakened popular unity. The state proved capable of expanding the
number and type of associations in civil society in order to promote
communitarian republicanism. It would prove equally capable of limiting alternative civic aspirations in order to defend the ambitious new
Commonwealth.

# ~ 2

# *Fragmentation and Contestation*

THE FREEDOM OF ASSOCIATION was not protected by the 1780 constitution under Article Six. According to Federalists, only the state could determine which associations and corporations to sanction because the state alone represented the community. When individuals formed an association independent of the state, Federalists labeled them partial voices—those of a minority—that ought to be discouraged. Even as Federalists used the state to promote new associations and corporations, Massachusetts citizens discovered that their leaders were willing to use state power to prevent the proliferation of those groups that might threaten the new Commonwealth.

In his Farewell Address of 1796, outgoing President George Washington perhaps best stated the Federalists' position. The first president's administration had weathered many challenges to the new Union, including the rise of organized opposition and the violence of the Whiskey Rebellion. President Washington warned citizens against forming associations that promoted diverse interests. "The very idea of the power and the right of the people to establish government presupposes the duty of every individual to obey the established government," Washington wrote, adding:

All obstructions to the execution of the laws, all combinations and associations, under whatever plausible character, with the real

design to direct, control, counteract, or awe the regular deliberation and action of the constituted authorities, are destructive of
this fundamental principle, and of fatal tendency. They serve to
organize faction, to give it an artificial and extraordinary force;
to put, in the place of the delegated will of the nation the will
of a party, often a small but artful and enterprising minority of
the community; and, according to the alternate triumphs of different parties, to make the public administration the mirror of
the ill-concerted and incongruous projects of faction, rather than
the organ of consistent and wholesome plans digested by common
counsels and modified by mutual interests.

Washington believed the new government represented the people's
will, and thus deliberation (and therefore the public sphere) ought to
be limited to "constituted authorities," or elected officials. He told
citizens not only to set aside their parochial interests but that the new
government "has a right to concentrate your affections" to ensure its
success.[1]

Many citizens challenged the Federalists' efforts to concentrate their
affections and to limit deliberation to elected officials. They argued
that their right to associate was fundamental to republican liberty. But
that was not all they said. They also offered an alternate vision of civil
society. Western farmers and then leaders of the new Republican Party
argued that the voice of the people could be heard in civil society and,
moreover, that the people had an obligation to associate to oversee
their leaders. Federalist claims that the state spoke for the people was
a dangerous innovation that could undermine republican government.
President Washington had it backward.[2]

THE AMERICAN REVOLUTION had been carried out by
voluntary associations—conventions, congresses, and committees of
correspondence and of safety. As British authority evaporated, these
associations claimed to speak on behalf of the sovereign people. The
members of these associations—none more so than the delegates to the
Continental Congress—endowed themselves with an authority higher
than that of government itself. In Lockean theory, when governments
are dissolved, society remains. Patriot leaders argued that the interests of society—of the people—were embodied in the associations and

assemblies that resisted the British. Following ratification of the state constitution in 1780, however, these extralegal associations and assemblies were no longer necessary. Having formed a new government, the people's will could be expressed by their legitimate representatives. Nonetheless, many citizens continued to assemble in conventions to protest the new Commonwealth's policies. State leaders worried that these assemblies would undermine the new regime just as they had done in the Revolution.

During the Revolution, Massachusetts royal governor Thomas Hutchinson argued that self-created associations and assemblies were "tending to mutiny and rebellion."[3] Calling Boston's town meeting a "mock Assembly," he believed that the British must "end these most illegal and destructive combinations."[4] Hutchinson recognized that the various associations and assemblies were becoming "in everything but in name . . . a house of representatives."[5] His observations were correct; the assemblies and conventions had evolved into organs representing "the people" in civil society. Provincial congresses, town meetings, county conventions, and committees of correspondence and of safety all functioned as quasi-sovereign bodies following the dissolution of royal authority. Over time, these assemblies came to be seen as direct expressions of the people's will. In a few short years, *de facto* sovereignty was transformed into a superior sovereignty in constitutional theory: the people assembled in civil society became the constituent sovereign from whom all governments derived their authority. From this premise followed a new conclusion: only conventions of the people could draft constitutions since governments must be subordinate to the people. In his critique of Virginia's Revolutionary constitution, Thomas Jefferson argued that if legislatures could draft constitutions, what one legislature did another could undo. Constitutions should be compacts in which the people in civil society established their government.[6]

The Massachusetts General Court confronted this innovation in constitutional theory when its 1778 constitution was soundly defeated by voters. In early 1777, a committee of the House of Representatives recommended electing delegates to a special constitutional convention. The legislature rejected the recommendation, and in June the House and the Council resolved themselves into a constitutional convention. The people opposed the proposed constitution for many reasons, especially the lack of a bill of rights. Many westerners also argued that the new constitution favored eastern interests because of how it apportioned representation. Following its rejection, citizens in Berkshire County refused to allow the state's courts to reopen. They argued that without a constitution Massachusetts remained in the state of nature and therefore the General Court had no authority to enforce law.

The "Berkshire constitutionalists" admitted that the current situation was "very Extraordinary" and that they did not consider the General Court to be "Usurpers & Tyrants," as the British had been. Until the people sanctioned a new government, however, the General Court could not claim to speak on their behalf. "The whole Legislature," the residents of Pittsfield told a General Court committee, "is insufficient to give Life to the fundamental Constitution of such state, it being the foundation on which they themselves stand." If the legislature could act prior to ratification of a new constitution, that would make "the legislature greater than the people who send them."[7] In February 1779, in response to overwhelming popular demand, the General Court agreed to call the nation's first constitutional convention. Legislators acknowledged the superior authority of conventions of the people and admitted the right of the assembled people to create a new regime.

Many leaders believed that ratification of the 1780 constitution solved the problem of the government's authority. Unless the new government violated the terms of the social contract, citizens could now be expected to obey its dictates. Not everyone agreed. The Revolution taught Americans that conventions were effective institutions to express popular discontent. Even after the new constitution went into effect, conventions assembled with regularity, especially in the western counties where the constitution remained illegitimate in the eyes of many citizens. The conventions posed a theoretical problem for the Commonwealth's leaders: how could "the people" continue to assemble if they had already approved a constitution and delegated their authority to a new government? The problem stemmed from the nascent state of the theories of assembly and association. Both delegates to the conventions and Massachusetts's elected leaders spoke as if the conventions represented the unmediated voice of the sovereign people. The Commonwealth and the conventions thus competed for the exclusive right to represent the people.[8]

Western disaffection with the new constitution was compounded by economic depression following the end of war. Western farmers sought debt relief from eastern creditors, including increasing the availability of paper money and changing the General Court's pro-creditor policies. Many western farmers believed that the constitution must be altered to shift westward the balance of power in the legislature.[9] Westerners argued, as they had during debates over ratification, that representatives ought to be apportioned by towns, not population. To petition the General Court for redress, westerners met in conventions at least twenty times between 1781 and 1786, most often in Hampshire, Berkshire, and Worcester counties.[10]

In 1784 Boston's newspapers condemned the conventions as unlawful assemblies. Commenting on conventions in Plymouth and Worcester counties, one writer concluded that "the people are seized with . . . a rage for revolution." "There was a time," the writer continued, "when the government had a distinct interest from the people," making "county conventions and smaller committees . . . a necessary substitute in the room of government." Following ratification of the constitution, however, "government has the same interest as the people." The General Court was composed of the people's elected representatives, not the King's appointed henchmen. More important, only the General Court represented the true interest of Massachusetts, the conventions being "partial assemblies" representing local, and thus special, interests. Instead of speaking for the people, the conventions threatened their sovereignty.[11]

The writer concisely articulated the challenge facing Massachusetts leaders. They believed that conventions were appropriate only when the people had no constitutional alternative. Critics of the conventions distinguished between Massachusetts following 1780 and the status of the colonists under Britain, but their language also implied that the freedom of assembly was unnecessary within republics. In his charge to a grand jury in Middlesex, state supreme court justice Francis Dana made this case explicitly. In 1780, he argued, the people delegated authority to deliberate the common good to their representatives in the General Court. The constitution authorized no other "body of men with delegated powers to deliberate and determine upon publick affairs; and to vote and resolve for others." Yet westerners continued to establish "smaller bodies of men in the form and semblance of representative bodies." The conventions, Dana concluded, drew "away mens [sic] minds from their duty and obedience to that constitutional authority, to which they have engaged by the solemn compact of government."[12] Even future Republican leaders thought that the conventions went too far. James Sullivan—who would become Massachusetts's first Republican governor—wrote Samuel Adams that he wished "that the idea of a county convention being a legal body could be exploded," a view with which Adams concurred.[13]

Delegates to the conventions defended their legitimacy and the right of citizens to assemble to deliberate and express judgment on public policies. A Middlesex convention meeting in August 1786 noted that the constitution "justified . . . their present mode of meeting" and that such meetings were necessary whenever "a people feel themselves oppressed."[14] If conventions were legitimate only during revolutions, the freedom of assembly was an empty right. It made little sense that the people would have sacrificed their right to assemble and to petition the government.

Convention delegates had more difficulty overcoming the problem of competing sovereignties. Delegates were usually elected by town voters and claimed to speak on their behalf, much like a representative assembly. The conventions' actions exacerbated the problem. As if replaying the script of the Revolution, a Worcester convention appointed a "committee to correspond with all the other counties" in order to collect "the sentiments of the whole."[15] To worried observers it looked as if the conventions were constituting themselves into sovereign bodies just as other conventions before them had done. It did not help that the conventions published long lists of grievances that, like the Declaration of Independence, seemed to be making a case for independence.[16] Such an outcome was not beyond the realm of possibility. Throughout the American west, residents sought to establish new states where older ones claimed sovereignty. The only successful case was Vermont's bid against New York, but similar conflicts plagued many states.[17] In August 1778, following the General Court's rejection of the proposed constitution, the residents of Berkshire argued that unless the Court called a constitutional convention they would be forced to turn to "other states," which, they believed, "would gladly receive us."[18] In Maine, a convention met in September 1786 and advocated the creation of "an Independent State."[19] Massachusetts leaders worried that unless they defended the Commonwealth's authority the state might disintegrate.

The cold war turned hot with the outbreak of Shays's Rebellion in August 1786. Daniel Shays and his cohorts closed the courts in Northampton to protest the government's tax and currency policies. Political leaders were convinced that the conventions' rhetoric reflected their intent to overthrow the government. The rebels, on the other hand, believed that their actions were consistent with the principles of 1776; throughout the Imperial Crisis, conventions had been held and courts were closed when the royal government pursued policies deemed oppressive to the community. In a September 1786 petition presented to the justices of the Courts of Common Pleas and General Sessions in the town of Worcester, the rebels declared themselves "the body of people collected for their own good and that of the Commonwealth," implying that they represented the unmediated sovereign will of the people.[20] As Richard D. Brown argues, the Shaysites "did not see themselves as rebels but as reformers who were using methods that had been vindicated by the Independence movement."[21]

By shutting down the courts with force or the threat of force, the rebels challenged the Commonwealth's authority to enforce the law, just as colonists had done when they closed the royal courts in 1774. Governor James Bowdoin called an early session of the legislature in order to respond to the rebellion. Bowdoin had no doubt that the Shaysites hoped "to dissolve our excellent constitution." Moreover, he believed that the General Court was "the only body" that could redress public grievances. All other bodies, he argued, "are anti-constitutional, and of a very dangerous tendency." Like other critics of the conventions, Bowdoin did not elaborate what role the freedom of assembly might play in a republic. The General Court agreed with Bowdoin's assessment. In the legislature, they pointed out, "the major part" of the people are represented whereas in the conventions, "nine-tenths of the state are not represented." The conventions therefore could not speak for the people. A minority must not be allowed to endanger the common good. With the legislature's support, Bowdoin called out the militia to put down the rebellion, meeting force with force.[22]

Violence effectively de-legitimized the conventions. Massachusetts leaders did not recognize the right of citizens to bear arms against a legitimate republican government. As Alexander Hamilton would later put it when reflecting on the rebellion, "Where the whole power of the government is in the hands of the people, there is less pretense for the use of violent remedies in partial or occasional distempers of the State. The natural cure for an ill administration in a popular or representative constitution is a change of men."[23] Although it is doubtful that the Shaysites actually sought revolution, there was little doubt following the rebellion that the Commonwealth would enforce the sovereignty of the whole over the parts. Fundamentally, the people could not oppose "the people." The Commonwealth's supporters believed that the only appropriate way for citizens to express opposition to government policies was for towns to instruct their representatives, since only representatives had the right to speak on their constituents' behalf.[24] Other voluntary gatherings, except those incorporated by the state or otherwise given its official sanction, usurped the people's authority. In contrast, the delegates to the conventions claimed that the conventions were a constitutional alternative to rebellion.[25] So long as both sides claimed to represent the voice of the people—while disagreeing about where the people's voice was located—conflict remained unavoidable. To the conventions and to the rebels, the people were distinct from the state and could represent themselves in civil society. To the Commonwealth's leaders, the new state government was the only legitimate agent of the people.

⁓ EVEN IF they did not claim to represent the people, self-created voluntary associations were considered dangerous because they fragmented the community. Massachusetts leaders were determined that only associations that united the people—that provided a cement to hold them together or in some other way promoted the common good—be permitted. In the last decades of the eighteenth century, two particular associations, the Society of the Cincinnati and craft unions, both confronted these limits to the freedom of association.

The Society of the Cincinnati was a voluntary association established and governed by its members without any public oversight. Although the Cincinnati's members claimed to speak only for themselves, the society's very existence threatened the state's ability to manage civil society. The Cincinnati was a fraternal association of former Continental Army officers and their descendants. Citizens across the nation worried that the officers sought to form a "hereditary peerage" that would subvert republicanism. In response, the Cincinnati emphasized their charitable goals: providing aid to indigent former officers and their families and, like the Freemasons, promoting fraternity and the social affections. To skeptical observers, however, the Cincinnati "cloak[ed] their design under a pious name of raising a charitable fund."[26] At the federal Constitutional Convention in Philadelphia in 1787, Massachusetts delegate and future Republican governor Elbridge Gerry supported the electoral college to prevent "one set of men dispersed throughout the Union & acting in concert," such as "the Society of the Cincinnati," from taking advantage of the "ignorance of the people."[27] To Gerry the Cincinnati looked like a dangerous organization of military officers that might convert their friendship and status into political power, as the army had done when the English attempted to create a republic in the seventeenth century. Ideally, friendship cultivated ties of affection that forged an imagined community; in the case of the Cincinnati, however, friendship might lead powerful elites to promote their own interests and not the common good.

The Cincinnati's case was harmed because it was a voluntary association. Lacking a charter, the society lacked legitimacy. It was "self-created" and beyond state control. The Cincinnati elected their own officers, held their own meetings, and performed other activities usually reserved for corporations, but without a charter the state could not limit the association's power. To make matters worse, the Cincinnati's organizational structure copied the federal union's. The society had its own constitution, was divided into state-level chapters, and elected a national president. It looked to many like a shadow government.[28]

Although many of the Cincinnati's members would become Federalists, state leaders remained wary of it. In response to public criticism, the Cincinnati's titular head, George Washington, penned a widely reprinted circular in May 1784. Washington sought to reconcile the society with the imperatives of republicanism. He first argued that hereditary succession should be abolished. He then urged state chapters to have their "funds placed under the immediate cognizance of the several Legislatures, who should also be requested to grant charters for more effectually carrying our humane designs into execution." Washington hoped to transform the Cincinnati from a national and dangerous voluntary association to a number of state-level corporations in order to convince the public that the society posed no threat and that its members were willing to be governed by state laws. Incorporation would also grant the society public sanction.[29]

Despite Washington's prestige, the Massachusetts General Court refused to consider incorporation. A legislative committee appointed to examine the society had reported in April 1784 that

> for any class of men to form themselves into a select Society, and convene expressly for the purpose of deliberating upon, judging of, and adopting measures concerning matters, proper only for the cognizance of the legislative and their determination thereon, or of such other bodies as are known in the constitution, or authorized by the laws of the land, favours of a disposition to become independent of lawful and constitutional authority, tending if unrestrained, to *Imperium in Imperio*, and consequently to confusion and the subversion of public liberty.[30]

As with conventions, Massachusetts legislators could not conceive of a public sphere independent of the state in which diverse groups of citizens participated in the deliberative processes that shaped public opinion. They saw such activities as corruption pure and simple. The committee therefore recommended that the Cincinnati be formally "discountenanced." The General Court defended its right to speak for the people without any mediation from other groups in civil society.

Artisans faced similar hurdles to the Cincinnati in their own efforts to form associations. The Commonwealth's leaders believed that self-created artisans associations threatened the government's ability to manage the economy. Voluntary artisans associations, like guilds in the Old World, would create a monopoly that regulated prices and wages in their own interests instead of the public interest. Since the settlement of the Bay Colony, Massachusetts had disavowed craft guilds in order to preserve communal unity.[31] In 1776 Adam Smith had condemned guilds for promoting "the corporation spirit" and stifling prosperity in order to protect their members' corporate interests.[32] Federalist leaders were therefore determined to uphold the principles of Article Six and protect the common good from self-interested associations.

As in other cities Boston's artisans were organized by craft. At the top of each craft stood master craftsmen followed by journeymen and apprentices. In theory all members of a craft shared the same interests and masters could therefore speak for those below them. With industrialization in the nineteenth century, journeymen would become wage workers with their own class interests. In the late eighteenth century, however, the ideal of craft unity remained powerful.[33] Master craftsmen had tried to organize several times since the Revolution. In March 1785 they formed a mechanics association, drafted a constitution, and boasted more than eighty-five mechanics as members within three weeks. Their officers were the most successful and prestigious craftsmen in Boston, including their first president, Paul Revere. The association laid down general rules to govern master-apprentice relationships. In 1795, and again in 1796, they petitioned for incorporation and were turned down. They would not receive a charter until 1806.[34] According to a later comment by one of their members, Benjamin Russell, Federalists viewed the association as "a combination of sordid Tradesmen" who associated to "extract exorbitant prices for labour and fabricks" at the public's expense.[35]

Whether they were composed of elite army officers or craftsmen, Massachusetts leaders uniformly denounced these self-created voluntary associations and refused them legal privileges. They worried that such associations would divide the community into competing interest groups, each putting its own good ahead of the common good. When Philadelphia's journeymen cordwainers organized a labor union in 1806, one Massachusetts Federalist commented: "Cooperation and concert are so useful to a multitude, pursuing a common end, that we frequently find brethren of the same craft constituting communities, enacting by-laws, and sanctioning them by the severe penalties of ignominy and ruin to the disobedient. These associations frequently contravene the right and are very vexatious to other classes of citizens . . . Wise policy dictates that they should be repressed."[36]

⌒ To FEDERALISTS, conflicts over county conventions exposed the danger of permitting assemblies to speak for "the people," while debates over the legitimacy of the Cincinnati and artisans societies suggested that self-created voluntary associations threatened to divide the community into competing interests. In both cases a minority promoted its own interests and threatened the common good. The emergence of the Jeffersonian Republicans and their political organizations in the 1790s combined the two threats. Republicans' partisan societies not only were self-created but they claimed to represent the voice of the people in civil society.

During the 1790s Republican opponents of President George Washington's Federalist administration formed "democratic societies" throughout the new nation to protest the administration's "monarchical" policies. At the federal level a coalition coalesced around Secretary of State Thomas Jefferson. The nascent Republican Party worried that President Washington, under the influence of Treasury secretary Alexander Hamilton, sought to establish a powerful national government that would not only subvert the autonomy of the states but would also corrupt the republic's founding principles. Hamilton supported a national bank to coordinate economic policy for the nation, proposed incorporating a Society for Establishing Useful Manufactures to encourage inventions and manufacturing, and wanted to use the federal government's credit to tie citizens' financial interests to the new nation. Republicans concluded that Hamilton planned to use monetary policy to lure wealthy Americans into an alliance with the federal government just as the Crown had used sinecures in England. Moreover, Federalists under Washington favored strong ties to Britain over America's Revolutionary ally France. To Federalists, access to British trade was vital to America's well-being. To Republicans, Federalists violated not only America's treaty obligations to France but its moral ones as well. Republicans considered Hamilton's policies as tending toward corruption. It was necessary to organize to resist them.[37]

The formation of the first democratic societies in Pennsylvania in 1793 ushered in two years of debate over the role of associations in public life. Over the course of this debate, Massachusetts leaders would rethink many of their assumptions concerning the relationship between themselves and the people. Although the societies had faded away by 1796, their implications were far-reaching. The societies cleared space for organized partisan conflict and, as parties became a permanent fixture in American politics, it became more difficult for any leader to claim that the Commonwealth was composed of a single harmonious people.[38]

Massachusetts Republicans were composed of various groups, including former opponents of the Constitution and Salem merchants who felt locked out of the channels of power in Boston. Massachusetts Republicans concluded that Hamilton's policies were being duplicated by state leaders. Corporate charters were being handed out as patron-age, and they were equally corrupting as Hamiltonianism. Many Republicans were angry at Federalist unwillingness to charter any corporation that competed with an existing one, effectively insulat-ing Federalist institutions from competition. They accused Federalists of using corporations to serve their own interests. Other Republicans were primarily concerned with the distribution of power. If corpo-rations and the state were co-dependent, leaders' private and public interests could never be disentangled. Instead, in civil society and in the market, a small set of elites could rule over the people with their special legal privileges. Republicans portrayed the Federalist concep-tion of civil society as one that placed the economic, political, and institutional welfare of a small group of elites ahead of the people's, a clear violation of the spirit of Article Six.[39]

Republicans proclaimed that the true voice of the people could be heard in civil society. Challenging the Federalist claim to speak for the people, Republicans argued that citizens must organize in civil society to ensure that leaders continue to promote the common good and not their own. In January 1794 the Massachusetts Constitutional Society proclaimed that under a constitution that protected the freedom of assembly "there can be no necessity of an apology to the public, for an association of a number of Citizens." Already, however, Federalists had condemned the societies and prophesied that they would lead to anarchy. The Constitutional Society denied any revolutionary intent. Their only goal was to protect the people from their elected leaders. Political clubs, they stated in a public address, are "the great bulwark . . . against the artful designs of men." The societies would "harmonize the public mind" by publishing "authentic information."[40] Like the delegates to county conventions in the 1780s, the democratic societies conflated themselves with the people. It can hardly be "treason," they argued, "for *the people* to convene themselves together."[41]

Federalists believed that the clubs' claims to represent the people undermined the rule of law. Once again the central issue was where to locate the people's voice. As one writer explained, if the clubs represent the people, the result would be an impossible *"Imperium in imperio."*[42] Federalists reminded the public that since the people had "freely del-egated *a part* to act for the *whole*" through the principle of represen-tation, "no *individual man*, and no *body of men*, is *independent of that sovereign will.*"[43] Federalists across the nation reiterated, "There is but one order, and that, *the people*." A political club, far from embodying the vox populi, was a "*self-created body*, which . . . has *assumed* the office of *discussing* public measures for other people."[44] While the "clubbists pretend to be advocates for the people," one writer argued, in reality they sought to influence public policy in "a way in which neither the people nor their representatives can have any agency."[45] Like Bowdoin in 1786, Federalists insisted that "the real *Democratic Societies* in *America*, are the people legally assembled in town meetings; and the true *Republican Societies*, are the Federal Government and the Legislatures of the several States."[46] Republicans were a faction that acted as if their own factional interests were the same as the common good. According to the Rev. David Osgood, "The moment a man is attached to [a] club, his mind is not free," but committed to serving a special interest.[47]

The debate over the democratic societies gained a sense of urgency following the outbreak of the Whiskey Rebellion in western Pennsylvania during the summer of 1794. Western Pennsylvania's farmers considered the federal excise tax on whiskey oppressive. They gathered in conventions and assemblies to protest the implementation of an unjust tax. During the months prior to the rebellion, farmers had also engaged in various forms of mob activity to prevent federal agents from collecting the tax.[48] Most Federalists blamed the democratic societies for fanning the popular flames of rebellion. Massachusetts Federalists had already seen parallels between Shays's Rebellion and the probable outcome of the democratic societies' agitation. The Whiskey Rebellion made that conclusion evident to national leaders as well. In September 1794 President Washington announced his intent to use the militia to quell the rebellion. Washington condemned "combinations against the Constitution and Laws of the United States" and exhorted "all individuals, officers, and bodies of men, to contemplate with abhorrence the measures leading directly or indirectly" to the rebellion.[49] In a message to Congress, Washington was even more explicit. He argued that "certain self-created societies" were responsible for the violence.[50]

Washington's words provoked a national debate about the legitimacy of voluntary political associations. In Congress, Republican leader Representative William Giles of Virginia refused to accept Washington's interpretation. Giles noted that many associations were self-created, including Baptist and Methodist churches and, with a clear sense of irony, the Society of the Cincinnati. To link voluntary associations with rebellion was absurd, and to condemn the democratic societies for being self-created was to condemn all voluntary associations.[51] By focusing on the voluntary aspect of associations, Giles helped Americans distinguish between the eighteenth-century freedom of assembly and the emerging freedom of association. Assemblies of the people in their sovereign capacity were quite different from individuals voluntarily associating to promote their own ends, as citizens did every day in churches. Federalist members of Congress were more supportive of Washington's position. Yet even Massachusetts's Fisher Ames, who called the societies a "poison" in the body politic, was willing to accept Giles's logic. The freedom of citizens to get together to discuss politics, Ames agreed, is different from "the abuse of the right" for rebellious purposes.[52]

The Whiskey Rebellion forced the members of the democratic societies to launch a vigorous defense of their freedom to associate. In doing so they distinguished between the lawful activities of voluntary associations and the unlawful activities of the rebels. The societies emphasized their commitment to law and order and accepted their legal obligation to bow to the will of the majority as represented by elected officials.[53] Although the societies had never preached disobedience to the law, the rebellion spurred them to define what constituted obedience. Massachusetts Republicans asked their critics to "produce one instance wherein" the clubs broke a law or violated the constitution. By accepting the distinction between themselves and the people, the Republicans made an important innovation. They acknowledged that voluntary associations in civil society should not claim to speak for "the people." The Pennsylvania society stated that they "felt themselves, as a portion of the people, bound by the acts of the legal representatives of the whole."[54] In December 1794 a Massachusetts writer struck a sarcastic tone, mocking the "wonderful discovery . . . that the Democratic societies are not the People; that is, that a part is not the whole," concluding, "it required no Ghost to announce this *solemn truth*."[55] Whether or not it required a ghost, the societies had initially claimed to speak for the people and only the Whiskey Rebellion and the Federalists' response convinced them to say otherwise.

The Republicans' new position enabled them to defend the freedom of association. "The *right* [to associate]," Republicans adamantly proclaimed, "cannot be destroyed."[56] Challenging the Federalists' corporatism, Republicans argued that the societies posed no threat precisely because they were partial interests. "If," one writer asked, voluntary associations "speak only for themselves, on public measure, where is the crime?"[57] Federalists refused to accept this expanded conception of the freedom of association. They would continue to use state power to limit who could associate and on what terms. Far from legitimizing voluntary associations, the Whiskey Rebellion only reminded them how dangerous these associations could be.

The real victims of the Republicans' rhetorical shift were the rebellious farmers, who found themselves without any powerful political allies. Western Pennsylvania's farmers believed, like the Shays rebels before them, that their proceedings were compatible with the principles of 1776 and Anglo-American plebian traditions of collective action. In the eighteenth century, crowd and mob activity was, as Pauline Maier writes, "an extralegal arm of the community's interest" that checked public policies that went beyond tolerable bounds. During the Revolution, crowds and mobs were often led by prominent local leaders.[58] Following the Whiskey Rebellion, however, Republicans realized that to protect the freedom of association they would have to disavow the farmers. The freedom of association, they concluded, requires obedience to law; older traditional forms of collective action must no longer be tolerated.[59]

The members of the democratic societies were the first to grapple with how the freedom of association could be made safe for a republic. They overcame the limits of geographical thinking and argued for the existence of a public sphere in which voluntary associations could exist so long as their members deferred to the higher authority of the law. Pennsylvania farmers unfortunately found themselves on the wrong side of this evolving intellectual and legal understanding. Yet the idea of a public sphere composed of diverse groups, each representing partial interests, was primarily a response to the Rebellion. It would soon pass as Republicans reasserted their claim to speak for the entire people.

EVER SINCE the publication of Richard Hofstadter's 1969 *The Idea of a Party System*, students of early American history have known that despite the existence of intense and acerbic political conflicts between Americans, Revolutionary-era statesmen despised political parties.[60] One manifestation of this sentiment can be seen in debates over the legitimacy of the democratic societies. Both sides originally sought to speak for "the people" in order to avoid being labeled a partial interest, or, in the word of the time, a faction. Hofstadter argued that within the English Whig tradition—the same one so influential to the Commonwealth's founders—political parties, like corporations, were condemned for promoting their own interests instead of the people's interest. As the influential Bolingbroke wrote, "Parties, even before they degenerate into absolute factions, are still numbers of men associated together for certain purposes and certain interests, which are not . . . those of the community by others."[61] Article Six prohibited legal recognition of such groups. Yet for a brief moment in the early 1790s the members of democratic societies had turned Bolingbroke's formulation on its head, arguing that parties were legitimate precisely because of their partial nature. The democratic societies had made virtue out of a vice.

The moment did not last. Leaders in both parties clung to antiparty ideals. James Sullivan, who would become the state's first Republican governor, hoped that new president Thomas Jefferson would make "every exertion . . . to destroy the lines of party distinctions."[62] In his 1801 inaugural address, President Thomas Jefferson urged Americans to "unite with one heart and one mind." The partisanship of the past decade was, he hoped, the exception rather than the rule. Virtuous republican citizens ought to share the same principles, Jefferson believed. Despite party labels, he reminded Americans, "we are all republicans, we are all federalists." To Jefferson and his Republican allies in Massachusetts, the Federalist Party did not embody this national consensus. They were instead a minority cabal who sought to use their political power to serve themselves at the cost of the people's liberties. In response Republicans had been forced to mobilize in civil society. Now that Republicans were in charge, harmony had been restored between the people in civil society and their government. If American leaders ever again violate the people's trust, Jefferson, mindful of "the blood of our heroes" that had been sacrificed to achieve independence, hoped Americans would "hasten to retrace our steps and to regain the road which alone leads to peace, liberty, and safety." In other words, Jefferson argued that American citizens were naturally Republicans. Federalists had stolen power from the people and it was up to Republicans like himself to restore "the people" to their rightful place.[63]

Federalists also denied the legitimacy of partisan conflict. They believed that virtuous leaders must serve the common good. Republicans threatened to replace committed and honest leaders with popular demagogues like President Jefferson. As late as 1808, John Adams, although he was thankful that New England was "again converted to federalism," believed that neither party could "pursue the true interest, honor, and dignity of the nation" so long as the "selfish spirit of the leaders" came before the common good. In a partisan environment, "party is substituted for that nation and faction for a party."[64] To Federalists like Adams, leaders must place the commonwealth above themselves. Unlike the Jeffersonians, however, Federalists did not argue that the common good emerged from the unfiltered voice of the people. The state must instead play an active role in ensuring that citizens put the common good ahead of their own petty interests.

Despite the rhetoric, the Commonwealth was slowly being undermined by partisan competition. Politicians were forced to acknowledge that citizens did not speak with one voice. A new generation of political leaders would understand that voters, not an abstract common good, determined the outcome of elections. In response both Republicans and Federalists would construct elaborate party organizations to run candidates for office.[65] The disconnect between the intellectual ideal and on-the-ground reality set the tone for early national political conflict. As Ronald P. Formisano writes, "The period from the 1780s to the 1820s possessed a split personality: intensely passionate in partisan conviction but inhibited by powerful anti-partisan assumptions about the nature of politics and society."[66]

WHILE MANY Americans still accept, and even celebrate, the antiparty ideals of the Founders, these same ideals spurred Massachusetts Federalists to limit the rights of voluntary dissenting churches. The American Revolution, it is often thought, did away with religious oppression, especially because of the First Amendment.[67] To Federalist leaders, however, dissenting churches posed no less a threat to the Commonwealth than did other voluntary associations. By forming subcommunities, they divided the citizenry into competing denominations and weakened the unifying power of the public religious system.

The Congregational clergy supported efforts to strengthen the public system. In response Republicans, who supported expanding the rights of religious dissenters, denounced the clergy's involvement in politics. Republicans argued that public churches were supposed to unite the community but, by taking sides in partisan conflicts, the clergy undermined their ability to do so. From the Federalist perspective, however, the clergy were not taking sides in partisan questions but, like themselves, were protecting the common good from factional interests. Ministers were public servants and it was their job to promote the common good. Debates over the public role of the clergy, in tandem with the larger conversation about the rights of voluntary associations, galvanized Federalist support for the public religious system, support that came at the expense of other religious groups.[68]

Baptists and Universalists quickly learned that the legal rights of their churches would be limited under the 1780 regime. Baptists had opposed Article Three of the 1780 constitution because it permitted the state to interfere with religion and, according to them, by definition violated the freedom of conscience. Their fears were warranted. According to Federalists, all citizens should support public churches just as they supported public schools. The growing number of Baptist, Universalist, and in the early nineteenth century Methodist churches threatened the public religious system's effort to promote shared values and the social affections.

Soon after the constitution was ratified, Baptists tested Article Three in hopes that courts would limit its authority and, by extension, the new Commonwealth's reach. In 1783 Baptist churchgoer Elijiah Balkcom sued the tax assessor of East Attleborough for illegally collecting taxes from him to support the parochial Congregational church. At issue was whether colonial laws requiring dissenters to file certificates with local tax assessors remained in effect. Despite Attorney General Robert Treat Paine's arguments in the parish's favor, the court was convinced that the certificate system implied the subordination of one denomination under another in violation of the new constitution.[69] Isaac Backus and other Baptists were exuberant, proclaiming that the decision "overthrows the superstructure of the establishment."[70] Their victory was short lived. In the 1785 case *Cutter v. Frost*, the state supreme court determined that only incorporated churches could be recognized under Article Three. All other bodies were purely voluntary and had no legal existence.[71] The ruling permitted town and parish officials to deny taxes to voluntary churches while requiring Baptist churches to seek incorporation if they wished any legal rights. Baptists had to choose between their commitment to the separation of church and state and their need to hold property and receive their communicants' taxes.[72] The ruling demonstrates the central role access to incorporation would play in defining the freedom of association.

The *Cutter* decision drew on the case of *John Murray v. First Parish of Gloucester.* At issue was whether Murray, a Universalist minister, was ordained properly, and thus whether his church was legitimate under Article Three. Theophilus Parsons, arguing for the parish, claimed first that Universalism was a threat to public morality, a position the court rejected because the state had no authority to determine church doctrine. But this did not mean that the state had to recognize all churches. Instead, according to Murray's lawyer James Sullivan, the court ruled that "no teacher but one who was elected by a corporate society" could receive any tax support under Article Three.[73] The court overruled the *Murray* decision in 1786 but the legal status of dissenters remained precarious. That same year the General Court passed legislation granting corporate privileges to parishes while remaining silent on voluntary churches.[74] On the other hand, at least six court rulings by 1804 upheld the rights of voluntary churches.[75] In practice most dissenters were dependent on the whim of local tax collectors. In 1796, for example, Baptists in Harwich were imprisoned and their property seized to pay religious taxes.[76]

Federalists responded to this legal confusion by imposing clear limits to the freedom of association. In colonial law and practice, church deacons had been considered a quasi-corporation in order to perform the church's earthly functions. In 1786 the legislature passed an act declaring that the residents of every "parish and precinct are hereby declared a body corporate" with all the legal privileges of other corporations.[77] The act's primary goal was to establish new procedures for parochial governance and the duties of parochial officers, yet it made clear that only parishes and other municipal bodies had corporate privileges. In 1800, in an even more draconian measure, the General Court determined that only churches connected with existing "Towns, Parishes, Precincts, Districts and other bodies politic" could receive "their accustomed privileges and liberties," while unincorporated voluntary churches would receive none. In a subsequent clause the act mandated that "every corporate" church in the state must support a minister and could collect local taxes.[78] By explicitly delineating the rights and duties of incorporated churches, the General Court implicitly denied them to voluntary churches.

In 1807 voters gave Republicans control of both houses of the legislature and elected James Sullivan governor. Dissenters hoped that Republicans would grant voluntary churches the same legal privileges as incorporated ones. Despite his own hostility to corporations, Sullivan believed that religious freedom required the state to protect the legal rights of all churches. Sullivan had defended the rights of voluntary churches in both the *Cutter* and *Murray* cases although neither Sullivan nor his party promoted disestablishment. Despite his past support of dissenters, Sullivan, in the words of historian William G. McLoughlin, trod a path "squarely between" Federalists and dissenters. In June a bill was introduced exempting all dissenters from local religious taxes if they belonged to another church "whether incorporated or unincorporated." The proposal would have granted self-created voluntary churches privileges usually reserved for incorporated ones. Federalists labeled it the "infidel bill" and it was tabled until 1808 when, although Republicans remained in charge, it was rejected 127 to 102. Sullivan seems to have made no comment encouraging the bill's passage.[79] Despite its failure, the Rev. William Bentley, a Republican, wrote in his diary that "the increase of sects must eventually make this law necessary."[80]

As of 1808 neither Republicans nor Federalists were willing to accept the intellectual ramifications of permitting voluntary associations—even religious ones—to receive corporate privileges. Republicans, no less than Federalists, remained committed to the principles of Article Six. Although Republicans believed that Federalists used state power to promote Congregationalists' special interests at the community's expense, they did not support the proliferation of incorporated special interests.

Baptists and Universalists refused to accept these limits to their freedom of association. In 1810 the important case of *Barnes v. Falmouth* reached the state supreme court. Thomas Barnes, the Universalist minister of an unincorporated church, sought the taxes paid by his congregants. Instead, Theophilus Parsons, now Federalist chief justice, handed down an eloquent and controversial defense of the public religious system and the threat private associations pose to the common good. Parsons upheld the long-standing doctrine that Article Three applied only to incorporated churches because a charter was a public franchise. Since the collection and distribution of taxes was a sovereign prerogative, it made no sense to permit unincorporated associations to take advantage of the state's taxing power. The state supported churches to better secure "all the social and civil obligations of man to man, and of citizen to the state." Ministers were civil servants. Although no person could be compelled to attend public worship, to confuse attendance with tax obligations "seems to mistake a man's conscience for his money." Religious corporations, whether parishes or chartered churches, must be supported like any other state activity, by taxes. As the preacher of a purely voluntary association with no legal existence, Barnes was denied access to taxes.[81]

By 1810 dissenters were a large voting bloc.[82] Seeking to capitalize on dissenters' frustration, Republicans portrayed *Barnes* as a grave threat to religious freedom. Republicans argued that if every church "must make application to the government for civil incorporation, would not this place it in the power of political rulers to determine whether there should be such a public body in the Commonwealth as a church of Christ?"[83] They noted that in 1780 there had been no incorporated religious societies; the framers could not have intended to limit Article Three's application to corporations.[84] In the wake of *Barnes*, Republicans once again secured an electoral majority and elected Elbridge Gerry governor. In his address to the legislature, Gerry commented:

> A late solemn decision of our Supreme Judicial Court, has limited the right of protestant teachers of piety, religion and morality, to demand the taxes paid by their respective hearers, for the support of public worship, to those of incorporated societies; and has produced a great excitement. This may render, indispensable, an attention to the subject; and further provisions, to encourage, by every possible mean, the liberty of conscience in relation to religious opinion and worship.[85]

Republicans were once again in a position to extend religious freedom of association. Their goals remained ambiguous, however. Not all

Republicans favored the proliferation of corporations. To others, incorporation was the most effective mechanism to protect the religious freedom of association. Governor Gerry embodied this tension. In 1787 he had criticized the Cincinnati for being self-created; now he advocated expanding the number and rights of self-created associations.

⌒ IN THEIR QUEST for the freedom of association, Baptists and Universalists were unwittingly part of a much larger partisan debate over the role of corporations and associations in public life. Before dissenters could earn the freedom of association, they would have to convince leaders that the freedom of association was a right and, more important, that the proliferation of voluntary churches would not destroy the Commonwealth. Their quest would gain support from divisions among elites over how to control the state's corporate institutions in a partisan environment. Until then, religious minorities, like other minorities within the Commonwealth, found their rights limited in the interest of communal unity.

# ~ 3

# The Political Transformation
# of Civil Society

In 1780 Massachusetts leaders had imagined a commonwealth in which all the institutions and associations of civil society served the common good. During the final two decades of the eighteenth century, Federalist leaders had implemented their vision by extending the state's legal, rhetorical, and financial support to public religion, public education, the arts and sciences, and fraternal associations, as well as to corporations committed to internal economic improvement. But even as Federalists increased the state's involvement with and support of civil society, it found its vision challenged by insurgencies with different ideas of civil society. Had challenges to the Federalist conception of civil society remained localized, it is conceivable that the Federalist vision would have taken hold. The rise of sustained partisan conflict during the 1790s, however, destroyed any hope that the Federalist Commonwealth, with its state-dominated civil society, would survive.

In this chapter, partisan debates over corporations serve as a window into how elites thought about associations more generally, whether corporate or voluntary. But to churchgoing citizens these debates were more than just a window. To many ordinary citizens, gaining corporate privileges meant being allowed to form their own churches and other voluntary associations. State legal structures affect how outsider groups gain access to public privileges.[1] Historians have pointed out that marriage can be viewed as a private voluntary association of individuals, but its legitimacy and the legal privileges granted to households require state action.[2] So too with voluntary societies. The state may never have been able to eliminate all undesirable voluntary associations but its laws defined which groups received legal benefits and, by extension, what kinds of associations were considered legitimate. Arguments about the freedom of association revolved around the status of corporations because one of the primary ways that Federalists had determined who should gain access to civil society was by controlling the chartering process.

Federalists had always argued that all the state's associations and corporations were public institutions. When Federalists controlled the state and its corporations they saw little reason to distinguish between the two spheres of activity. Republicans also believed corporations to be public institutions; they worried that private corporations would amass wealth and power and threaten popular self-government. Yet as control of the state's elected offices became more contested, leaders in both parties found it in their interest to abandon the ideals of Article Six in order to maintain control over their own institutions in civil society. Grudgingly, both parties acknowledged that in a pluralistic society it made sense to extend a certain level of legal protection to nonprofit institutions. In a partisan environment, the freedom of association was the best way to protect one's corporate interests from hostile leaders. As party leaders shifted positions over time, they transformed the corporation from a public agency into a private association and granted new privileges to private corporations that were essential to the legal and institutional development of American civil society.

THE FOUR YEARS between 1810 and 1814 were watershed years for civil society in Massachusetts. State leaders confronted the problem of whether minorities should be permitted to control corporate institutions when the state was controlled by a rival majority. And, ironically, it was the Federalists who now found themselves in a minority position and had to adapt their own communitarian ideas to new realities.

In the 1810 election voters gave Republicans control of both houses of the legislature and elected Elbridge Gerry governor. Federalists panicked, worrying about not only their electoral losses but also what untrustworthy Republicans would do to the various institutions Federalists controlled, none more so than Harvard College. When the constitution was drafted in 1780, its framers had hoped that public oversight would guarantee Harvard a central place in the state's civic pantheon. It now meant that a hostile party would have a majority on Harvard's Board of Overseers. Republicans had long complained that Harvard was controlled by Federalist partisans and Unitarian sectarians. Harvard was supposed to be a public institution but it was governed by a religious and, after 1810, a political minority. Republicans argued that for Harvard to serve its public mission it must be controlled by the majority. To Federalists looking for a way to retain their college, the principles of Article Six suddenly became a liability.

It is not clear what changes Republicans would have imposed on Harvard. Some Republicans hoped to replace Harvard's classical curriculum with a modern one better suited for republics.[3] Republicans also resented the Harvard Medical School and the Massachusetts Medical Society's joint monopoly over licensing doctors. Finally, since the appointment of the Unitarian Rev. Henry Ware as professor of divinity in 1805, orthodox Congregationalists, who remained Calvinists and considered the Unitarians' commitment to reason and the sciences dangerous, had been complaining that Harvard was controlled by a minority sect and therefore was no longer suited to educate the state's future ministers.[4]

Whatever may or may not have happened, lame-duck Federalists guaranteed a fight when, in March 1810, they removed the senate from Harvard's Board of Overseers, reduced *ex officio* representation, and added fifteen ministers and fifteen laymen to the Board.[5] By removing public oversight and placing effective control in a self-perpetuating board, Federalists hoped that Republicans would never get a chance to destroy their beloved college. They also raised the specter of a powerful corporation beyond the state's control that promoted its own interests at the people's expense, the very thing they had spent the last three decades trying to prevent.

The 1810 act was difficult to defend. Federalists had long complained about partisanship but, as John Quincy Adams wrote his mother, the act "arose from party motives." Adams worried that absent public oversight, Harvard would lose the political and financial support that came from "attaching the public authority of the

State and the ministers of religion to the welfare of the College."[6]
What Adams admitted privately the Republican press broadcast far
and wide. Appealing to both orthodox Congregationalists and dissenters, Republicans labeled the 1810 act "proof of the most outrageous intolerance."[7] They feared leaving the "exclusive regulation of
this seminary, to a particular body of men" without "some *check* by
the superintendence of the senate."[8] Republicans portrayed Harvard
as under control of a *"hierarchy* or *conclave"* and asked "nothing more
than to restore our College to its former station."[9]

The heart of the debate was whether a public institution could be
controlled by a minority party once it had been voted out of power.
Harvard was a public college and its trustees were public officeholders,
Republicans correctly asserted. Remaining true to the original intent
in 1780, Republicans reinstated to the Board of Overseers the senate
and the six local ministers who had been removed by Federalists.[10]
Although Republicans believed in public oversight, they also realized
that if the legislature could alter Harvard's charter all corporations
risked being altered by future legislatures. This was not a remote fear.
Now that they had come to power, Republican partisans sought access
to corporate privileges long denied them, especially in the lucrative
realm of banking. Like other corporations, banks in the post-Revolutionary era were considered public institutions. Republicans had
long been frustrated that Massachusetts's banks were controlled by
Federalists. After winning the election, some Republicans hoped to
allow all existing bank charters to expire and to replace them with a
single, publicly controlled State Bank. But powerful Republican merchants, namely the Crowninshields of Salem, wanted their own banks.
As a result, Republicans, in a compromise with Federalists, ended up
renewing existing bank charters and incorporating new ones for their
own co-partisans. Because they invested in banking, Republicans had
self-interested reasons to protect corporate charters from subsequent
legislatures.[11] Republicans therefore were concerned about how they
went about reasserting the state's control over Harvard. Rhetorically,
Republicans' heated language pitted "the people" against a dangerous corporation controlled by a minority faction. The details of their
argument exhibit more caution.

The founder of any charitable institution retained some authority
over it, Republicans proclaimed. According to English and colonial

law, the original donor to any charitable institution could visit it to
ensure that its trustees were carrying out the donor's intent.[12] In Harvard's case the state was the donor and had a legal right to oversee the
college's affairs. Therefore the 1810 act must be repealed, not because
it threatened the Commonwealth, but because it unconstitutionally
violated the state's property rights. Some Republicans suggested that
any changes to Harvard's governing board would violate the contract
between the college and both its original and subsequent donors, all of
whom had assumed that the college would remain publicly controlled.
If Republicans were right, all the college's funds were put at risk by the
Federalists' actions.[13] Finally, Republicans argued, the six local ministers removed by Federalists from the Board of Overseers had a vested
right to their offices.[14]

Republican arguments made charters grants of privilege that, once
granted, were unalterable. "The *essence of every contract*, charter or constitution," according to one Republican, "is the primary ground on
which their *inviolability* and *legitimacy* are to be preserved; and every
attempt to *alter, change*, or *weaken* their *fundamental basis* is considered,
not only in law, but in equity, as an unjustifiable act, and can never be
entered as a plea to destroy their original principles."[15] Aware that their
hold on the state was precarious, Republicans sought to reassert public
control over Harvard while ensuring that their own corporate institutions would remain safe if and when Federalists returned to power.
In the process of keeping Harvard public, Republicans weakened the
state's control over its corporations.

Federalists were forced to defend their actions before a skeptical public. Moreover, not all Federalists were convinced that the 1810 law was
the right thing to do. Harvard's president confessed that "the example
of change will do more hurt than the nature of it will do good."[16] Even
more than Republicans, Federalists were committed to unity between
the state and civil society. When pushed to the wire, however, Federalists no less than Republicans were willing to turn to property rights
and charters to keep Harvard under their control.

Federalists had a narrow legal line of defense. The final section of
the 1810 law altering Harvard's charter stated that it would not go into
effect without Harvard's consent, since charters could not be altered
without violating the property rights of corporate proprietors.[17] Harvard corporation member and state Chief Justice Theophilus Parsons

wrote a memorial defending this principle. Parsons was in an awkward position. In an 1806 case concerning the right of a turnpike company to interfere with ancient public roads, Parsons had ruled against the corporation, agreeing instead with his partisan rival James Sullivan that charters must be construed to protect "the existing rights of the public, or individuals." But, Parsons had then added, corporations' rights must also be protected and "cannot be controuled [*sic*] or destroyed by subsequent statute."[18] The same year that Federalists altered Harvard's Board of Overseers, moreover, Parsons would rule in *Barnes v. Falmouth* that churches were public institutions that received corporate privileges only because they served the common good.

Parsons struggled to maintain the balance he had drawn in 1806 between defending corporate charters and protecting the public interest. Lacking the language to differentiate between public and private corporations, Parsons did not make a case for the separation of college and state. Instead, he echoed the Republicans' argument that charters, once issued, granted rights to their recipients that the state must respect. The new members of the Board of Overseers, Parsons wrote, had *"acquired rights, of which they cannot be deprived, but by their own consent."*[19] This admittedly weak position was the best that Federalists could do because they remained unwilling to abandon their communitarian principles and make a case for turning Harvard into a private institution. Thus, despite their disagreements over Harvard's status, both Republicans and Federalists seemed to agree that in a partisan environment the state must respect charters in order to protect minority rights from elected majorities, a major erosion of the principles the Commonwealth's founders had articulated in Article Six.

Federalists' troubles were compounded by a concurrent debate over the Harvard Medical School and the Massachusetts Medical Society's (MMS) control over licensing doctors. The MMS was established in 1781 and the medical school a year later. Initially, relations between the two institutions were choppy, as the first sought to limit access to the medical profession while the second graduated increasing numbers of physicians. Over time they reached a consensus in which either a Harvard diploma or letters from the MMS would qualify a doctor to practice medicine and to use the MMS library. Their political problems began when Dr. Benjamin Waterhouse, Harvard's only prominent Republican faculty member, was passed over for a new professorship of natural philosophy. Waterhouse was a respected physician known for introducing a smallpox vaccine from Europe to the United States. Subsequent conflicts, including a decision to move the medical school from Cambridge to Boston over Waterhouse's objections, isolated him from his colleagues. He became convinced that hostility toward him was part of a more general conspiracy of Federalists against Republicans.[20]

The Republican press supported Waterhouse. Appealing to public opinion, Waterhouse played innocent victim to Federalist tyranny.[21] Blaming Theophilus Parsons and other college officers, he vented against a "medical combination leagued together to bury him."[22] Parsons denied that Harvard was controlled by scheming Federalists, prompting Waterhouse to comment, "We will, however, venture to say, neither the under graduates nor yet the officers of college will be able to read this, without roaring out with laughter!—They know,— we *all* know, that Harvard College is a castle, or fortress, garrisoned chiefly by the disciplined troops of the Essex Junto," a leading group of Federalists.[23] Other critics complained that Federalists refused to grant medical licenses to worthy Republican doctors and "used every means of maintaining their petty despotism" in medicine.[24]

Waterhouse teamed up with other embittered colleagues to propose a new College of Physicians. They petitioned the legislature for a charter, stating that "two literary and scientific bodies produce more than double the advantage of one."[25] Governor Gerry agreed:

Many institutions of this Commonwealth which have promised great benefit to the publick, would have met with much more success, had similar corporations been established. When one only of any kind is permitted, it too frequently happens that a majority of the individuals composing it, indulge their private views and interest, to the exclusion of men of the most enlarged liberal and informed minds; and thus destroy the reputation and all the usefulness of the society itself. The multiplication of such institutions has a tendency, not only to prevent this *evil* ... but to produce a competition, and to promote in the highest degree the utility of such establishments.[26]

On the surface Gerry's comments are quite conventional, tapping into long-standing fears of corporate monopolies. Yet Gerry's comments reflect intellectual change as well. Anticorporate rhetoric usually sought to prevent corporations. Gerry, on the other hand, hints at a different conception of civic life, one in which private institutions proliferate and competition between them ensures that none could abuse their power. This idea would reach full expression among Jacksonian Democrats in subsequent decades.

One Republican connected the dots between various spheres of Federalist corporate activity. Federalists, the writer noted, resisted the new College of Physicians on the same grounds "used by your party in opposition to the State bank and religious bill." Regardless of whether the issue was medicine, banking, or religion, Federalists sought to retain control of the state's corporations even as they lost political power. Federalists, the writer concluded, exhibit "the true spirit of monopoly."[27] Monopolies were dangerous in a republic because they could use their exclusive privileges to serve their interests even if doing so threatened the people's welfare.

After Republicans restored the old Board of Overseers in 1812, Harvard corporation members were uncertain what to do next. They denied the new Board any authority over the college. They contemplated going to court to defend their corporate privileges but decided against it, perhaps because many Federalists were uncertain whether their actions were legal.[28] Republicans decided against incorporating a new medical school, focusing instead on regaining control of Harvard.[29] Harvard's status thus remained in limbo until Federalists returned to power in 1814. Federalists immediately rescinded the 1812 act and established—with the consent of Harvard—a new Board of Overseers that included both the additions they had made in 1810 and, once again, the senate.[30] With Federalists back in power, the close ties between college and state had been restored and Federalists hoped that the previous four years did not set a precedent. To cement the ties between colleges and the state, the General Court appropriated bank taxes over the next ten years to Harvard and in lesser amounts to Williams and Bowdoin.[31] This would be the last time the state would offer direct aid to Harvard. By the time the act expired, the status of the state's nonprofit corporations would be dramatically different.

Neither Republicans nor Federalists were comfortable with the innovations they were making. In fact, in debates over the incorporation of the Massachusetts General Hospital, both parties affirmed their commitment to public oversight of nonprofit corporations. Federalists sought a charter for the new hospital to provide needed services in Boston and clinical education for new doctors. In their original petition all the proprietors would have been Federalists. Republicans added members of their own party and a Board of Visitors composed of the governor, lieutenant governor, speaker of the house, the chaplains of both houses, and twelve self-perpetuating laymen. In the midst of conflicts over banks, churches, and Harvard, Republicans reasserted the importance of public oversight of corporations in civil society. For their part, Federalists were willing to accept public oversight in return for a charter. Both parties accepted that the state should retain some control over corporations.[32]

On the whole, however, Republicans weakened the state's control over civil society despite their worries about powerful private corporations. Their arguments about Harvard's charter exposed their commitment to the sanctity of corporate charters. Republicans also realized that their religious supporters expected Republicans to do something for them. Following *Barnes*, Republicans had promised dissenters that they would protect religious freedom and break the Federalist-Congregationalist monopoly. In order to grant dissenters' churches legal status, Republicans freely incorporated them. During the two sessions under Republican control, the legislature incorporated twenty Baptist and sixteen other dissenting churches. By comparison, the previous Federalist legislature had chartered only one Baptist church and, between 1790 and 1810, an average of only 2.5 Baptist churches had been incorporated each year.[33] By increasing the number of incorporated churches, Republicans gave more citizens a stake in protecting corporations from the state.

In 1811 Republicans went a step further by passing the Religious Freedom Act.[34] The act reiterated the constitutional right of all citizens to choose which church received their religious taxes but added that a church need not be incorporated. The act extended the religious freedom of association to all citizens. Rather than depending on the whim of legislators, judges, or town officials, dissenters could now form their own voluntary religious associations with all the privileges of those incorporated by the state. After 1811 voluntary churches proliferated and could no longer be considered abhorrent. Yet voluntary churches challenged the connection between church and state and, by extension, the state's control over civil society. If any church is legitimate, how could the public religious system claim to represent the moral community? Although Republicans had constructed a sphere of free associational activity, it existed side by side, and in tension with, the parochial system.

⁓ SURPRISINGLY, orthodox Congregationalists emerged among the most adamant supporters of the freedom of association during the 1810s and 1820s. Originally committed to a strong public church, and philosophically committed to communitarian republicanism, their conversion was essential to undermining the public religious system and with it the Federalists' theory of civil society. Just as the Republican victory in 1810 convinced some Federalists that the state might need to extend a higher barrier between civil society and the state, so Federalists' policies in religion convinced their former ministerial allies that their goals may be served better by an independent civil society.

Orthodox Congregationalists did not embrace Jeffersonian principles. Far from it; their decision was purely pragmatic. Orthodoxy had long been fighting the forces of liberal Unitarianism. Liberals sought to reconcile the Bible with the Enlightenment, often by playing down those aspects of the Christian tradition that were not compatible with reason and advanced thinking in the natural and human sciences. Orthodoxy, on the other hand, sought to sustain the Calvinist emphasis on salvation by faith alone. They opposed the liberals' effort to question God's word.[35] As the theological lines between orthodox and Unitarian Congregationalists became more clearly defined, orthodox ministers desired to go their own way. They discovered, however, that the current system compromised their institutional and spiritual needs. The institutional infrastructure of the state would need to change to meet new realities.

In many Massachusetts parishes the majority of church members—those who had experienced conversion and been admitted to full membership—were orthodox, but liberal Unitarians maintained parochial majorities by recruiting uncommitted nonmembers from the parish.[36] In response, orthodox ministers initially sought to separate control of the church from the parish. To the public religious system's Federalist and Unitarian defenders, the church was part of the community and ought to be controlled by it. There should be no distinction between residents of the parish and church members. In theory, however, the distinction had existed since the colonial era. The church was considered a spiritual institution made up of the converted. The corporate status of the church via the parish was simply a way to give a spiritual entity worldly existence. In colonial times parishioners had usually deferred control over church affairs to members. After the Revolution, parishioners increasingly sought a hand in church affairs, especially the choice of a minister.[37]

Orthodox leaders hoped that the courts would enforce the distinction between the parish and the church but the courts proved unhelpful. Instead, orthodox Congregationalists found themselves in a situation similar to dissenters prior to the Religious Freedom Act. In 1812 the state supreme court invalidated a voluntary orthodox church's effort to receive a charitable bequest made to the parish. In the absence of a charter, the court ruled, "there existed no society."[38] That same month in the case of *Burr v. First Parish in Sandwich*, Chief Justice Theophilus Parsons handed down an opinion he admitted "may have a general influence." The court ruled that parishes were municipal bodies and that all residents in a parish who did not belong to another church had the right to elect parochial ministers. To Parsons, ministers were civil servants elected by citizens not the church.[39]

In the next nine years orthodox Congregationalists brought four more cases before the state supreme court and lost every one. Their struggles demonstrate how important corporate law was for ordinary citizens seeking the freedom of association. The most important of the four cases was *Baker v. Fales*, or the Dedham case, decided in 1821. At issue in the case was who should control church property following a schism between orthodox and liberal church members. Orthodox Congregationalists had formed a separate voluntary society but argued that they represented the original church. Liberal members responded that the parish, not the church, controlled all church property. New chief justice Isaac Parker upheld precedent. The parish was a public body and thus citizens "must have the right to have the minister of their choice." Orthodoxy's effort to control church affairs "would tend directly to break up the whole system of religious instruction" because citizens "would never consent to be taxed for support of men, in whose election they had no voice."[40]

As the Dedham case was being decided, debates over the corporate rights of orthodox churches spilled over into Massachusetts's 1820–1821

constitutional convention, called in large part to manage the separation of Maine from Massachusetts after Maine gained admission into
the United States as part of the Compromise of 1820. Dissenters and
some Republicans urged disestablishment. Orthodox leaders had the
more conservative goal of extending the provisions of the 1811 Religious Freedom Act to themselves. Federalist Daniel Webster countered that the state had a responsibility to provide moral education
for all citizens.[41] Unitarian minister Leverett Saltonstall worried that
extending the freedom of association would offer "every inducement
to people to cherish discontent and division." The primary goal of the
1780 constitution, he reminded listeners, was to "promote harmony."[42]
The convention proposed incorporating the provisions of the Religious
Freedom Act into Article Three; but to balance this expansion of the
freedom of association, it also proposed to permit the state to compel
unincorporated churches to support "public teachers," ensuring that
even voluntary churches would be treated as public institutions. In
an awkward compromise, delegates combined the principles of both
*Barnes* and the Religious Freedom Act. In counties with large dissenting populations—Bristol, Worcester, Hampshire, and Berkshire—the
amendment was opposed by large margins, perhaps because it granted
the state new authority over voluntary churches, undermining the very
benefits many citizens desired.[43]

Following the Dedham decision orthodox ministers reconsidered
their commitment to the public religious system. The Rev. Lyman
Beecher, New England's most prominent Congregationalist minister,
urged his colleagues to seek disestablishment rather than to allow their
churches to be controlled by voters. Beecher moved to Massachusetts
from Connecticut in 1826 to take over Park Street Church in the heart
of Unitarian Boston. As a member of the Standing Order in Connecticut, Beecher had vociferously opposed disestablishment there in
1818. Beecher discovered that disestablishment was actually a blessing
in disguise. Despite worrying that the "injury done to the cause of
Christ was irreparable," he concluded that disestablishment was *"the
best thing that ever happened to the State of Connecticut."* "Cut loose from
the dependence on state support," orthodox churches were forced to
rely "wholly on their own resources and on God." Beecher hoped to
bring some of the same spirit of self-reliance to Massachusetts.[44]

As early as 1819, Beecher had condemned the Massachusetts supreme
court's decisions concerning ecclesiology. By allowing the parish to

govern church affairs, Beecher argued, the state wrongly asserted its authority over a religious community and corrupted the church's purity.[45] In additional essays and sermons over the next decade, Beecher reiterated this argument. In 1827 Beecher and his allies established a new magazine, *The Spirit of the Pilgrims*, to advocate the orthodox cause. The magazine argued in favor of legal recognition for voluntary churches.[46] Corporate privileges, orthodox writers concluded, were vital to religious freedom. Without corporate privileges no church "could preserve itself, and its interests," including such fundamentals as determining the terms of communion and who should be minister.[47] By denying orthodox churches corporate privileges, the state reduced them to slavery, every church "bound to some parish, and she must humor the parish in every thing, or she is at once stripped of all." The parish had become the church's "civil master."[48]

Orthodox leaders won an important legal victory in 1822 when the state supreme court ruled that the resident of one parish who joined an orthodox church in a neighboring parish should be released from paying his local taxes. By allowing people to join churches regardless of residence, the court weakened the parish's claim to represent all residents. In a rare occurrence, the chief justice dissented, fearing that the decision might undermine the rationale for the public religious system.[49] Federalists and Unitarians remained convinced that the public religious system was no different from the militia or public schools. The question was how to make men "better citizens" and to "secure the good order and preservation of the government."[50] Orthodox citizens, however, were moving closer to the position of Republicans and dissenters, their traditional opponents. If religious freedom meant the right to form and to control one's own churches, the freedom to associate and to receive corporate privileges must be extended to all citizens.

AT THE 1820–1821 constitutional convention, some delegates also raised the issue of Harvard's status and asked why citizens should tolerate Harvard being controlled by a Federalist-Unitarian minority. They accused Federalists of seeking to place the college "above the control of the State government."[51] This time, Harvard's defenders had a new ace up their sleeve. In 1819 the U.S. Supreme Court had handed down its *Dartmouth College* ruling that corporate charters were protected by the contract clause of the U.S. Constitution. Following *Dartmouth*, one Boston delegate declared, the people of Massachusetts could not "deprive the University of its chartered rights."[52] Delegate Joseph Story, who as a justice on the Supreme Court wrote a concurring opinion in *Dartmouth*, agreed, stating that the Board of Overseers as established in 1814 "was as immovable as the constitution itself."[53] Some concerned delegates wondered what made Harvard a public college if its charter rendered it immune to public control.[54]

The *Dartmouth* decision changed the terms of the debate. Suddenly all corporations, whether old or new, could look to their charters to protect their rights against state legislatures seeking to control them. Ironically, Dartmouth's lawyer was Daniel Webster, who was simultaneously defending the public status of Massachusetts colleges and churches. By the time the case was decided by the U.S. Supreme Court, Webster and Story helped undermine the intellectual case for the Federalist vision of civil society.

The *Dartmouth* decision was not the federal government's first entry into the post-Revolutionary debate over the status of corporations. Congress and the president had long debated whether the federal government was permitted to establish corporations. Under the Washington administration, Alexander Hamilton convinced Congress to incorporate the Bank of the United States, but the decision spurred Thomas Jefferson and others worried about Federalist ambitions to protest. As president, Jefferson argued that the federal government did not have the power to establish corporations, rejecting, for example, Charles Willson Peale's request that Jefferson urge Congress to incorporate Peale's natural history museum. Although all of America's first six presidents desired a national university, Republicans consistently denied Congress the power to establish one. (Jefferson and Congress bypassed this constitutional limit by chartering the U.S. Military Academy in 1802, relying on the federal government's authority to provide for the common defense.[55]) Neither President James Madison nor President James Monroe believed that the Constitution permitted the federal government to incorporate roads for internal improvements, although Monroe pleaded with Congress to pass a constitutional amendment granting the government necessary powers.[56] Following the nation's financial disasters during and after the War of 1812, President Madison did ultimately accept the necessity, and thus the legitimacy, of a national bank, but by the late

1820s the new Democratic Party under Andrew Jackson would raise new concerns about the bank's constitutionality.

The Supreme Court proved more supportive of corporations than did the legislative and executive branches. In *Fletcher v. Peck* (1810) the Court had ruled that a state of Georgia land grant to private investors was a contract that the state must respect.[57] In the 1815 case *Terrett v. Taylor*, the Court extended *Fletcher v. Peck* to corporations.[58] At issue in *Terrett* was whether the Episcopal church of Alexandria, Virginia, could continue to hold its glebe lands despite legislation returning all glebe lands to the public domain. In his opinion for the Court, Justice Story argued that all grants made to the church since the Revolution were binding. Private corporations, Story argued, could lose their property only through misuse or nonuse, both of which required judicial, not legislative, action. Public corporations, which he limited to "counties, towns, cities, &c.," were subject to legislative alteration.[59] As a private corporation in Virginia, the Episcopal church had property rights that the state could not violate without due process. To Massachusetts Federalists, the decision could only have reinforced their commitment to the *Barnes* doctrine. They did not want their state's institutions to be turned into private corporations.

The Dartmouth controversy began in New Hampshire in 1816 when Republicans gained control of the state. Prior to 1816, Dartmouth's president John Wheelock, son of the college's founder, had been battling the college's trustees for control of curriculum and faculty. The trustees and the faculty aligned against Wheelock, leading him to appeal to the then-Federalist legislature for redress.[60] In the interim, the trustees deposed Wheelock and appointed a new president. Wheelock's case was taken up by Republicans and helped bring them to power in 1816. Like their Massachusetts compatriots in 1810, New Hampshire Republicans assumed that their electoral victory would grant them control over Dartmouth. There was one problem. Unlike Harvard, the only *ex officio* representation on Dartmouth's Board of Trustees was the governor; the rest of the board was self-perpetuating, allowing Dartmouth to remain under Federalist control. Republicans decided that Dartmouth's charter should be altered in order to grant the state more control, but doing so meant contradicting arguments made by their party in Massachusetts during the Harvard controversy. Republican Governor William Plumer believed that changing

Dartmouth's charter was justifiable because Dartmouth, like Harvard, was supposed to be a public institution. Like other corporations, Dartmouth had received its charter in return for its public service:

> As it [Dartmouth's charter] emanated from royalty, it contained, as was natural it should, principles congenial to monarchy. Among others, it established trustees, made seven a quorum, and authorized a majority of those present to remove any of its members which they might consider unfit or unacceptable, and the survivors *to perpetuate to the board by themselves the electing of others to supply vacancies.* This last principle is against the spirit and genius of a free government. Sound policy therefore requires that the mode of election should be changed, and that the trustees in the future should be elected by some other body of men.[61]

At first glance Plumer's words appear as nothing more than partisan rhetoric. In a monarchy all citizens were not equal, and monarchies tolerated giving special privileges to certain classes that were not available to others. Democracies could not permit the rise of a noble class that relied on corporations to perpetuate its power. But Plumer implicitly understood a larger change. When Dartmouth was incorporated in the colonial era it had been assumed that all its trustees would be public men. The charter did not make explicit provision for public oversight because colonial leaders did not distinguish between political and corporate offices. Both grew out of their status as members of the colonial gentry.[62] After the Revolution, corporations continued to be seen as public institutions and their officers public servants. When Republicans came to power in 1816, however, a new set of leaders controlled the government. The charter had always intended to place state leaders on the Board of Trustees but did not anticipate electoral democracy. Plumer hoped to formalize a relationship between Dartmouth and the state that had functioned *de facto* before the rise of partisan competition.

    Thomas Jefferson endorsed Plumer's position. In an 1816 letter to Plumer, Jefferson affirmed Plumer's "sound principles," continuing:

> The idea that institutions established for the use of the nation cannot be touched nor modified, even to make them answer their

end, because of rights gratuitously supposed in those employed to manage them in trust for the public, may perhaps be a salutary provision against the abuses of a monarch, but is most absurd against the nation itself.

Jefferson recognized that not everyone agreed that the public should control public institutions. He criticized "lawyers and priests" who supposed that "preceding generations held the earth more freely than we do," and acted as if "the earth belongs to the dead and not the living."[63] In a democracy the people must remain in control of their institutions.

Republicans altered Dartmouth's charter to place it under the state's control by expanding the Board of Trustees and adding a state Board of Overseers.[64] In response Federalists were once again forced to turn to the rights inherent in charters. In doing so they went beyond Theophilus Parsons's defense of Harvard to proclaim that Dartmouth was and had always been a private institution. The legislature, Federalists now averred, could neither alter the charter nor claim the right to visit the college without violating the personal and property rights of the trustees, who had inherited their rights from the original founder Eleazer Wheelock. In granting the trustees legal right to Dartmouth's property, Federalists implied that trusteeship should no longer be considered a civil office.[65]

In August 1816 the new and old boards of trustees convened separately because the old trustees refused to recognize the legitimacy of the new ones. Unable to assemble a quorum, the new trustees dismissed their meeting. That winter Governor Plumer and the Republican legislature reduced the number of trustees necessary for a quorum and made it a crime for any person to act as an officer of the old Dartmouth.[66] The old Federalist board was now backed into a corner and faced punitive fines if they continued to act under the old charter. They decided to fight and, in order to "assert their corporate rights," turned to the judiciary.[67] The New Hampshire supreme court, composed entirely of Republicans, heard the case in 1817. The question facing the court was whether the 1816 alterations to the charter were lawful. If the corporation was public, as Republicans argued, then the state was free to alter it. If Dartmouth was a private college, however, the state had to respect its charter rights. In a partisan context both sides now agreed that there ought to be a distinction between public and private institutions but disagreed on Dartmouth's status.

Chief Justice William Richardson ruled against the old trustees on the ground that Dartmouth's charter had intended to create a public institution. Public corporations, according to Richardson, were those "created for public purposes and whose property is devoted to the object for which they are created." It followed that "the office of trustee of Dartmouth College is, in fact, a public trust, as much so as the office of governor, or of judge of this court." Richardson insisted that Dartmouth's charter must be interpreted according to the time when it was granted. In the eighteenth century Dartmouth would have been considered a public corporation, its property intended for the benefit of New Hampshire's people.[68]

Federalists appealed to the U.S. Supreme Court, claiming that the 1816 act violated the contract clause of the Constitution and thus the principles of *Fletcher v. Peck*. The New Hampshire supreme court determined that *Fletcher v. Peck* applied only to cases where property was at stake and thus was irrelevant to public institutions.[69] The Supreme Court disagreed. Federalist Chief Justice John Marshall wrote the Court's opinion in *Dartmouth College v. Woodward*. Marshall had no doubt that Dartmouth's charter was a contract that vested property rights in the trustees: "In every literary or charitable institution, unless the objects of the bounty be themselves incorporated, the whole legal interest is in trustees and can be asserted only by them." Dartmouth's Board of Trustees had the same legal capacity to take and to use property as any natural person, limited only by the terms of the charter, the nature of the gift, and general laws. The decision clarified the ambiguous status of charitable corporations by embracing the New Hampshire Federalists' definition. A corporation, Marshall asserted, must be considered "an artificial being."[70]

Marshall's opinion reflects the changing status of corporate trusteeship. In the past, corporate trustees and public officeholders had been the same people. With the rise of partisan competition, as William Plumer also understood, corporations were often governed by different men with different ideals than those who governed the state. This point was made before the Court by Daniel Webster. "The case before the court," Webster stated, "affects not this college only, but every college, and all the literary institutions of the country."

"It will be dangerous, a most dangerous experiment," he continued, "to hold these institutions subject to the rise and fall of popular parties, and the fluctuations of political opinions." If charters could be altered whenever a new party rose to power, "colleges and halls will be deserted by better spirits, and become a theatre for the contention of politics."[71] Marshall agreed, and interpreted Dartmouth's charter as if it was granted in the nineteenth rather than in the eighteenth century. Dartmouth's trustees "are not public officers, nor is it a civil institution." Marshall treated the trustees' actions as private in a way that would have been foreign to the trustees themselves a few years earlier. Plumer was correct that the charter intended to include state leaders as trustees, as had been the case until Federalists started losing elections. Nonetheless, Marshall refused to allow older conceptions of trusteeship to creep into his decision. Instead he counterfactually suggested that the trustees had always acted as private individuals overseeing a private corporation. Marshall separated the actions of private civic institutions in civil society from the state.

In a concurring opinion, Joseph Story seconded Webster's and Marshall's claims. Story denied that "if the uses of an eleemosynary corporation be for general charity, this alone would constitute it a public corporation." Story argued that although all charitable corporations promoted public ends, most were endowed and governed by private trustees overseeing private property. "The fact, then that the charity is public," Story wrote, "affords no proof that the corporation is also public." Instead, as Webster hoped, corporate trustees should be granted the autonomy to pursue civic objectives in civil society without worrying about partisan politics. The decision liberated trustees from the state and allowed them to promote civic goods and ideas that might conflict with those of state leaders.

*Dartmouth* effectively razed the Federalists' vision of a civil society managed by the state in the name of the people.[72] Corporations and their officers could now act as private persons. The decision legally separated public and private realms of activity, or the state from civil society. This was more than many Federalists had wanted. Webster's and Story's arguments contradicted their own claims during Massachusetts's constitutional convention. Partisan conflict had forced Federalists to alter the legal status of corporations before they had come to terms with the existence of an independent civil society composed of private associations. Their intellectual confusion can be seen from two articles that appeared in the January 1820 edition of the Boston *North American Review*. One author praised the *Dartmouth* decision for protecting corporate rights, while another article written by future Whig governor Edward Everett celebrated Virginia's patronage of the University of Virginia since education should be publicly supported and not dependent "on single and private bequests of rich individuals."[73] While New Hampshire Federalists retained control of their college, they forced Marshall and other Federalists to recognize that in a pluralistic environment they preferred sacrificing their old ideas about civil society to giving up control of their institutions. They still lacked new ideas to make sense of the legal changes they had helped create.

DARTMOUTH SET a precedent Massachusetts would have to follow. To Republicans, the *Dartmouth* precedent meant that rather than exert greater state control over Federalist institutions they would need a new strategy to prevent powerful now-private and legally protected corporations from threatening the public interest. Although no coherent set of ideas would emerge until the formation of the Democratic Party after 1828, Republicans moved piecemeal toward a new conception of civil society. In 1812, during the controversy over the Harvard Medical School, Governor Elbridge Gerry had suggested that permitting corporations to proliferate and to compete might better serve the common good than allowing one set of people a monopoly.[74] By introducing competition, no institution would be allowed to control the provision of civic goods for their own private gain. After winning elections in 1823, Republicans decided to act on this new idea and incorporated the Berkshire Medical Institution with a five-year public subsidy in order to create an alternative to Harvard. Federalists, in contrast, suggested that even though certain civic institutions were legally private, the common good would still best be served if the state continued to support them by insulating them from needless competition.[75]

Republicans' and Federalists' divergent views came to a head during debates over whether to incorporate Amherst College. Amherst opened in 1821 as an orthodox seminary. Two years later its proprietors asked the legislature for a charter. In a novel and bold innovation, Amherst's proprietors framed their request around the freedom of association. Just as orthodox ministers demanded corporate privileges for their churches as a matter of right, so they argued that Amherst's charter should be granted "not merely as a favor from Government, but as a *right*, which all free citizens, enjoying equal rights and privileges, might under similar circumstances reasonably expect would be granted." The legislature, they continued, "was unquestionably bound to give them a charter—*an instrument acknowledging their rights.*"[76] Federalists rejected the petitioners' argument. The Commonwealth's priority was "to support the institutions founded under their authority." Harvard and Williams would be threatened by competition from the new school. Federalists flatly dismissed the claim that "any body of men" could associate and, "under the plea of claiming equal privileges, demand *as a right* that the government shall lend its countenance."[77]

Following Republican electoral victory, Amherst's proprietors asked again in 1824. This time Amherst's president changed tack and invoked the traditional justification for a charter, "the broad basis of the public good."[78] Amherst's request produced a lively debate in the state House of Representatives. Federalists argued that "multiplying colleges" would "destroy the unity of effort in the public, which is necessary for their success."[79] One pro-Amherst legislator invoked Adam Smith, leading another Federalist to respond that he did "not object to the *principle*, but deny the conclusion which he draws, that another College is needed at Amherst. When he can show me in Smith, or Ricardo, or any good writer upon 'political economy,' that there are not students enough in a country to support one existing College in a *reputable* condition, if you erect another, both will have students enough, and both will thus flourish, by mere force of competition, I shall be ready to hear him."[80] Federalists remained unconvinced that allowing private corporations to multiply and to compete would better serve the common good than a state-managed civil society that favored a few institutions.

Republicans granted Amherst a charter in 1825 with a clause stating that the state made no promise to support the new institution.[81] That same year, a ten-year state grant to Harvard and Williams expired and, despite Harvard's petitions, no more money was forthcoming.[82] The only higher educational institution to receive state aid was the Berkshire Medical Institution, chartered specifically to break the

Harvard Medical School's monopoly.[83] Massachusetts's commitment to its state-run civil society was quickly eroding.

Republican efforts to undermine Federalist monopolies in civil society extended to religion. Baptist minister and Republican legislator Charles Train introduced a House bill amending the Religious Freedom Act to permit Congregationalists to establish their own churches. Train's actions reflected Baptists' long-standing desire to undermine the public religious system, but Train also appealed to disenchanted orthodox Congregationalists. Speaking to both constituencies, Train declared that "the old practice of vesting towns with corporate powers as a parish is one of the greatest evils that ever infested Massachusetts."[84] In January 1824 Republicans extended to Congregationalists the same freedom to associate with corporate privileges granted to dissenters in 1811. The parochial church no longer held a monopoly over Congregationalists in a given territory. The parish, while remaining a municipal body with taxing privileges, would have to recognize the right of all citizens to form their own churches.[85]

⌢ Following their 1823 defeat, Federalists in 1825 joined with moderate Republicans to form the National Republican Party. The union was orchestrated by Daniel Webster and other state leaders. The new coalition nominated Levi Lincoln Jr., the son of Thomas Jefferson's attorney general, for governor and Marcus Morton for lieutenant governor. Lincoln held office for a decade during which Nationals hoped finally to end partisan conflict and reinvigorate the communitarian vision of the post-Revolutionary decades.[86]

Whatever Nationals may have wished, conflicts under Lincoln proved divisive. The number of charters granted to Massachusetts citizens had increased dramatically since the Revolution. Few charters sparked as much debate as Amherst's did, but each charter still had to pass through a legislative committee followed by approval from the legislature and governor. General incorporation laws, and thus the freedom to associate, existed only for libraries (1798), aqueducts (1799), and now churches (1811 and 1824). An 1809 act outlined the general legal privileges of manufacturing corporations but it did not permit new corporations to be formed without legislative action.[87] Despite this cumbersome process, Massachusetts had more than 800 business corporations by 1830, compared to 450 in Pennsylvania and even fewer elsewhere.[88] Oscar and Mary Handlin argue that the proliferation of corporations weakened the link made in Article Six between an act of incorporation and the common good.[89] As Amherst's supporters noted, the more charters that were granted, the more arbitrary and unjustified it appeared when one's own was turned down. By continuing to require special legislative acts of incorporation, however, the legislature could at least maintain the fiction that charters were granted only when they served the common good.

Governor Lincoln sought to strengthen Article Six by limiting the number of new charters. He was not opposed to corporations; in fact, he supported limited liability laws for corporate shareholders and encouraged corporations that promoted internal improvements. But Lincoln worried that the more the number of corporations grew, and the wealth they controlled increased, the more difficult it would be for citizens to manage the common wealth.[90] In 1827 Lincoln did something no previous governor had done: he used his veto to reject the legislature's incorporation of the Salem Mozart Association, which promoted music appreciation. Looking back on Lincoln's veto, Robert Rantoul, an anticorporation Democrat, commented, "If there ever was a harmless corporation, this was one."[91] Lincoln, however, felt it was time to remind citizens that corporate charters should be granted sparingly precisely because charters, once granted, must be forever respected. Lincoln worried that corporations kept resources "locked up from individual control . . . subtracted from the mass of transmissible wealth, to be applied only to the purposes and objects to which it was originally destined." Although Lincoln would ultimately become a Whig, he reflected his father's Jeffersonianism and concluded that the public interest required that charters be granted carefully to prevent a small elite from amassing control of the state's wealth through private corporations.[92]

That same year Lincoln also vetoed the legislature's incorporation of a new bridge over the Charles River. He argued that the new bridge would compete with the existing Charles River Bridge, undermining the benefits the Charles River Bridge corporate proprietors were entitled to from their investments. Even as Lincoln worried about the dangers of too many corporations, he was committed to protecting the privileges of those that already existed. He worried that if the state undermined the privileges of the existing Charles River Bridge, the state would have a difficult time finding private investors for future public improvements. Perhaps it was precisely because he recognized that corporate charters, once issued, must be respected that he was wary of incorporating associations for any and every purpose.[93]

In March 1830 National Republicans opposed the incorporation of the American Temperance Society (ATS) on different grounds from Governor Lincoln's veto. Reaching back to the Revolutionary idea that all corporations must serve the common good, Nationals argued that the ATS, an orthodox institution that had broken off from the existing Massachusetts Society for the Suppression of Intemperance, would divide citizens into competing groups rather than promote social unity. When the ATS petitioned for a charter, a Worcester legislator proposed that the legislature force the ATS to allow any person who paid dues to become a member. State representative Horace Mann supported the amendment in order to prevent the ATS from being controlled by "any sect or party." If orthodoxy were allowed to control the ATS, they would use it to serve their agenda and not the Commonwealth's. In response, the ATS's supporters argued that orthodox citizens should have the same rights as all citizens. All associations, they suggested, were controlled by particular groups or sects. To limit charters on the supposed basis of the common good was an intolerable conceit in a pluralistic society. The question was delayed several months and the charter granted only when the ATS acquiesced.[94]

Finally, in the midst of a growing opposition to corporations from both the Democratic and the Antimasonic parties, the legislature in 1831 passed "An Act Concerning Corporations," limiting the reach of the *Dartmouth* decision. All new corporate charters, legislators determined, could be "amended, altered, or repealed at the pleasure of the legislature, and in the same manner as if an express provision to that effect were therein contained; unless there shall have been inserted, in such act of incorporation, an express limitation as to the duration of the same." The law threatened the protections the Supreme Court extended to corporations in 1819 but the law's actual influence was probably limited. National Republicans and, later, Whigs believed that corporate charters must be safeguarded, not only to protect property rights, but also to encourage investment. If charters were not respected, investors would not support commercial or nonprofit institutions. The law's context was thus most likely politics rather than a sincere effort by the legislative majority to overturn *Dartmouth*.[95]

⁓ DEBATES OVER Amherst, the Mozart Association, the Charles River Bridge, and the ATS, as well as the 1831 Act Concerning Corporations, reflect leaders' uncertainty over the state's relationship to civil society following *Dartmouth*. While partisan conflict had convinced both parties that the state should respect the distinction between private corporations in civil society and public corporations founded and governed by the state, this position was one that both parties backed into, not always intentionally, in response to immediate interests. Party leaders had learned that in a pluralistic society corporate rights must be protected, but the arguments they had used to defend their positions were often made in the heat of the moment. Under the National Republicans, the state seemed to be drifting between accepting the post-*Dartmouth* reality and seeking to revive the communitarian agenda of the Commonwealth's founders.

In such a state of confusion, new ideas were needed. Political and religious conflict had fomented significant legal change but ideas had not kept up. During the second party system, Democrats and Whigs would develop more coherent rationales to justify or limit the influence of the *Dartmouth* decision and its protection of private nonprofit corporate rights. By then, however, elite party leaders no longer controlled the debate. Instead, as the situation at the top changed, so did the situation at the bottom. If the political transformation of civil society made it legally possible to separate civil society from the state, orthodox ministers, angered by the increasing reticence of political leaders, would unleash an even more important social transformation of civil society.

# ~ 4

## Forging a Grassroots Public Sphere

As MASSACHUSETTS's political elite struggled to come to terms with partisan conflict, ministers were transforming civil society from below. Frustrated by larger changes in American society, ministers launched a crusade to reform American society and culture. Rather than turn to the state, they now turned to ordinary citizens. They combined a Jeffersonian emphasis on the people with the Federalists' communitarian moral principles. In essence, ministers borrowed from the Jeffersonian toolbox in order to combat the rise of Jeffersonian liberalism. They realized that state governments were becoming increasingly hostile to church-state alliances and, moreover, that those alliances had more costs than benefits. Organizing citizens, they discovered, could be a more effective way of mobilizing public opinion in favor of specific policies. Ministers spurred America's first massive grassroots organizational efforts and greatly expanded the number of voluntary associations just as political leaders were breaking up the legal basis for a state-controlled civil society.

It is well known that the United States witnessed an explosion in the number of voluntary associations during the 1810s and 1820s, but how this happened is not understood. This is not because voluntary associations have lacked historical interest but because the spread of associations is usually seen as the product of something else, such as modernization[1] or democratization.[2] Other historians have looked at voluntary associations to understand the rise of the middle class and middle-class ideology rather than how Americans learned to use them for political purposes.[3] The origins of America's voluntary tradition merit more investigation. Associating was a new form of technology. Ministers, whether in churches or as traveling missionaries, taught ordinary Americans what sociologist Elisabeth S. Clemens calls new "organizational repertoires," or skills and techniques for using associations to shape public affairs.[4] Forming associations and corporations had once been the preserve of urban elites. Ministers taught ordinary citizens how to do the same. Political historians have explored how party leaders developed new tools to inspire voters to come to the polls and to identify with particular parties or candidates.[5] Historians of the book have investigated how the circulation of texts spread knowledge that was reinterpreted in local contexts.[6] Building on these two approaches, this chapter will answer how and why ordinary people became involved in voluntary associations.

Ministers were unwitting agents of democratization by giving citizens who may have already believed that they had a right to participate in politics the means to do so. Before associations could become useful, people had to be taught how to use them; they had to learn new civic skills.[7] The men and women who joined voluntary associations defined new roles for citizens in a democracy. In learning how to volunteer, ordinary people learned to think and to act as citizens. They ensured that citizenship in a democracy would not be confined to voting and to office holding. The revivals of the Second Great Awakening converted thousands who then desired to reform the nation. People who had never before joined an association signed up to fight immorality and to distribute Bibles and tracts. In time some of these brave citizens would join the fight against slavery and in favor of female suffrage. While religion provided the ends, voluntary associations provided the means.[8] The social transformation of civil society dramatically altered America's political culture. Citizens in civil society now defined many of the issues before voters, from prohibition to the expansion of slavery. At the time of American independence, civil society was not preordained to become a vibrant zone for independent civic activity. Although few Americans were volunteers in 1776, by the 1830s it could truly be said that America was a nation of joiners.

POLITICAL HISTORIANS rightly argue that political parties were one of the most important institutions through which ordinary people, mostly white men, engaged in politics. In their need to gain votes, parties transformed individuals into citizens. Parties relied on the press and on such local activities as banquets, parades, and organized militias to foster a sense of partisan identity among their followers. As citizens read newspapers or participated in local partisan events, they came to think of themselves as vested and engaged members of the political nation. By the antebellum era, intense two-party competition spurred increased voter turnout as parties recruited greater numbers of the people to win elections and, in turn, as more and more citizens came to see elections as critical moments in their collective lives.[9]

By bringing thousands of Americans into the political realm and by helping them take on new political identities, parties both took advantage of and encouraged Americans' confidence in their equality, turning what Alexis de Tocqueville called Americans' "passion for equality" to political purposes.[10] Parties also transformed the American public sphere by encouraging public debate and by helping citizens realize their right to participate in it. Because so much good research has already been done on this topic, this chapter will take the democratizing influence of parties for granted and focus instead on the less well known but equally important role of evangelical voluntary associations in bringing about a similar transformation for an even larger number of Americans. Evangelical ministers actively recruited both men and women, reaching deeper into the citizenry than did parties.

The success of voluntary associations was itself due to political parties and their role in American governance. During the antebellum era political power was held and contested by parties. Thanks to an expanded electorate, parties were also closely tied to their constituencies. Although party leaders retained a degree of autonomy from voters, and parties both reflected and shaped voters' preferences, the relatively close and direct links between parties and voters meant that grassroots organizing to alter public opinion could directly influence the halls of power.[11]

Massachusetts ministers turned to voluntary associations at first to further the Federalist cause. Following the Dedham case, however, orthodox Congregationalists became frustrated by the Federalists and their National Republican successors' efforts to control the public religious system, which, they determined, favored minority Unitarians over orthodox Congregationalists. They became convinced that voluntarism better served their interests than did state support.[12] As important, many ministers, inspired by the Second Great Awakening, thought it possible to create a truly Christian nation. They knew it would not be easy, however. The separation of church from state in most parts of the nation was proof enough that old assumptions about the role of religion in public life were withering. The market revolution and the rise of party politics brought about even greater challenges. They worried about the individualistic libertarian world they saw developing in Jacksonian America. Ministers reminded Americans that Protestant Christianity requires citizens to place their duties to God above their own interests and greed. Ministers hoped to reinforce the teachings of the church at a time when many Americans seemed more interested in getting ahead in the market.[13]

Orthodox ministers were the most active early organizers but they were not alone. Unitarians were involved in early charities and patronized such elite institutions as Harvard and the Boston Athenaeum. They were also active in Bible, temperance, and peace societies and essential to the antislavery movement. Both black and white Baptists supported moral and antislavery societies. Although Methodists were important organizers in other states, their numbers were smaller in Massachusetts. In places like the manufacturing town of Lynn, where they had a sizeable presence, Methodists organized moral reform and temperance societies. Many orthodox-controlled state and national associations also included diverse membership at the local level. Cooperation between denominations was not always possible, however, and orthodox Congregationalists, Baptists, Methodists, and Unitarians each formed their own missionary, tract, and education societies. Interdenominational cooperation encouraged the growth of mass national movements, while rivalry spurred church leaders to establish their own associations. These dual tendencies helped increase the overall number of associations.[14]

Associations spread by emulation, each group following the example of others. One might argue that voluntary associations, once their form and function were understood, proliferated by what sociologists Paul DiMaggio and Walter Powell call "institutional isomorphism." This isomorphic process had two stages. First, ministers employed the corporate form in new ways; they adopted what had been a state-created structure and made it the institutional basis for American civil society. In the next stage, the success of initial voluntary associations encouraged more and more citizens to organize themselves, ensuring that the corporate form of the voluntary association reached deep into American society.[15]

Turning to voluntary associations, ministers embraced a new vision of the role of citizens in society. Rather than defer to political and social elites, ministers argued that each citizen has a moral obligation to get involved by joining an association. These efforts would take on cosmic proportions as ministers and their middle-class congregants formed and joined thousands of voluntary associations.[16] From moral reform to antislavery, Massachusetts citizens learned to use associations to frame the political agenda. The Revolutionary generation had assumed that the common good would be mediated through the state and its leaders, but orthodox ministers discovered the power of organizing beyond the state's reach. Many ministers anticipated the dawn of a new age. According to Lyman Beecher, "By voluntary efforts, societies, missions, and revivals . . . [ministers] exert a deeper influence than ever they could by queues, and shoe-buckles, and cocked hats, and gold-headed canes."[17] The common good, another suggested, would be secured not by the state but by citizens acting through "societies for promoting domestic and foreign missions, bible societies, tract, moral, education, and charitable associations."[18] By the 1820s, when one minister proclaimed the present is "the age of benevolent associations," the proliferation of associations was considered a sign of both Christian and civic progress.[19] In civil society orthodox leaders hoped to recruit an army of converts. As public opinion changed, political leaders would be forced to follow. Before voluntary associations could exert their full influence, however, citizens would have to learn to join.

No person better expressed the hopes ministers assigned to voluntary associations than Bowdoin College's president Jesse Appleton. Speaking before an 1813 audience in Bath, Maine, Appleton explained that "when several persons coalesce for a particular purpose, that purpose is more likely to be attained, than when pursued by individual efforts." Not only could associations channel the limited efforts of individuals but, more interesting, voluntarism produced a greater commitment on the part of individuals than they held before joining. When people join an association "for a particular object, that object rises in their estimation. From the circumstances of their union, it acquires a degree of importance, and excites an interest, previously unknown." Appleton echoed his contemporaries in expressing the novelty of association, noting that prior to the nineteenth century, "the methods, most suitable for this purpose, were unknown." The present age, however, provided clarity to the Bible's claim that "two are better than one; because they have a good reward for their labour" (Eccl., iv., 9).[20]

Since few Massachusetts residents had much experience with associating, ministers had to develop new tools to spread how-to knowledge. Perhaps the most important tool was the annual report.[21] On its own, the annual report was not new. Officers in corporations were often asked to prepare annual reports for their members or shareholders and, as in the case of banks, to submit reports to the legislature exhibiting their activities and accounts. As the number of voluntary associations increased, and as they became increasingly dependent on donations from middle-class supporters, however, their most important constituency was no longer the state government nor a small set of elite proprietors. Instead, associations needed to report their achievements to a broader public. As reports circulated more widely, they took on a common form. Most included a narrative of the past year's activities and a treasury report. Reports listed donors and members to give them a sense of ownership in the larger project. The narrative combined celebratory language to show success with frustration in order to justify requests for more money and effort.

Ministers relied on annual reports to teach people about associations. Ministers read them before their congregations, educating listeners on how associations were structured and what they did. In time, reports helped create translocal communities united by print.[22] The earliest reports to serve this purpose in Massachusetts were those of the Royal Humane Society and other British societies. Reading these reports, gentlemen in Boston, Salem, and Newburyport were inspired to establish similar associations. This knowledge was in turn spread throughout the state by way of the new groups' reports. Through its reports, a new organization made its work and worth known to all citizens. As the Rev. Abiel Holmes remarked in an 1804 speech before the Massachusetts Missionary Society, "With what diligence and success it has prosecuted this benevolent and pious design, its annual Reports may inform you."[23] In speeches throughout the state, commentators noted the importance of the annual report to spreading information.[24] The directors of the Hampshire Missionary Society believed that if ministers read the society's annual report before all the congregations in the county, ordinary people would be inspired to make contributions.[25]

When the Massachusetts Society for the Suppression of Intemperance first met in 1813, its directors were unclear how best to use their annual reports. At their first annual meeting, they said little about distributing the report, noting only that it was "submitted & accepted" by the Board of Directors. By their third annual meeting in 1815, however, the directors voted to print two thousand copies of a circular address along with "as many of the Report as the committee with the advice of the Board shall think proper" in order to encourage residents across the state to establish their own temperance societies. The following year, the directors voted to print another two thousand copies of the address, this time with the annual report attached, and, importantly, to have twelve copies sent to each auxiliary society connected with the Temperance Society and two to each town in the state, one of which was for the parochial minister and the other for that town's social library. The number of reports grew continuously throughout the next ten years. The directors wanted the reports "circulating as extensively as may be," illustrating the central place the annual report held in their effort to create a network of societies pursuing a common agenda. By 1826 the Society was printing six thousand copies of its annual report and asking clergymen of every denomination to read it before their congregations. The Society's annual reports did much more than simply report facts to a board of directors. The circulation of annual reports publicized the temperance cause and encouraged others to establish their own societies.[26]

The spread of information about associations served two important purposes. The first was a general increase in knowledge about associations, vital to the creation of the auxiliary system (see below). In addition, associations relied on annual reports to "operate upon the members, as encouragement to proceed, with promptness and vigour, in the benevolent work, in which they are engaged."[27] Addressing their reports to a public audience, directors hoped that they could "with a better grace call upon our fellow citizens for their cooperation."[28] Annual reports were central to the success of associations, as measured by increased membership and donations in both local and statewide associations. No wonder the directors of the Middlesex Bible Society were happy to report at their fifth meeting that "the fourth annual report has been published, and, in conformity with the desire of the Society, expressed at the last meeting, circulated with care throughout the county."[29]

The circulation of annual reports was supplemented by their republication in newspapers and magazines. The annual report was a new form of literature which contemporaries considered worthy of review and discussion. Jeremiah Chaplin believed that the extracts of letters from missionaries "published in our Magazine" provided proof of the Baptist Missionary Society's successful work.[30] The directors of the Temperance Society placed an advertisement in newspapers informing readers of their decision to deposit copies of their annual reports in libraries across the state.[31] Following its 1833 annual meeting, the directors instructed their secretary to "publish the proceedings of the meeting in the daily newspapers."[32] Some magazines and newspapers also worked in tandem with associations to promote a cause. The American Board of Commissioners for Foreign Missions relied on the *Panoplist and Missionary Herald* to communicate news about its missions and activities and, in turn, used profits from the magazine to support its own activities.[33] In 1820 the *Panoplist* urged members of "the Congregational Churches of New England to form themselves into auxiliary societies."[34] Temperance journals were also gainfully employed throughout the nation to support the work of local associations. Other journals, such as the orthodox Congregational *Boston Recorder* and *Spirit of the Pilgrims*, and the Unitarian *Monthly Anthology* and *Christian Examiner*, all provided excerpts from the publications of, and celebratory discussions of, their favored institutions. In other cases magazines provided a site for debate. Both the *Christian Disciple* and *Christian Examiner* used reviews of annual reports to critique orthodox associations. Magazines and newspapers therefore provided an important means both to spread the knowledge of associations and to spur discussion about their proper role in society.[35]

Annual reports were central to creating trust between associations and their increasingly dispersed constituencies. In earlier charities annual reports were presented at meetings attended by members who knew each other well. The reports of new statewide and national associations were distributed across vast distances, and donations had to be collected from people directors did not know. The challenge of doing so should not be underestimated. In an era before most people were familiar with associations, citizens had no reason to be confident that money donated to an association in Andover or Boston, much less New York City, would be used appropriately. In some cases incorporation provided an answer. One of the first acts by many associations was to seek a charter and to publish it either separately or in the next year's annual report. Charters created legal obligations that directors hoped would build confidence. Directors of associations also sought to convince possible donors that their money would not be misused by pointing out that their accounts were readily available in their annual reports. The Hampshire Missionary Society reassured its public, "We aim that you feel every security for our faithfulness," and thus "[our] accounts will be communicated for public information."[36] Responding to rumors in the press that charities misused their funds, the Rev. Benjamin Wadsworth said such a statement would be "utterly groundless" if applied to the Society for Promoting Christian Knowledge. Each year, Wadsworth noted, the treasurer gives a statement of accounts, is audited by a committee of the directors, and "a regular report of the proceedings is annually published, setting before the world to what purpose every cent has been expended."[37] One speaker went so far as to say that the public circulation of voluntary associations' accounts made them "better guarded" than the treasuries of "states and kingdoms."[38] Hyperbole aside, there can be no doubt that the distribution of annual reports helped develop trust between associations and a broader public.

In addition to their annual reports, the directors of a new association would often publish a circular address to the public, which included the constitution of their society and an account of the society's origins.[39] The initial steps in establishing an association were to draft a constitution, elect officers, and establish regulations. By publishing constitutions, directors provided others a model to follow. The constitutions of most societies were remarkably similar because new organizations usually copied the example of an existing society. Constitution making was itself an important new skill, and organizers sought advice when forming new associations. When the Rev. Jedidiah Morse decided to establish the Massachusetts Society for Promoting

Christian Knowledge, the nation's first tract society, he wrote to the secretary of England's Religious Tract Society seeking information on its constitution and asking for copies of tracts that could be easily redistributed.[40] Young Federalists gathering to form Washington Benevolent Societies in towns across the state wrote the Boston society asking for "a copy of your Constitution as a model for ours."[41]

As knowledge about associations grew, buttressed by the celebratory rhetoric of their boosters, people throughout the state started to form their own groups. Most followed the same process, publishing a constitution, a list of officers and members, and a circular address.[42] The Massachusetts Missionary Society was soon followed by missionary societies in Northampton and Hampshire. The Evangelical Missionary Society of Worcester and Middlesex counties acknowledged not only the existence of other societies, but their desire "to emulate the pious zeal of those, who have gone before us in the benevolent work."[43] The establishment of the Massachusetts Bible Society in 1809, itself modeled on its British and Philadelphia counterparts, spurred the formation of Bible societies in Maine, in the city of Salem, and in Berkshire, Bristol, Hampden, Merrimack, and Middlesex counties.[44] The new societies admitted that they followed "the noble example of the capital of the Commonwealth."[45] A similar process was followed by other associations, with a state-level organization, often based in either Boston or Andover, providing an example for others.

By the 1830s the circulation of annual reports, journals, newspapers, and constitutions had familiarized large segments of the population with voluntary associations, how they were structured, and how to organize them. This knowledge, though relatively simple, was not before widely known. As more people learned how to form associations, the number of associations increased dramatically, spreading from urban centers into the hinterland. By familiarizing people with associations, annual reports and other publications laid the groundwork for the development of an evangelical "Benevolent Empire" that linked associations across Massachusetts into statewide and national networks.

〰 ONE OF THE most important developments of the early nineteenth century was the creation of the auxiliary system, which tied like-minded associations together around parent institutions at the state or national level. The auxiliary system, like the annual report, was a new technology whose utility, once learned, was pursued with fervor.[46] Since few people volunteered in the eighteenth century, it was not common practice for people in small towns and rural areas to come together in associations. This ignorance helps explain why speakers before various associations were constantly using celebratory language, reflecting not only their own excitement but also their hope that their words would spur others to follow suit. Before they could follow the example of others, however, ordinary people had to learn what to do when forming an association. Annual reports and published constitutions initially provided much of this information, but the development of the auxiliary system was an important catalyst to spreading this knowledge throughout the state and nation.

Most associations formed before 1810 functioned more or less autonomously and their numbers were limited. In the 1810s and 1820s, however, state and national organizers decided that a federal system composed of a central, or parent, institution, working in tandem with hundreds of local auxiliaries, would better promote the ends of their associations. This push for a system of like-minded groups was not preordained. Local attachments and jealousies worked against the creation of statewide, much less national, networks. It was also not immediately clear that charitable and benevolent work could best be undertaken by central associations. While associational leaders usually celebrated the formation of new associations, they did not initially seek to tie them together. Once they did, the center-auxiliary system significantly affected both the spread of the knowledge of association and the ability of associations to raise revenue to support their activities.

The initial impetus for centralization was the logic of association itself. If individuals could accomplish more in association than alone, imagine what a union between associations might accomplish! In addition, organizers may have been inspired by the federal structure of the republic, which combined local, state, and national units.[47] The orthodox founders of the New England Tract Society in Andover in 1814 hoped that by "directing and combining all the energy and activity which can be brought into operation, in this cause," they could create an institution "on a plan of operations sufficiently extensive and permanent" to meet the population's needs.[48] Likewise, the directors of the American Education Society, which provided scholarship aid for needy ministerial students, reminded the public that their goals were large and daunting "and would doubtless baffle the attempts of individuals, or a few local unconnected Societies." Although local education societies had been established throughout the state, the directors argued that "experience sanctioned" their confidence that "a large, well informed, active Society commands more of the public confidence, and is more efficient, than many small Societies."[49]

The real push to establish a network of like-minded associations in Massachusetts began in 1813 with the formation of the Massachusetts Society for the Suppression of Intemperance. The Temperance Society was explicitly designed to "hold the place of a parent institution, and to operate in a systematic connection with auxiliary societies." Moral societies had been formed in various parts of New England, but the establishment of the Temperance Society marked the first attempt to develop formal interaction between these associations.[50] Similarly, the New England Tract Society hoped "to aid [other] such societies wherever they are formed" and "to multiply their numbers" until "the salutary influence shall be felt in every village of New England."[51] Both the Temperance and the Tract societies' directors believed that that their work would be furthered not by centralization alone, but by cooperation between center and periphery.

By 1820 a host of state, regional, and national institutions had been established. In addition to the Temperance Society and the New England Tract Society, Massachusetts's Congregational leaders helped establish the American Board of Commissioners for Foreign Missions in 1810, and renamed the Tract Society the American Tract Society in 1823, illustrating the expanding reach of its operations. Lyman Beecher and his allies also established the American Temperance Society in 1826 and the General Union for Promoting the Observance of the Christian Sabbath in 1828. Other important institutions at the national level included the American Bible Society, the American Home Missionary Society in New York, and the American Sunday School Union in Philadelphia. Together these organizations created a network of evangelical associations seeking to promote common ends across the nation.[52]

One of the first institutions to organize at the national level was the American Bible Society. The initial impetus came from the directors of the New Jersey Bible Society. When the Massachusetts Bible Society first learned of the plan to create a national institution, they resisted it.[53] Supporters of the national institution responded that although the United States could boast 108 independent Bible societies, without union their efforts were duplicated and wasted.[54] In 1816 delegates from many regional societies met in New York City to organize the American Bible Society. Neither the Massachusetts nor the Philadelphia Bible societies sent any official representatives. In attendance, however, was Jedidiah Morse, who helped draft the new society's constitution and returned home an ardent supporter. In their address to the nation, the directors of the American Bible Society echoed the emerging belief that "concentrated action is powerful action" and proposed the creation of an auxiliary system modeled after that of the British and Foreign Bible Society. Local auxiliaries should organize themselves and adopt constitutions in which they would agree to supply any surplus income to the national institution "after supplying their own districts with the Bible." Like the Temperance and Tract societies, the American Bible Society sought to balance local needs with those of the national institution.[55] Perhaps this moderate stance proved sufficient for the directors of the Massachusetts society, which in 1817 reported "satisfaction" at having joined the national network.[56]

More likely, the directors of the Massachusetts Bible Society may have learned a lesson that their peers across the nation were also discovering. Extending the logic of association to a greater scale created formal pathways to channel money into larger pools governed by central boards. State and national institutions could play an important part in encouraging new associations and, if successful, these new associations could raise large amounts of revenue for their parents. The directors admitted that immediately after the formation of the national institution about two hundred new members had joined the Massachusetts Bible Society "and very considerable donations have been obtained." Rather than allowing the national society to bypass them, the directors decided that they should act as "the medium of aid, from this quarter, to the American Institution," collecting and distributing the money of their state's auxiliaries.[57] Localities were indeed quick to respond to the American Bible Society's requests. The directors of the recently established Berkshire Bible Society noted that before the national society, many Bible societies had been formed, but "in a detached and unconnected manner." This led to "a want of system in their exertions." Following 1816, however, the new national institution had placed "under its banner a great number of auxiliary institutions." Observing this phenomenon, Berkshire's citizens were roused from their own "inactivity" to establish an auxiliary to aid the national cause.[58] It soon became clear to the Massachusetts Bible Society's directors that auxiliaries united around parents would, in the words of a Bristol Bible society, be "the small rivlets" that would unite into "Larger Streams."[59] Having learned the advantages of union, the Society quickly joined the trend toward centralization.

Deciding to establish parent institutions was not enough; there also had to be a sufficient number of auxiliaries located throughout the state, region, or nation to support the system. As Theda Skocpol argues, it is a myth that voluntarism in the nineteenth century was localist. This myth, according to Skocpol, owes more to our own romanticization of "small-is-beautiful" than to the facts. As she rightly points out, translocal organizers were central to the proliferation of associations.[60] Although some parent institutions united preexisting local societies, others, such as the General Union for Promoting the Observance of the Christian Sabbath, were established first. Regardless of which came first, all parents subsequently encouraged the formation of new children. One of the Temperance Society's primary goals was to make "arrangements for the formation" of local societies. The directors urged their members to "exert their influence" in their respective locations. They also asked each local association to submit annual reports to the parent institution.[61] The New England Tract Society provided a set of guidelines by which existing local moral societies could become auxiliary members. They also hoped that "where no such society exists—a Tract Society may be formed." Knowing that the knowledge of association was limited, the directors enclosed a sample plan of association.[62] Other Massachusetts associations followed suit. The executive committee of the Massachusetts Peace Society proposed the establishment of "Branch Societies" in 1817, and also included a sample plan to aid local organizers.[63] By 1833 the New-England Anti-Slavery Society had organized twelve local auxiliaries to collect signatures on petitions and to build local support for abolitionism. Between 1832 and 1833 the society grew from seventy-two members to more than two thousand, and spurred the establishment of local societies throughout New England. By the end of 1834 there were ninety-seven local societies, most of which were auxiliary members.[64] Even more impressive, the American Temperance Society claimed five thousand chapters and a million members by 1835.[65] Directors of parent associations learned that the success of their cause depended on grassroots support.

In addition to circulating addresses and plans, parent associations hired agents to travel around the nation organizing auxiliaries. By 1817 the American Board of Commissioners for Foreign Missions had hired eight agents for this purpose.[66] Between 1820 and 1830 the American Bible Society hired more than forty agents. By organizing meetings and having face-to-face contact, the Bible Society's agents served as human faces to a distant institution.[67] The American Education Society's constitution charged its Board of Directors with the responsibility of hiring agents to make annual collections from churches and to establish "auxiliary Societies in towns, counties, and distant regions," as well as female cent societies and young men's associations.[68] Whether paid or not, agents, along with missionaries hired by denominational missionary societies, were quite successful in teaching citizens how to associate. For example, during a two-month trip in 1820 the Presbyterian minister Ward Stafford from New York organized twenty-two marine Bible societies in New England's port towns.[69] Using hired agents the American Anti-Slavery Society boasted more than thirteen hundred auxiliaries and a quarter of a million members around the nation in 1838.[70] While many of these associations may have been short lived, they taught their members new civic skills.

Directors of parent associations quickly discovered that the auxiliary system could raise more revenue than relying solely on elite subscribers and their membership dues. While elite benefactors never stopped playing an important role in supporting American evangelical associations, more and more revenue was generated by local auxiliaries. In 1814, for example, the American Board of Commissioners for Foreign Missions took in $1684.17 from local foreign missionary societies and $940.65 from other charitable associations, making up the major part of that year's income.[71] By 1817 the directors of the American Board noted in their annual report that they had received aid from 47 foreign missionary societies, 116 other societies (usually female cent societies), and 136 children's education societies, about 300 altogether. These numbers are staggering enough considering that before 1810 there were few voluntary associations, but even more so when one imagines the excitement of the Board's directors watching their treasury grow.[72] Other associations had similar experiences. In dire need of income, the directors of the American Education Society issued an appeal to the public to form associations in 1818. The following year they reported that their prayers had been answered and that "new societies were formed; new benefactors were secured; and old societies and benefactors increased their contributions."[73] County associations also relied on auxiliaries in the towns. The Religious Charitable Society in Worcester consisted of seventeen local branches by 1814, while the Hampshire Missionary Society drew from twenty-two local female societies.[74]

At the national level, the American Bible Society's annual reports document the income generated from local auxiliary societies. Local societies contributed either by donating directly or, more often, by purchasing Bibles printed by the Society for local distribution. By circulating its annual reports widely, every Bible society in the nation could see how it compared to others, and how its monies were being used by the national institution. By 1820 the Middlesex County Bible Society's proprietors believed that "the prosperity of the National Institute depends essentially upon the assistance afforded by its Auxiliaries."[75] This is exactly the message the American Bible Society wished its auxiliaries to receive. National organizations embraced ever-increasing numbers of local associations during the 1820s and 1830s; by 1837 the Bible Society claimed more than nine hundred auxiliaries, the American Board counted sixteen hundred in 1839, while the American Tract Society included over three thousand.[76] By promoting the formation of thousands of auxiliaries, the directors of state and national associations had tapped into a hitherto unknown resource composed of largely middle-income persons around the nation.[77]

To encourage middle-class people to form and to join auxiliaries, state and national leaders had to convince them that their local efforts were worthwhile. Relying on celebratory language, directors of associations made it clear that the charitable work of ordinary people was vital to success, and by reporting even the smallest donations in their annual reports they exhibited the importance of every dollar raised. No group received more attention from state and national directors than women, whose local associations soon became one of the most important wells for associational energy and income.[78] One of the earliest associations to discover the importance of women in Massachusetts was the Hampshire Missionary Society. In a circular address of 1803, the trustees circulated a plan to form a "FEMALE ASSOCIATION, for the purpose of raising a fund, for the purchase and charitable distribution of the Holy Bible and other pious Christian writings among the needy inhabitants of the new settlements of the United States." They were clearly not the first to do so, for they acknowledged that "various Associations of a similar nature are, already, instituted by the virtuous of your sex in New-England."[79] The female society quickly became an important source of annual revenue. In 1805 they supplied $280 to the male society, out of a total of $960, and by 1816 the annual contribution had grown to roughly $600, composing about 30 percent of annual donations. It is no wonder that the directors of the Hampshire Missionary Society "anticipate[d] growing benefits to the missionary cause from the future activity and zeal of pious females." The female society, in turn, was itself the parent of several local societies, allowing it to tap into even more sources of revenue.[80] In 1824 the Rev. Elias Cornelius acknowledged the important role of women in carrying out the work of the Salem Society for the Moral and Religious Instruction of the Poor. "The Society," he stated in a pamphlet, "have been greatly assisted by the exertions of benevolent females." Not only had women "rendered very important personal services" such as instructing Sabbath scholars and running the female adult school, "but they have formed themselves into an Auxiliary Society, which affords annually a valuable addition to the funds."[81]

Charitable women throughout the state also formed "cent societies" to raise revenue for charitable causes. Some, such as the Brookfield Female Bible Cent Society, were tied specifically to a particular cause, while others contributed more generally. Cent societies reflected the culmination of two trends in Massachusetts voluntarism. The first was the realization that small donations added up; the second was that women were a valuable source of energy and money. Speaking before the members of a Brookfield society in 1815, Thomas Snell reminded them that "however small the particular items may appear, many thousands of dollars have been collected and appropriated to the most benevolent purposes" through the work of cent societies. "Indeed," he continued, "the fair sex, promise to furnish more pecuniary aid in the country than the gentlemen."[82] Female societies provided much income to the American Board by 1814, and were the largest source of revenue for the Massachusetts Society for Promoting Christian Knowledge in 1816.[83]

Women raised money in various ways. For elite women, of course, surplus income was not a problem, and such early associations as the Boston Female Asylum, just like their male counterparts, were dependent on the largesse of wealthy benefactors. The cent societies and the associations auxiliary to the new parent associations established during the 1810s and after, however, were often composed of middle-class women who might have enough surplus income to pay their local membership dues but not enough to make substantial donations.[84] These women contributed time. They gathered in sewing circles or other such groups to produce items for sale. According to the Female Reading and Charitable Society in Worcester's first parish, about fifty "Young Ladies, divided into several Associations" would gather twice in every month. While one woman read, the others "engaged in some useful employment," the profits of which were "devoted to the objects of the Society." Through these labors and "an annual subscription," the women of the society supported a "heathen child" as well as the "wants of several poor."[85] In another Massachusetts town, according to the orthodox journal *Panoplist*, the members of a female auxiliary society would gather to braid straw, providing an annual income of fifty to sixty dollars. The *Panoplist*'s reporting once again demonstrates the importance of print to spreading the knowledge of association. By meeting together, middle-class women, especially young women, could raise money for a cause.[86]

As more auxiliary associations were established, greater numbers of people became familiar with their form and practices. Soon it became common for people to organize and to join associations, especially those linked to a state or national effort, deepening the reach of the new voluntary culture. The novelty of volunteering is reflected in a statement by the Auxiliary Foreign Missionary Society of Boston. Noting the recent proliferation of foreign missionary societies into "almost every town in New England," the Society admitted that it would take some time before the officers of these new organizations would become "familiar with the routine of their duties, and acquiring a facility in their discharge." Volunteering was a new experience, and the basic duties of running an association needed to be learned by both officers and members. Desirous of success, they hastened to add that "every individual connected with any association should, as soon as possible, become familiar with the duties incumbent upon him or her in the stations they respectively fill."[87] By publishing model constitutions, circular addresses, and annual reports, organizers were optimistic that the skills of voluntarism could be effectively employed by middle-class persons in union with state, regional, or national parents.

⌇ THE NUMBER OF voluntary associations of all kinds grew by 760 percent in Boston, and by more than 5,000 percent in the rest of Massachusetts and Maine between the 1760s and the 1820s, far outstripping the state's population growth, and this was just the beginning.[88] The emergence of new state and national networks inspired thousands more people to enter their local public spheres but also significantly eroded older versions of localism. Instead of the town being a single corporate entity, citizens were broken up into multiple groups, each pursuing different objectives. While there were many overlapping memberships, class, religious and political divisions also resulted in distinct memberships in different associations.[89] National networks tied the members of local voluntary societies into larger and larger groups of like-minded persons. These groups formed "imagined communities" linked through print culture across space. By reading annual reports and magazines, ordinary people thought of themselves as members of new communities.[90] Local citizens imagined themselves sending missionaries to India and Ceylon, struggling to spread the Word in the American West, and alleviating the sufferings of black slaves. This work was made tangible by their interaction with agents and by their own local activities. Joining meant coming to meetings, listening to speeches, distributing Bibles and tracts, and thus performing locally the work that one supported nationally and globally. To understand the significance of this change, we must take seriously Thomas Bender's claim that communal identity is composed of the "network of social relations in which the individual is embedded."[91] As more Massachusetts residents came to think of themselves as members of the temperance or antislavery communities, their civic activity was premised on their commitment to a cause as much as to a place.

Despite breaking up local communities into translocal like-minded groups, the auxiliary system reinforced the importance of meaningful local activity. Local associations had to be governed, annual meetings had to be held, and Bibles needed to be distributed. Local voluntary labor was not simply a function of the directives of national leaders, but existed in cooperation with them. Although state and national parents were vital to organizing citizens in towns across the state, the auxiliary system functioned because citizens had local work to accomplish. In turn, citizens gained a new commitment to their own communities that was reinforced by their membership in translocal networks.[92]

The continued vitality of localism can be seen in the problems faced by the American Education Society (AES) and the American Bible Society. In 1818 the AES explicitly challenged the "*locality* of feeling, which limits the view of good men to their own vicinity." Localism, the directors complained, is "unfriendly to the accomplishment of any great, public object, where concentration of efforts is required." While local auxiliaries should be encouraged, the AES considered their only function to be fund-raising, and thought that they should relinquish control over beneficiaries, a privilege the local societies had long enjoyed.[93] The American Bible Society confronted similar issues. The Bible society movement was one of the most successful of all the evangelical charitable efforts, in part because its auxiliary system was based on both local and national efforts. As the Massachusetts Bible Society well understood, local societies provided "a convenient opportunity to a large and valuable class of our fellow citizens, to contribute their mites, and gratify their benevolent and pious wishes, who cannot afford to become regular members."[94] Initially, the American Bible Society followed this model. In their 1816 circular address, the directors underscored the importance of local Bible distribution and asked only that the surplus income of auxiliaries be donated to the national institution. By the late 1820s, however, the American Bible Society had invested heavily in printing and a hired staff, and their livelihood depended on the income generated by donations from and book sales to local auxiliaries. These societies were often unreliable, and the Bible Society turned to paid agents, who urged localities to be more vigilant, and carried Bibles and other books for sale throughout the nation. Increased financial complexity required both the American Education Society and the Bible Society to move beyond the auxiliary system, shifting toward a more bureaucratic and centralized form of organizational management.[95]

Bureaucratization made local voluntary work less meaningful, and as major charities came to rely on their local auxiliaries primarily to raise funds, local volunteers proved less willing to play a passive role. As the Massachusetts Bible Society had noted, the success of the system depended on meaningful activity at the local level in combination with a strong central institution. Increasingly, middle-class women and men turned their attention to other causes in which their labor would be considered more productive. While the number of charitable societies (including missionary and Bible societies) increased rapidly after 1800, their numbers were declining by 1820. In their place arose associations committed to new reforms, from moral, temperance, and sabbatarian societies to, by the 1830s, antislavery.[96] Each of these new movements required local activity, whether to mold public opinion, to maintain the propriety of their own members, or to lobby to enforce or to change laws at the local, state, and national levels. The auxiliary system was satisfying only when local volunteers had a stake in the parent societies' efforts, both through their imagined participation via annual reports and magazines and by more concrete local activity.[97]

⌒ VOLUNTARY ASSOCIATIONS transformed how ordinary citizens conceptualized their civic roles and obligations. In the eighteenth century members of charities had been elite public trustees. By contrast, the new associations were composed of middle-class members with little prior public standing. The shift from elite trusteeship to mass membership did not completely eradicate older ideas, however. Although the earlier charitable associations gained their public legitimacy from the status of their members, they endowed membership with a civic role that was now claimed by middle-class joiners. As a result, the "office" of member allowed ordinary people to enter the public sphere as citizens. Engagement with civic life became a direct result of joining rather than the other way around.

Organizers accommodated the new members by changing the terms of membership. In a hierarchical society that valued consensus, joining an association in the decades following independence often required the assent of the entire membership. In this way the number of members could be limited, and access to an association was reserved for those persons whose public status could not be challenged. In Salem, the Female Charitable Society's constitution mandated that "one dissenting vote" would preclude the admission of a new member. Other associations had similar rules. The constitution of the Massachusetts Society for Promoting Christian Knowledge required that potential members first be nominated by a member of the elite Board of Directors. The nominee would then need the approval of three-fourths of the Board before he could be reported to the next meeting of the whole society, at which time three-fourths of the current members must also acquiesce.[98]

As voluntary associations spread into the small towns and rural areas of the state, it became more difficult to erect such high barriers. Although "town fathers" served the same role at the local level as their more elite counterparts in Boston or Salem, small-town associations, at least on paper, made membership contingent on dues paying rather than on complex rules. When the Religious and Charitable Society of Worcester was established in 1812 as an auxiliary to the American Board, it opened its membership to "every person, male or female, who shall subscribe to the constitution." Rather than limit membership to those who had prior standing in the community, membership could be had for a small fee. Similarly, the Bible Society in Bristol encouraged "any inhabitant of the county of Bristol" to join.[99] The elite office of public trustee was being replaced by the democratic office of member.

Following the development of the auxiliary system, state, regional, and national associations encouraged the shift from trusteeship to membership. When the directors of the Massachusetts Peace Society proposed a plan to create branch societies in 1817, they also decided that members of the branches be *de facto* members of the parent institution.[100] Two years later the Middlesex County Bible Society determined that any person who paid their annual dues should enjoy the privileges of membership.[101] When the Massachusetts Society for the Suppression of Intemperance was established in 1813 its original constitution required that new candidates be nominated and approved by two-thirds of the members present at the annual meeting. In 1817, as the number of temperance and moral reform societies was expanding rapidly across the state, the society voted to amend its constitution to permit "any person" to become a member simply "by subscribing the

Constitution, and paying Two Dollars for the use of the Society."[102]
In 1833 it decided that the officers of all county auxiliaries were to be
*ex officio* members of the parent society.[103] Offices once reserved for an
elite few were now made available to most citizens.

In addition to easing membership rules, parent societies also sought
to increase their interaction with auxiliaries. One method of doing
so was by circulating annual reports and other publications. In these
reports parent societies listed their members, either as individuals or
as auxiliary societies, as well as the contributions of each. In 1819 the
directors of the Middlesex County Bible Society proposed that all persons who pay their annual fee "shall be recognized and published in
the Annual Report as such, and enjoy all the privileges of members."[104]
In the Massachusetts Temperance Society's 1832 annual report, the
directors not only celebrated the "the formation of State, County,
Town, and Village Temperance Societies, comprising, it is said, a million of members" throughout the nation, but decided to publish a list
of all member associations. In 1824 the Society voted to provide each
member with a copy of one of its tracts and, perhaps due to internal
divisions within the temperance movement, they voted in 1833 to provide each member with a copy of its constitution.[105] The writers of
annual reports also tried to provide readers a sense of participating in
a larger cause. The American Education Society asked its auxiliaries
to submit reports of their activities so that "a complete view of the
combined operations of the Society in different parts of the country
may be given in its Annual Reports." They even hoped that "a representative from each Branch, and County Auxiliary Society, [would]
attend the Annual Meeting of the Parent Society, and, when practi-
cable, that a representative from the Parent Society attend the Annual
meetings of such District Societies."[106] Through their representation
in membership lists, treasurers' reports, and narrative accounts, the
members of local societies gained stronger attachments to the parent institution. As the proprietors of the Baptist Missionary Society
of Norfolk well understood, the reports were now published "for the
benefit of its members."[107]

Middle-class women were probably the most affected by changing ideas of membership. While there had been a few female societies
before the 1810s, these were largely limited to elites and many were
adjunct to male societies.[108] These early associations provided valuable

lessons about what women could contribute and were an impetus for
bringing more women into voluntary work. The Boston Female Asylum and the Salem Female Charitable Society were among the first in
Massachusetts to rely exclusively on women's labor. By forming associations, elite women were claiming a role for themselves in the culture of public trusteeship. When the Boston Female Asylum sought
incorporation in 1803 the legislature suggested that the Asylum have
a male Board of Trustees, which the proprietors of the Asylum successfully resisted.[109] Such state paternalism should not detract from
the new role elite women were coming to play in public life. In 1803
Thomas Barnard noted that although in the past women "encouraged
charitable associations by their persuasive efforts to soften the harder
hearts of men . . . They, at the present time, *associate themselves*, for the
purpose."[110] By the 1830s, Barnard's comments were certainly accu-
rate. In 1838, when the Boston Female Anti-Slavery Society decided
to sponsor lectures by the Grimké sisters, one officer of the society
commented that while the men thought that the lectures were "altogether in their hands," women "stepped in and informed them that we
should *transact* this business and they, finding we were not to be guided
by their superior wisdom, gave in." Women were entering the public
sphere on their own terms.[111]

Even as women were gaining new identities as citizens, their civic
roles were premised on their gender. Aiding their entry into public
life was the belief that women were naturally inclined toward certain
charitable activities. Both the Boston Female Asylum and the Salem
Female Charitable Society provided aid and education to female
orphans, a role that many commentators believed was "the proper
business of women," an extension of "the feelings of mothers."[112] Both
men and women discovered that the benefits of association could be
effectively carried out by women and that "virtue, far from being
exclusively appropriate to men, is peculiarly adapted and ornamental
to the *female* sex."[113] While this language sounds sexist to the modern
reader, it helped women overcome the objection that voluntary work
"'*far out step'd the modesty*' of sex!"[114] In their speeches before female
associations, male ministers reminded women that it was both their
natural role and their Christian duty to participate in voluntary work.
The affinity between women and social reform was reinforced by the
feminization of the Congregational church. Women had long been

the majority of church members in New England. Following 1800, women composed from 65 to 75 percent of new members. The revivals of the Second Great Awakening, the continued exclusion of women from formal politics, and the spread of female voluntary associations all contributed to this increase. Local associations were often based in churches, so becoming a member of one often led to joining the other.[115] Ministers therefore went out of their way to encourage women to become even more active. By the 1820s, reform work was an integral part of a middle-class woman's identity.[116]

The transition from trustee to member did not always go smoothly. By joining associations, women took on roles once reserved for elite men. Joining also granted women a stake in public affairs that, over time, led some to embrace such radical causes as antislavery and female suffrage. For some women, volunteering at the local level was satisfaction enough. Moreover, by proclaiming their right to join as an extension of their status as virtuous women, many women reinforced the importance of the separation of female citizenship from male citizenship, making it less likely for them to urge political equality.[117] For others, many of whom were Quakers and Unitarians, limits on female civic activity were frustrating.[118] As Lori Ginzberg argues, although women initially entered the public sphere to pursue goals compatible with their own feminine virtues, the very fact that they served as members and officers in associations meant that they were assuming roles traditionally reserved for men.[119] In response to the increasingly public agitations of the Boston Female Anti-Slavery Society in the 1830s, one newspaper writer expressed regret that women "should have come forth from their retirement—from the holiness of the fireside, the protection of their household goods—to mingle in scenes like this."[120] The orthodox General Association of the Massachusetts Congregational Churches, which generally supported female voluntarism, condemned activists as "a shame and scandalous offense against propriety and decency."[121]

The growth of abolitionism in the 1830s brought these tensions into the open. The abolitionist movement brought together not only men and women but blacks and whites. Abolitionists therefore challenged the ability of elites to control who could speak in the public sphere and what they could say. Debates over the status of women within the movement were intense. As Theodore Dwight Weld wrote to Angelina

Grimké, "Why! folks talk about women's preaching as tho' it was next to highway robbery—eyes astare and mouth agape." As radical as he was, Weld urged the Grimké sisters to focus on abolition instead of women's rights, but, as Grimké responded to Weld and to John Greenleaf Whittier, even abolitionist ministers tried to silence women. One minister in Groton, Grimké wrote, "said, he would as soon be caught robbing a hen roost as encouraging a woman to lecture."[122]

In 1839 female delegates were first admitted as equals to the annual convention of the American Anti-Slavery Society. A year later, with the support of William Lloyd Garrison and other radicals, Abigail Kelley was elected to serve on the society's governing committee. A substantial number of delegates responded by walking out to form a new society. Even more famously, Elizabeth Cady Stanton and Lucrecia Mott were angered when they were refused access to the floor at an 1840 antislavery convention in London. They returned to the United States ardent supporters of equal rights and were the primary organizers of the Seneca Falls Convention in 1848. Learning to think and to act as citizens, advocates of female suffrage demanded full membership in the civic community.[123]

Other women disavowed the emerging suffrage movement, believing that the moral authority of their activities depended on the separation of civil society from the state. By being denied the vote, women embodied this separation. (For the same reason, some male abolitionists such as William Lloyd Garrison also refused to dirty their hands with politics.[124]) Political parties compromised purity of principle for electoral success, compromises that could be avoided in civil society.[125] As radicals increasingly demanded equality for women both within the abolition movement and without, more moderate antislavery advocates abandoned the Massachusetts Anti-Slavery Society to form the Massachusetts Abolition Society. The Boston Female Anti-Slavery Society also divided in 1840. Moderate women formed the Massachusetts Female Emancipation Society, auxiliary to the Abolition Society, while radicals resuscitated the older organization.[126]

Whether pro- or antisuffrage, participation in voluntary associations politicized women. Women came to think of themselves as citizens and learned the organizational skills necessary to enter public life. The conflicts signified not only the tensions created when thousands of new women (and men) entered the public sphere as citizens for the first time, but also that the knowledge of association could be turned to new uses beyond the control of any one group.[127]

Similar questions existed about the civic role of African Americans. The northern African American community relied on diverse associations to provide social, economic, and political support at a time when they were kept out of the nation's formal institutional and political life. Out of necessity, African Americans formed a rich network of charities and aid societies earlier than many white Americans. When it came to reform, they adopted the associational form to support such causes as temperance and antislavery.[128] African Americans had organized the antislavery Massachusetts General Colored Association in 1826 to oppose the colonization movement. When William Lloyd Garrison established the New England Anti-Slavery Society in January 1832, it was unclear how whites should relate to blacks. Garrison took the radical option, embracing the right of the General Colored Association to become auxiliary to his organization in 1833, and subsequently allowing blacks to become full members. A handful of African American women were already members of the Boston Female Anti-Slavery Society.[129]

Although African Americans were better off in Massachusetts than in other parts of the Union, they were not considered full participants in public life. Even in mixed associations whites often tried to maintain separation. In Boston a white female antislavery advocate expressed "dismay" when a black member sat in the white section of a meeting hall. In Fall River a female antislavery association almost disbanded when African Americans tried to join.[130] With the exception of Garrison and his radical followers, most white middle-class citizens, and many blacks themselves, preferred to allow African Americans to continue to form parallel but separate associations.[131] The African American community also divided over the propriety of reform. Some black Baptists, like some of their white Baptist brethren, believed that personal salvation and piety were more important than social activism. As more and more African Americans joined the reform movement, Boston's black churches, especially the prominent African Church, divided over the relationship between religion and reform.[132]

Young white men and women were also directly affected by the emergence of voluntary associations. On college campuses, in small towns, and in growing cities, ministers reached out to youth. Youth were more likely to be converted during revivals and, unlike their parents, to grow up familiar with voluntary associations. Many young people first learned the skills of voluntarism by joining children's auxiliaries.[133] Volunteering was also one of the few legitimate social activities for middle-class youth. When young women gathered in associations or in sewing circles, they served their god's cause while socializing with friends. Ministers also targeted young men. Throughout the nineteenth century, young men left their rural and small-town homes to find work in the city where they faced new temptations, including gambling, liquor, and sex, without the moral security of the families and churches they left behind. Evangelical ministers believed that voluntary associations would promote moral order and provide young men more pious leisure activities. Young men aspiring to middle-class respectability agreed, and joined moral reform associations, self-improvement societies and, in the 1830s, lyceums.[134] By 1833, dozens of young men's societies had been established in Boston alone.[135] Not all young men responded to the evangelical call, turning instead to Masonic lodges, militias, or fire companies, where a boisterous cult of manhood gave them a sense of belonging.[136]

Some men also became active reformers. Young men, often from poorer backgrounds, could receive scholarships from the American Education Society (itself dependent on the donations of local male and female education societies) to attend Andover or other seminaries. Upon graduation they might be hired as missionaries for the American Board or the American Home Missionary Society, or as agents for the American Bible Society, and travel around the country or world spreading the Word and encouraging the formation of new societies. Later in life they would themselves become the members and patrons of charitable and reform associations.[137] The rising generation—both men and women—considered volunteering an extension of citizenship.

⌒ BY THE LATE 1820S, the voluntary association had become the primary tool citizens used to make their voices heard in the public sphere. American leaders confronted the consequences of the changing landscape of American democracy during the Antimasonic movement of the early 1830s. Middle-class citizens turned their organizing efforts against political elites, forcing party leaders to respond to the demands of ordinary citizens. To many observers, Antimasonry made clear both the democratic possibilities and the dangers of the social transformation of American civil society. Antimasonry was a new kind of political movement made possible by the new civil society. The majority of Antimasons were self-organized middle-class men and women with little prior political experience. They originated in western New York's "burned-over district," where ministers had trained citizens in the tools of grassroots organizing. Citizens relied on their new knowledge to foster a popular movement that symbolizes the fundamental transformation of America's political culture.[138]

The immediate origin of Antimasonry was in what might have otherwise been an obscure and forgotten incident but, thanks to citizens' new civic skills, served as the impetus for a mass political movement. In 1826 in western New York, William Morgan disappeared and many concluded that he had been murdered by Freemasons. Morgan, who had been a Mason, had decided to expose the fraternity's secret traditions, despite having sworn himself to silence. A Masonic mob attempted to burn down Morgan's publisher's press. Morgan himself was arrested on specious grounds and, after his bail was mysteriously paid, he was released and never heard from again. Although some claimed to have seen Morgan in Canada, and even Turkey, many other Americans concluded, perhaps with reason, that the Freemasons had murdered Morgan in order to protect themselves from public scrutiny.[139]

Organizing "people's committees" in towns throughout the North, Americans demanded that the Freemasons be held accountable. They were convinced that the Masons, an elite association, were setting themselves up as a shadow government. In Masonic lodges, Antimasons claimed, America's elite politicians made secret deals that were beyond the public's control. If anything, the new civil society was premised on enhancing popular control over politics; the Masons seemed to challenge the new civil society's democratic ideals.[140] That Masons were often tried before jurists and juries composed of fraternity members, and that the few who were convicted for Morgan's kidnapping received very light sentences, was proof that Masons "HAVE ERECTED THEMSELVES A DISTINCT, AND INDEPENDENT GOVERNMENT."[141]

Antimasonry was more than a political movement; it was a moral crusade. The movement's evangelical middle-class base believed that Masons were an obstacle in their goal to create a more Christian

America.[142] By the 1820s, Freemasonry had expanded beyond its Federalist elite roots and now included many middle-class persons as well as Jeffersonian Republicans. Working together, leaders of both parties hoped to limit the influence of Christianity in American public life, Antimasons averred. They attacked Masonic lodges as places "where men of all religions, or of no religion" took secret oaths together. They compared Masonry to "popery" because it kept "men in ignorance."[143] Antimasons considered Freemasonry "as anti-Christian as it is Anti-Republican."[144] Speaking before an Antimasonic convention in 1832, Massachusetts orthodox minister Nathanael Emmons condemned Freemasonry as the "darkest and deepest plot that ever was formed in this wicked world against the true God, the true religion, and the temporal and eternal interests of mankind."[145] Lyman Beecher was initially neutral toward Antimasonry, worrying that the issue would prove too divisive. In July 1831, as the movement gained traction among his followers, he came out in support before an Antimasonic meeting, supposedly bringing tears to the eyes of his listeners.[146] Beecher's support connected Antimasonry to the evangelicals' other reform movements.

Antimasons moved quickly into politics. They ran local candidates for office in 1829 and 1830. In 1830 they also held a national convention in Philadelphia and county nominating conventions throughout Massachusetts. In 1831 and 1832 they ran orthodox congressman Samuel Lathrop for governor, and in 1833 they almost undermined Whig control of Massachusetts by running John Quincy Adams.[147] There are clear links, moreover, between orthodox Congregationalism and Antimasonry's electoral success in Massachusetts. Between 1828 and 1832, the years of Antimasonry's growth, National Republican Governor Levi Lincoln was weakest in the orthodox towns of the west. In fall 1831, and again in 1832, Antimasons carried Hampshire County, while making large inroads in Franklin County. Antimasonry was also strong in the southeast, such as in Bristol County, which had a large Baptist population and was home to the Hopkinsian (ultra-Calvinist) orthodox Congregational Mendon Association. In the 1833 elections Antimasonry had its greatest victories, especially in the southeast. However, their strength weakened in the west. Both responses might be due to the fact that Antimasons that year chose to run Unitarian Adams for governor instead of Lathrop, an orthodox Congregationalist who supported disestablishment. Adams, while capable of pulling in more votes, also might have been less desirable to many orthodox voters.[148]

The new movement demonstrated that ordinary citizens, by organizing in civil society, could challenge elites' control of political life. In neighboring Vermont, Antimasons were for a short time the largest political party and captured the governor's office. Not surprisingly, both Whigs and Democrats reacted to Antimasonry with hostility. Leaders in both parties resisted the new movement not just out of interest but also from principle. Members of the new Democratic Party argued that no group in civil society should be allowed to force its agenda on the people. They accused Antimasons of seeking "to introduce a despotism as complete, odious and oppressive, as that of Ferdinand or Don Miguel."[149] National Republicans, reorganizing themselves as Whigs, argued that impassioned popular movements threaten democracy by promoting the "terrors of proscription." In a democracy, they argued, "opinion shall be free from political power as well as legal restraint."[150] Party leaders suggested that by forcing their goals onto the political agenda Antimasons threatened democracy itself.

Antimasons defended the right of ordinary citizens to shape public opinion. As Steven C. Bullock argues, Antimasons transformed the public sphere by placing "public opinion and conscience at the heart of their thinking."[151] One writer commented on critics' claims that the movement is "monstrous" because it seeks "to deprive masons" of political office. But, the writer wondered, was this not democracy in action? "If any class of citizens wish to bring about what they consider an important reform, if they wish to have laws passed to remedy what they consider political evils, have they not a right to be fairly represented whenever they hold a majority of votes?" The issue was one of "numbers," namely which party could gain the support of "public opinion."[152] The Antimasons' national committee defended voters' right to "denounce" men and principles they consider dangerous to society and to use the ballot box to reform society.[153] Each voter should vote his conscience, which would, in the aggregate, represent public opinion. More important, all citizens have a stake in the deliberative processes that shape public opinion.

Even as Antimasons defended the freedom of citizens to participate in deliberation, they threatened those same freedoms during a debate over whether the state should strip the Freemasons' Boston

Grand Lodge of its 1817 charter. In the process Antimasons also demonstrated the dangers of mass politics to minorities. The debate began in 1831 when Boston Masons petitioned the legislature to increase the amount of property they could hold under their charter. They had already commenced building a new lodge the previous year, and realized that its value when completed would exceed the amount of property their charter permitted.[154] That same year, Masons launched a defense of their own freedom to associate in a letter signed by twelve hundred brothers.[155] As construction of the new lodge proceeded, Antimasons accused Masons of violating their charter and demanded that legislators look into the fraternity's affairs. By November 1833 more than six thousand citizens had signed petitions calling for a legislative investigation.[156]

In March 1833 the legislature decided to investigate. A debate emerged over whether the state should limit its examination to the specific legal issue of whether the charter had been violated or if its investigation should include questioning Masonic beliefs and practices. One legislator who, Antimasons noted, was a Mason proposed limiting the investigation "to the corporate powers, acts, and duties of the Grand Lodge." Another legislator agreed that "the Legislature has no more right to investigate the private concerns of the Grand Lodge, than they would have to institute an inquiry into the moral character of the members of a banking corporation." Democrat Robert Rantoul, also a Mason, argued that the investigation "should be confined to the question whether the Grand Lodge had violated their corporate rights." Antimasons wanted a broader investigation for two reasons. First, "they hold more real estate, than the Charter authorizes them to hold." But this technical rationale was secondary. The "principal one is that they hold principles and sanction practices which are dangerous to the State, injurious to equal rights, and come in conflict with the duties of civil officers and magistrates." Antimasons asked the state to examine the internal affairs of a private association to see if its values contradicted those of the moral majority.[157]

In January 1834 the Grand Lodge agreed to surrender its charter. Boston Masons pointed out that they had only asked for a charter once their charitable fund reached a level in which corporate powers would provide it better management and safety. The original purchase was within the terms of the charter, but they realized the new building would be worth more than they could legitimately hold, which is why they sought an amendment. The Grand Lodge acknowledged that they had recently received notice from the sheriff of a memorial presented to the legislature against them but they refused to discuss "the principles of Freemasonry, with prejudiced and abusive partizans." They called the legislative campaign "undeserved persecution and injury." By surrendering its charter, the Grand Lodge "relinquished none of its Masonic attributes or prerogatives." Masons would continue to associate "not of toleration; but of right" and they vowed not "to sacrifice a private institution . . . in order to appease a popular excitement."[158]

As the Antimasonry episode makes clear, by the 1830s citizens had learned new skills that enabled them to participate in public life. Ordinary people discovered that they could make a difference and that it was their responsibility as citizens and as Christians to do so. The result was a massive release of civic energy that set the tone and led to the many conflicts that defined Jacksonian and antebellum America.[159] By the 1830s leaders could no longer claim to mediate exclusively the will of the people; citizens had learned to organize themselves at the grass roots. Certainly, reformers sometimes went too far because they combined their faith in the people with their communitarian commitment to a moral social order. Historians have accused such reformers of seeking "social control," but there was never anything conspiratorial about their aims. They were openly and loudly seeking to shape American culture and politics, at times putting at risk the deliberative public sphere they had helped to create.[160]

Antimasons were dead as a party by 1836, but the questions they raised about the relationship between popular mobilization and democratic government were not. Political elites, many of whom were themselves Freemasons, concluded that mass movements might threaten the common good. This fear spurred the divergent efforts of both Whigs and Democrats to limit the influence of the grassroots public sphere. It is to their responses that we now turn.

# ~ 5

## The Elite Public Sphere

WHEN CONGRESS RENEWED a rule mandating delivery of the mail on Sundays, many evangelical ministers took it as a challenge to their effort to foster a more Christian America. The Sabbath, they argued, was sacred. The state was aligning itself against religion. In response, Lyman Beecher and his allies organized the General Union for the Promotion of the Christian Sabbath as a parent society and quickly mobilized a mass movement of middle-class joiners in auxiliaries throughout the North. By May 1829, 467 petitions had reached Washington urging Congress to repeal the rule; by 1831 the number topped 900. In his address to the General Union, Beecher made clear that the new organization's strategy was different from previous reform efforts. Rather than appeal to state leaders, Beecher argued, the General Union must first change "public sentiment."[1] Ministers mobilized citizens so effectively that for a few years the General Union claimed more than one percent of the American population. As Richard R. John argues, the General Union was "unabashedly democratic—and, indeed, almost populistic."[2]

Sabbatarianism was one of the first movements to demonstrate the grassroots public sphere's power. And it shocked many elite Americans, none more so than the Unitarian minister and future Whig William Ellery Channing. In an 1829 essay that anticipated later critiques of Antimasons, Channing noted that "everything is done now by Societies" but "no general principles" exist to judge them. Channing began with the assumption that citizens must resist the force of public opinion and follow their conscience. In mass movements, however, citizens "substitute the consciences of others for our own" and are "swept away by a crowd." Such citizens were little better than slaves. Organized mass movements were "at war with the spirit of our institutions," Channing concluded, because they allowed a powerful cadre of elite ministers to promote "as cruel a persecution" as in "despotism." Reformers' reliance on the "sway by numbers" would "create tyrants as effectively as standing armies." Grassroots voluntary associations enabled evangelicals to manipulate public opinion "tyrannically against individuals or sects," proving that "public opinion is often unjust." If they became too powerful, mass membership associations would become "a kind of irregular government created within our Constitutional government." Channing hoped that reformers would not allow their associations to be "perverted to political purposes."[3]

In the 1820s and 1830s, Channing, and others who crossed from Federalism to National Republicanism to Whiggery, confronted the challenges of a pluralistic society that differed greatly from the communitarian vision of the Commonwealth's founders. Although many leaders had hoped for a postpartisan "era of good feelings," the rise of the Democratic Party and the emergence of new political tensions over the role of the federal government, the national bank, internal improvements, slavery, and economic policy, once again divided Americans. Industrialization and immigration produced class and religious tensions that exploded onto the streets in riots throughout the urban North. After 1821 almost all male citizens in Massachusetts were granted the vote, requiring leaders to appeal not simply to abstract ideas about the common good but to the values and interests of a mass electorate.[4] As important, the proliferation of grassroots voluntary associations meant that more Americans were demanding that their particular values and interests be served. In such an environment, elites struggled to retain the civic ideals that had animated the Commonwealth's Revolutionary leaders. They sought new outlets for exercising civic virtue. Although they continued to argue for a common good that transcended specific interests, they now housed that good in private institutions "independent" of politics.

Whigs believed that in a pluralistic and competitive society virtuous citizens must exercise moral and intellectual autonomy, the quality of individuals who have the education and self-mastery to act according to universal principles. Dependent persons followed their self-interest and their passions or, worse, as Channing pointed out, the lead of a sectarian or partisan leader. Only by overcoming this dependence could republican citizens promote the common good. The ideal of autonomy built on the existing notion of virtue. A virtuous person had to have what nineteenth-century Americans called "good character," an internal principle of heart and mind. Each citizen had to learn how to use his or her intelligence and piety to govern his or her self. A virtuous citizen would resist the machinations of others, not to mention the myriad temptations in the nation's growing cities.[5] Autonomous, virtuous citizens would, according to Massachusetts Chief Justice Lemuel Shaw, use their "moral and intellectual powers" in the "disinterested devotion to public service." They should not seek nor be influenced by "the temporary applause of the multitudes."[6]

Whigs analogized from the individual to institutions. In their struggle to come to terms with pluralism, Whigs established new private institutions to promote their values. The Commonwealth's founders had originally sought close ties between civil society and the state. Whigs now desired to sever those ties in order to protect the autonomy of their own institutions. By declaring independence from the state, civic institutions, like good citizens, would be freed from self-interest, partisanship, and most important, public opinion.[7]

Protecting the private rights of nonprofit corporations, or their freedom of association, now became a necessary precondition for the public purposes those institutions served. In the *Dartmouth* case, Daniel Webster had argued that partisanship necessitated insulating nonprofit institutions from a state too closely tied to the passions of voters, a position with which both John Marshall and Joseph Story agreed. In response to criticism about Harvard's quasi-independent Board of Overseers, a Federalist writer in 1821 claimed that its charter protects it "against arbitrary interference, by any political or religious party in the Legislature."[8] In the midst of a battle over whether to grant the public greater control over the Boston Athenaeum, Josiah Quincy, one of its founders, proclaimed that it would be "unjust, unwise, and unprincipled" to place control of the institution in "a political body, annually shifting its members, and changing principles and policy with every turn of party or passion."[9]

Complaining about partisanship and public opinion was not enough, however. Whigs had to articulate a language to justify elite trusteeship in a democratic age. They also needed to foster a legal environment friendly to private but civic-minded institutions. Elites had to explain why important civic institutions should be governed by persons who were not responsible to, nor responsive to, the sovereign will of the people. Whigs created and defended an elite public sphere premised on principles opposite from the grassroots public sphere. Rather than follow the Rev. Beecher and rely on "public sentiment," Whigs hoped that their institutions would put doing right ahead of being popular.

THE FIRST THING Whigs had to do was to demonstrate the public status of their private institutions in the post-*Dartmouth* era. When Federalists won the *Dartmouth* decision, they effectively undermined their Commonwealth. Chief Justice John Marshall's classification of Dartmouth and its trustees as private destroyed older notions of public trusteeship. Before *Dartmouth*, corporate trustees were civil servants; after *Dartmouth*, they became private individuals. Federalists and then Whigs were never satisfied with this distinction. Instead, they came to rely on dual axes for determining whether an institution was public or private. The first, expressed in *Dartmouth*, concerned whether the institution and its property was owned by the state or by private trustees. The second was whether an institution served the common good. A private institution with a public mission could be considered public. By relying on purpose, Whigs endowed the private realm of civil society with a public mission. Whigs argued that legally private institutions, free from parties and sects, as well as desire for profit, could promote the common good. Autonomy from the state and the market became a badge of public status. Whigs made "self-created" activity, long a term of derision, the hallmark of good citizenship.

Elite Federalists and Whigs carved out a role for themselves as cultural stewards by establishing, patronizing, and managing private cultural and charitable institutions.[10] New ideas about stewardship emphasized the independence of institutional trustees from politics. No longer were trustees assumed to be the same men who held public

office. Whig philanthropists concluded that democratic politics corrupted the freedom of mind necessary to pursue intellectual inquiry,
and thus threatened their ability to use knowledge to promote the
common good. Education had long been considered a prerequisite
for freedom. In the 1830s education once again became one of the
most important ways to cultivate the intellectual and moral attributes of citizenship. An educated person would not be duped by the
machinations of partisan or sectarian leaders. But this could happen
only if educational institutions were themselves shielded from politics. Within private yet public institutions, a new set of offices was
established—from professor to doctor to trustee—that allowed elites
to serve a public trust.[11]

In the early nineteenth century, Massachusetts elites began to distinguish between politics and culture. In 1803 wealthy Bostonians
sponsored the *Monthly Anthology*, a literary journal committed to cultural affairs and to avoiding politics. The new magazine was published
by the Anthology Society, a voluntary association of gentlemen and
ministers. During the early 1800s the society's members did not draw
a clear line between cultural and political authority. In a democratizing society, however, they found their commitment to elite stewardship under attack. They sought to establish institutions that would
shelter their ideals from the forces of political democracy while also
ensuring elites a continued presence in public life. As Peter Dobkin
Hall writes, "To the Federalists, authority—intellectual, political, or
economic—was if founded upon the sands of public favor, no authority at all."[12] In 1807 members of the Anthology Society established the
Boston Athenaeum. The Athenaeum, like other corporations of the
time, was a public institution. Its founders included such well-known
Federalists as Harvard's president John Thornton Kirkland, the Rev.
William Emerson, Theophilus Parsons, John Lowell, Samuel Eliot,
John Davis, and Harrison Gray Otis. These men all believed that they
held a public trust. When they applied for a charter the proprietors
employed standard communitarian language. Elites had an obligation
to apply their wealth for "noble uses" and the state would gain much
from an institution committed to "a just estimate of the value of letters
and arts." The Athenaeum would be "a place of social intercourse" and
would strengthen "the ties, that bind men together."[13] But even as the
proprietors focused on the Athenaeum's public benefits, it was intended

to serve only certain portions of the public. Shares were priced at three hundred dollars each, well more than most citizens could afford—even today. If this was a public library, its proprietors had a narrow definition of who composed the public. From its inception, the Athenaeum's proprietors mixed communitarian rhetoric with elite exclusivity.[14]

Because the new institution was privately controlled and endowed, and access to it was limited, it occupied an ambiguous place as conflicts over the public or private character of corporations flared. Harvard and the Massachusetts General Hospital could point to public oversight to defend their public status and corporate privileges. The Athenaeum, along with the American Academy of Arts and Sciences, the Massachusetts Historical Society, and the Linnean Society, were less clearly situated in the public-private continuum. In 1816 the General Court appointed a committee to investigate the proper relationship between the state and its literary and scientific societies. The committee, headed by Josiah Quincy, noted that the institutions had little state support. The Athenaeum, they wrote, had received no aid other than its charter, adding that, "as this institution has, in appearance, the aspect of a private concern, your committee feel it incumbent upon them to state that it is, both in its origin and on the principles, on which it is conducted, almost exclusively, public. The object of its establishment was to lay the foundation of a great public library for the use and resort of all our citizens." Because it was funded by private wealth and served an elite clientele, the committee had to balance the Athenaeum's private origins with its public mission, especially when Federalist-controlled corporations were under attack by Republicans. Moreover, partisan attacks convinced Federalists not to seek too close a relationship with the state. When the committee polled the proprietors of the above institutions they discovered that "no direct contribution to their funds was expected" from the state. The committee hoped, however, that the state would help the institutions build a fireproof building to store their collections. They concluded by reminding legislators that it was the legislature's duty "to patronize and encourage the exertions of literary men."[15]

In the early 1820s the Athenaeum undertook a massive expansion under John Lowell's leadership.[16] The Athenaeum's proprietors hoped to prove that it served the common good. In 1821 the *Daily Advertiser* published an essay supposedly from a tourist visiting Boston. The visitor was impressed by the Athenaeum's collections but troubled to discover that many of its valuables were housed in a wooden building susceptible to fire. Importantly, the visitor added, while "it may be said that it is the property of the individuals, and that their omission can never reflect a discredit on the whole community," the truth was that the "it is the public who enjoy the benefit equally . . . and it is the town to whom in effect it belongs!" He concluded that if Boston did not see fit to endow a new building, he had little doubt that the community's wealthy philanthropists would step forward to help.[17]

The letter was followed by a series of essays by Lowell. Lowell acknowledged the Athenaeum's elitism but linked its exclusivity to its public worth. The Athenaeum was founded for "communicating and diffusing knowledge in our metropolis," particularly "to afford our *clergy*, our *young physicians*, and *lawyers*, and to *all our youth of studious habits*, the means of acquiring information which no library in town could furnish." Lowell continued, "The prosperity of every city depends much more on its *intellectual* improvements than on any other causes united."[18] Lowell also established a public lecture series to demonstrate the Athenaeum's commitment to the general public. But he felt no shame in admitting that the Athenaeum was privately managed and served an elite clientele, for those young professionals and students would, in turn, serve the common good. Lowell gave expression to a redefinition of "public" to include publicly minded, privately run institutions. In private, elites could continue to promote their values and teach others their vision of the common good.

A similar story can be told about the Massachusetts General Hospital (MGH). When it was established in 1810 its trustees emphasized its public status, commenting with pride on the state's contribution of land and convict labor to help build the new institution. They celebrated the large donations from the rich as well as smaller grants from others in the Boston community. In its charter the state retained the right to appoint members to the Board of Overseers. It was, like most other corporations of its time, public.[19] By the second decade of the nineteenth century, however, its public status was being questioned. Like Harvard, day-to-day control was in the hands of private managers. During its first forty years, twenty-seven members of the manufacturing group the Boston Associates served as trustees. When the MGH needed more funds in the 1840s it pulled from a small list of wealthy private donors, bypassing the state and the community, suggesting that the MGH's trustees no longer desired to have the state involved in the institution's affairs.[20] For political reasons elites continued to appeal to old ideas about what was public. The MGH's trustees, for example, noted that the hospital's asylum for the insane, like other "public establishments," was under the "constant inspection of men, whose duty it is to frequently visit and examine" the inmates. For this purpose the General Court appointed four out of the twelve trustees.[21] In 1829, echoing statements made about Harvard, the trustees exalted that they were "founded by the State" and that "the highest officers in our Commonwealth are its visitors and supervisors," a point repeated in subsequent years.[22] The trustees bent over backward to prove that theirs was a public institution despite being privately funded and managed. Increasingly, however, Whig institutions were *de facto* if not *de jure* private. And privacy became the basis of public virtue.

Debates over Harvard illustrate elite concerns about mass democracy. Harvard was supposed to be a public institution. Its charter had been affirmed in the 1780 constitution and public officials sat on its Board of Overseers. Nonetheless, since the initial conflicts over its charter in 1810, Federalists had struggled to limit the state's influence over the college. One result was that major public funding for Harvard effectively ended in 1824. In its place, elite benefactors, some of whom were members of the corporation, gave more generously and wished to protect their gifts from the state. Harvard was becoming private in other ways as well. Its tuition and other regulations effectively priced out poorer persons. Moreover, between 1805 and the Civil War every corporation member was Unitarian, with the exception of three Episcopalians. No wonder Republicans and then Democrats accused Harvard of catering to a rich religious minority. Despite consistently defending Harvard's public status, Whigs were aware that their college was now a private institution supported by private philanthropy.[23]

In his 1816 inaugural address as law professor, state Chief Justice Isaac Parker called Harvard the "faithful nurse" of the Commonwealth. He praised the "publick and private munificence," which together had made it a great institution. "Her fame," Parker continued, "rests on the broad basis of publick utility." Science, Parker concluded, requires "free inquiry." This was a new twist. Parker suggested that because Harvard was a scientific institution it had to be insulated from partisan or sectarian interests.[24] An 1821 newspaper article was more explicit. Supporting the Federalists' defense of Harvard's charter in the 1820 constitutional convention, the writer argued that the Republicans had it backward. Far from making Harvard a partisan or sectarian institution, the charter protected Harvard "against arbitrary interference, by any political or religious party in the Legislature, who might for their own purposes wish to change the government of it." Legislators' private agendas threatened the pursuit of truth. To remain publicly valuable Harvard needed to be insulated from the public.[25]

The most adamant defender of Harvard's autonomy was its president Josiah Quincy. Quincy was appointed in 1829 after having served as Boston's second mayor. A longtime Federalist and Unitarian, Quincy argued that what made Harvard great was its disinterested commitment to promoting and to teaching truth. In his 1840 *History of Harvard University*, which originated in the trustees' request that he prepare an address celebrating Harvard's bicentennial, Quincy traced Harvard's path from a religious seminary to a modern university. The moral of Quincy's tale was that Harvard had broken free of past prejudices. "At the present day," he wrote, "its condition and prospects are not materially affected by either religious sects or political parties, but are chiefly influenced by the spirit of improvement which prevails in the civilized world, and by the attention and efforts now directed to the general diffusion of knowledge, and the intellectual advancement of the human race."[26]

After the Dark Ages, Quincy wrote, the Catholic clergy controlled education and perverted knowledge to serve their goals. The Reformation sought to liberate knowledge, but in fact most colleges remained dependent on the clergy. Only in the modern age were successful efforts being made "to rescue the general mind from the vassalage in which it has been held by sects in the church, and by parties in the state; giving to that interest, as far as possible, a vitality of its own, having no precarious dependence for existence on subserviency to particular views in politics or religion." College administrators therefore had a "duty to yield nothing to any temporary excitement, nothing to the desire of popularity, nothing to the mere hope of increasing the numbers in a seminary, nothing to any vain imagination of possessing more wisdom than the Author of the human mind."[27] To its critics Harvard was a "nursery of sectarian and partisan politics."[28] To

Quincy, however, the real story was the effort by Federalists and then Whigs to protect Harvard from political and sectarian interference. Critics' efforts to gain control over Harvard proved that they placed politics ahead of science and culture.

In fall 1842 the Democratic Party elected Marcus Morton governor for the second time and, in January, they secured a majority in the senate, giving the Whigs' opponents a majority on Harvard's Board of Overseers. Democrats appointed a committee headed by their intellectual leader George Bancroft to visit the college. The committee examined minute details of the college's affairs. In 1844 Whigs regained control of the Board and, although they issued a mildly critical report of the corporation's management of the college's finances, sought to protect Harvard from its opponents. Bancroft, however, issued a minority report in February 1845 arguing that Harvard, a public college, was too expensive and cloistered to fulfill its constitutional mission. Whigs hoped to let the report die but Quincy decided to give a speech to the Overseers in response. Quincy attacked Bancroft's claims on empirical grounds, but then came to the core issue. Although Bancroft posed no immediate threat, his report had to be taken seriously since it came from a political figure. The problem, Quincy concluded, was Harvard's connection to the state. So long as the Board of Overseers included public officials, Harvard would be a slave to the changing whims of the electorate: "It is the fate of Harvard College to be cast by the constitution of its Board of Overseers, into the very troughs of a politico-theological sea, which has tossed that seminary in successive periods of its history, always to its injury, sometimes nearly to its destruction." Bancroft threatened Harvard's grand trajectory as Quincy laid it out in his *History*. Quincy urged replacing public officials on the Overseers with Harvard alumni. The college would then be self-governing, autonomous, and not subject to the "politico-theological sea" of democratic politics. It could then stand above the fray and focus on finding and teaching truth to future leaders.[29]

In 1854, following the debates of a constitutional convention the previous year, Whig representative George Washington Warren introduced legislation to sever any legal ties between the college and the state. Warren claimed that "the annual recurrence of the election of overseers by the legislature will have the tendency . . . to connect the college with party politics . . . so as to endanger its stability and impair its means of usefulness."[30] Warren's bill also included clauses to establish an independent Board of Collegiate Examiners to regulate all colleges in the state, and to allow Amherst to remove its five state-appointed trustees . Warren's bill was opposed by those who wished to preserve Harvard's privileged place at the top of Massachusetts's educational pyramid. Over the next decade, however, Harvard Corporation members disagreed constantly with the state-appointed Overseers over such questions as who had the authority to hire new faculty members. In 1856, when the Know-Nothing Party controlled the government, a Harvard committee argued, "The time . . . may arrive, when it might be hazardous to the best interests of the College, if not to the purposes of its foundations, to have this unlimited power placed in the hands of any public body, the most influential members of which are in great part appointed at political elections or by those deriving authority under them."[31]

In 1865 the General Court removed the Overseers and replaced them with a board elected by Harvard's alumni residing in Massachusetts. Although the state limited voting to its residents, Harvard was now controlled by its graduates. It was effectively a private organization. (Hedging their bets, legislators included a clause stating that the act was not "in the nature of a contract, or a charter" and might be repealed at any time. Williams decided to allow alumni to elect five members on its board of trustees in 1867.) But not until the 1870s, when Harvard's president Charles Eliot embraced Harvard's newfound status as a private institution, did Harvard's trustees come to terms with a label that had been resisted since the American Revolution.[32] By protecting the college's autonomy from the state, Harvard's supporters since the 1820s had invoked the specter of sectarian or partisan influence over an institution that its opponents considered sectarian and partisan. Relying on *Dartmouth*, they argued that colleges must be legally protected from legislatures. In the 1860s they finally followed the logic of their own arguments and removed Harvard from the state's direct control.

Achieving corporate autonomy required more than rhetoric, however; it took money. Elite institutions relied on the charitable gifts of wealthy patrons to build up their endowments. Paradoxically, declaring independence from state patronage and from the market required the capital generated by those most successful in the market. Unlike most grassroots voluntary associations, which relied on voluntary labor and a combination of elite patronage, individual donations, and membership dues, elite institutions received and invested endowment funds. But charitable law in the early United States did not necessarily support this strategy. Many states, especially in the South, sought to limit charitable bequests in order to prevent a few institutions amassing great wealth and power over several generations. New York's Jacksonians pursued a similar path when they limited the amount of property any corporation or trust could hold. "The earth belongs in usufruct to the living," Thomas Jefferson had declared to James Madison in 1789, and many Americans agreed. Large endowments allowed the dead to influence the present and, worse, augmented the power of the few over the many.[33]

Massachusetts, as well as Connecticut, was more favorable to charities and trusts. In 1817 Massachusetts legislators extended to state courts equity jurisdiction over wills and bequests and, during the 1820s and 1830s, jurists proved that they were willing to exercise these powers to enforce charitable bequests in order to further the interests of nonprofit institutions.[34] When the Massachusetts General Hospital launched its fund drive in 1844, it could be confident that the gifts it received from wealthy donors would be protected and put to the institution's use. Yet, as Scott Lien demonstrates in his dissertation, jurists limited the legitimate uses of charity according to their definition of the common good. In the 1867 case *Jackson v. Phillips*, as well as in similar cases in other states, the Massachusetts state supreme court determined that a charitable bequest could be enforced in equity only if the gift served the state's public policy goals. Thus, a gift to aid fugitive slaves could be enforced because Massachusetts had long opposed slavery. And, since the Civil War had ended slavery, the court used its *cy pres* power to redirect the gift toward freed African Americans. Another part of the same estate intended to aid women's suffrage was quashed since it was not compatible with the public interest. In other words, jurists distinguished between worthy and unworthy charitable uses and permitted some kinds to have greater legal privileges. Most Whig institutions fit the law's definition of worthy.[35]

Even if the law continued to distinguish between worthy and unworthy institutions, the state did not seek to silence dissenting voluntary associations, as leaders had in the 1790s and early 1800s. More important, so long as a charity was worthy, it did not have to be incorporated. Federalist and then Whig jurists abandoned the *Barnes* doctrine that the state could not recognize the existence of self-created associations. As early as 1815 the state supreme court determined that a charitable bequest to the unincorporated American Board of Commissioners for Foreign Missions (ABCFM) was valid since the charity served a legitimate public interest (the propagation of Christianity) and the members of the Board were easily identifiable. Yet, the court added, the court could not compel the implementation of the trust. After courts gained equity powers in 1817, they could compel enforcement. In 1842 the court ruled that gifts of charitable uses to the ABCFM and the American Bible Society, both unincorporated, were valid and must be implemented.[36] Unincorporated associations now not only were deemed capable of holding property and gaining legal personality in the courts, but were actively encouraged.

The federal courts struggled over whether they could enforce charitable bequests across state lines. This question was a political hot potato because many states did not follow Massachusetts's liberal policies toward charities. In the U.S. Supreme Court case *Philadelphia Baptists v. Hart's Executors* (1819), concerning the bequest of a Virginian to an unincorporated Baptist association in Pennsylvania, the Court under John Marshall determined that the gift could not be enforced since Virginia had repealed the Elizabethan Statute for Charitable Uses, which, Marshall wrote, was the basis for the legal recognition of trusts. In a subsequent federal circuit court decision, *Magill v. Brown* (1833), Justice Henry Baldwin rejected Marshall's reasoning because English courts had exercised equity jurisdiction before the passage of the Elizabethan law. The Supreme Court embraced Baldwin's interpretation in 1844.[37] Federal cases determined law in situations in which deceased persons sought to leave part of their estate to institutions or voluntary associations in another state, but most giving took place within states, and here state laws were paramount. By granting their court equity privileges and promoting philanthropy, Massachusetts encouraged the growth of private elite nonprofit institutions.

The proprietors of the Athenaeum, Harvard, and the Massachusetts General Hospital considered themselves civic-minded despite their narrow vision of who belonged in the public realm. Not all citizens had the wealth and education to be public servants. For those who did, private institutions provided a space where they could promote the common good. These institutions' public value was premised on circumscribing their private world from the democracy outside. The Athenaeum and Harvard, especially, played an important institutional role in a process by which culture and learning were becoming separated from politics by barriers of both access and ideas. As Peter S. Field argues, elite institutions such as the Athenaeum were not anachronistic aristocratic responses to a democratizing culture but were products of that very culture.[38] By emphasizing the autonomy of nonprofit civic institutions from politics, and by relying on charitable giving to build up corporate endowments, Whigs established an elite public sphere through which they could exert public influence and promote their conception of the common good regardless of which party controlled the state or the kinds of pressures being generated by evangelicals in the grassroots public sphere. By 1874 Charles Eliot could proclaim that private nonprofit institutions "having no selfish object in view, or purpose of personal gain . . . contribute to the welfare of the State. Their function is largely a public function; their work is done, primarily indeed, for individuals, but ultimately for the public good."[39]

WHIGS EXTENDED the principle of autonomy to occupations that served a public trust. Doctors, lawyers, and teachers, like nonprofit institutions, must be insulated from public opinion for them to perform their duties. Whigs argued that professionals, like private civic institutions, should not be beholden to special interests. In fact, some elites suggested that virtuous young men seeking to serve the public good should pursue a professional career in which they would not have to prostitute themselves to the public, as they would be obliged to do in politics. Harvard's treasurer Samuel A. Eliot proclaimed in 1860 that to overcome the "ambition for political distinction," young men should be encouraged to pursue "other objects, such as science, theology, and law," where they can serve the community without seeking "political power."[40] Because medicine, law, and teaching were professions of the highest civic importance, they required professionals whose training and moral character placed them above politics.

The ideal object of a profession is to establish the skills and values necessary for practitioners to apply their art both competently and

objectively. Nathan Hatch writes that professions encompass three
distinct elements. First, they must have a definable body of knowledge
available only through academic training. Second, they must serve a
public good that transcends the desire for pecuniary gain and limits
what professionals do to promote their self-interest. Third, professionals must be autonomous and self-governing. As Hatch notes, "Professionals are granted something of a monopoly over the exercise of their
work," often through "licensure and certifications."[41]

Medicine underwent one of the first professionalization movements.
Because medicine is a matter of life and death, there exists a clear rationale to institute uniform training and licensing. Still, the process of
professionalization must be placed within its larger context. The Massachusetts Medical Society (MMS) and the Harvard Medical School
acted as gatekeepers to the medical profession. Together they established the necessary credentials while privileging a rational biological
approach to medicine over more holistic ones. They also reinforced
one party's control over the profession. For these reasons, Republicans and then Democrats attacked the MMS for abusing its mandate
by placing partisan interests ahead of the public welfare. In response,
the MMS argued that it served a vital public need by ensuring that all
doctors were qualified. Knowledge and training, the MMS claimed,
were by definition apolitical.[42] Doctors connected their professional
autonomy to the institutions in which they worked. Doctors supported
the establishment of the Massachusetts General Hospital, where they
insisted on controlling medical practices. In tandem with Harvard,
the hospital reinforced doctors' claims that medicine requires expert
training in formal institutional settings.[43] Although the MMS never
established a legal monopoly over medicine before the Civil War, it
raised the status of the medical profession and made proper training
an expectation for practitioners.[44]

The legal profession followed a similar trajectory to medicine.
During the colonial era, aspiring lawyers apprenticed under a men-
tor and county associations regulated who could enter the bar. The
first bar association was established in Suffolk County. The Suffolk
bar decided in 1771 that aspiring attorneys must have a college degree
and serve a three-year apprenticeship; by 1800 these requirements
had been more or less accepted by other county bars. The nation's
first law academy was established in 1784 by Judge Tapping Reeve

in Litchfield, Connecticut, although several colleges offered law lectures. Many young men from Massachusetts crossed the border to attend Reeve's school since, before 1815, no Massachusetts college offered formal legal training. Many lawyers did not wish to give up the apprentice system because it allowed them to determine who could cross the bar. Increasingly, however, legal reformers argued that law is a science requiring formal education and that the ad hoc method of relying on busy practitioners was inadequate. Like medicine, legal reformers emphasized the importance of acquiring a strong foundation in a specialized branch of knowledge inaccessible to the public at large. In reviewing a proposal for reforming legal education in 1817, Joseph Story, who would be appointed to teach law at Harvard in 1829, hoped to "dissipate the common delusion, that the law may be thoroughly acquired in the immethodical, interrupted and desultory studies of the office of a practicing counsellor."[45]

Harvard appointed two professorships in law in 1815 and 1817, and named Chief Justice Isaac Parker to the first and Asahel Stearns to the second. These appointments mark the beginning of graduate legal study at Harvard. Parker, like Story, believed that the law is "a science for the few to understand and practice." County bar associations resisted the move toward a more academic and centralized system of legal education, and many county bars refused to admit attorneys who had not completed local apprenticeships. As a result, the Harvard Law School, as well as the Northampton Law School which ran from 1823 to 1829, languished. By 1829 there were only two law students at Harvard and the college asked its professors to resign. Whigs stepped in and changed the qualifications for being admitted to the bar in 1836. Lawyers would now be admitted by studying law for three years or passing an examination. Harvard law graduates could enter the profession upon graduation. Democrat Robert Rantoul Jr. complained that the new act unjustly restricted entrance into the profession. It also adversely affected the interests of the county bars. The act favored Harvard's interests, and supported the claims of Story and Parker that lawyers needed formal education that could best be gained in academic settings. The number of students studying law at Harvard increased every year after 1836.[46]

Teachers also sought to professionalize. At first the impetus came from outside. In 1827 James G. Carter urged the state to establish a

seminary to improve teacher education. In March 1838 a philanthropist offered Horace Mann, the new secretary of the state Board of
Education, ten thousand dollars to establish normal schools on the
condition that the state match his gift. Mann immediately appealed
to the legislature for money. It was Mann's good fortune that Carter
now sat in the senate as a Whig and was chairman of the committee on
education and could help authorize a state matching grant.[47]

In his first series of lectures as secretary in 1837, Mann had argued
that teachers should understand "the science, or philosophical principles on which this work is to be conducted; the art, or manner in
which those principles are to be applied."[48] Teachers should be scientific professionals instead of practicing amateurs, Mann wrote in his
fourth *Annual Report of the Board of Education*. He outlined the five
core qualifications of educated teachers. Teachers must be knowledgeable in their subject matter; have "an aptness to teach"; understand the
"management, government, and discipline of a school"; display "good
behavior"; and have good moral character.[49] In 1842 Mann argued that
"the spiritual world," like the material world, "is governed by fixed
and immutable laws" that could be discovered through research and,
when applied to education, were the basis of enlightened teaching. To
Mann, "we have as little right to expect good teachers without adopting adequate means to prepare them, as we have to expect beautiful
gardens and cultivated fields to spring up spontaneously in the wilderness." Normal schools would ensure that teachers, like doctors and
lawyers, received a high-quality professional education.[50]

Over the course of the next year Mann and his supporters opened
three normal schools in different parts of the state. To assuage concerns that the schools would serve sectarian interests, Mann went out
of his way to find orthodox Congregationalists to run them. Two of
the schools were run by Unitarians, but one in Worcester County was
headed by an orthodox minister who had taught at Bowdoin. Sectarian texts were banned from the schools. To shield the schools from
partisan politics, control of each was placed in independent boards of
trustees, replicating Whig nonprofit institutional strategies. Although
the normal school in Lexington was dominated by Unitarians, including Democrat and educational activist Robert Rantoul, the others had
more diverse boards.[51] Nonetheless, the schools were quickly embroiled
in both partisan and sectarian controversy.

The attack first came in an 1839 article by Democrat Orestes Brownson in the *Boston Quarterly Review*. Brownson argued that education is by definition political and religious since the purpose of education is to prepare young people for this life and the next. A good education could not avoid dealing with politics and religion. By avoiding them, or by pretending to avoid them, Mann and his colleagues either failed to provide a true education, or implicitly supported a Whig-Unitarian one. Herein lay the danger of normal schools. "Schools for teachers require in turn their teachers," but who would train teachers? Since education is political and religious, Unitarian teachers would espouse different values than orthodox ones. The Board of Education argued that the only Christian doctrines to be taught in the schools were those "common to all sects." To Brownson, this "means nothing at all" and "no sect will be satisfied." Similar distinctions divided Whigs from Democrats, Brownson added. Even if they avoided political and religious issues, Unitarians and Whigs would impart their philosophies of knowledge to new teachers. The Whig- and Unitarian-controlled normal schools would then establish themselves as an elite monopoly. "As soon as they can get their Normal Schools into successful operation," Whigs would "arrange it, if they can, that no public school shall be permitted to employ a teacher who has not graduated at a Normal School." The content of educational knowledge would no longer be controlled by the people but by a faction with special legal privileges.[52] Brownson considered Whig efforts to achieve professional autonomy as setting illegitimate limits to the people's authority.

When Democrat Marcus Morton became governor in 1840 he condemned the centralizing goals of the Board of Education, although he did not mention the normal schools by name. Democrats in the General Court, however, seized the opportunity to condemn them. An 1840 legislative committee on Morton's program to reduce government spending argued that the Board of Education posed a threat to the freedoms of locally controlled schools and suggested that the committee on education look into the matter. The education committee's chair, Whig Allen Dodge, was an orthodox minister hostile to the Unitarian-dominated Board. Dodge agreed with Brownson that the normal schools were implicitly sectarian. He worried that by granting the Board any control over curriculum and the training of teachers, Massachusetts would replicate the "absolute police" systems of France or Prussia. The committee majority, composed of two Whigs and two Democrats, recommended eliminating the Board of Education and the normal schools.[53]

The majority of Whigs defended both the Board and normal schools. Whigs claimed that the Board was composed not of partisans and sectarians but of "enlightened and philanthropic citizens" above party politics.[54] Two Whigs on the committee of education penned a minority report against abolishing the Board; the bill to abolish the Board failed largely on partisan lines.[55] In 1845 Governor George Briggs, a Whig, proclaimed that he "cannot entertain a doubt" about the public benefit of professional teacher education.[56] Two years later Briggs commended the normal schools for "putting forth a most beneficial influence in supplying the districts with competent and well-qualified teachers."[57] Looking back in 1846, Horace Mann observed that the critics of the normal schools "combined all the elements of opposition which selfishness and intolerance had created." Mann was convinced that normal schools were one of many necessary "improvements" that transcended the partisanship and sectarianism of their critics. Normal schools were "a new instrumentality in the advancement of the race" because they trained professionals. Since education was necessary in a free society, without good teacher training, the "Free Schools themselves would be shorn of their strength and their healing power."[58]

Like Josiah Quincy's defense of Harvard, science served as Mann's foil for sectarianism and partisanship. He traveled to Europe, where he studied the state of the art in pedagogy. In Prussia, Mann learned about child-centered learning. In 1843 he argued in favor of European pedagogical principles, especially the work of Johann Pestalozzi. Education must actively engage a child's interest, Mann concluded, or children would not be motivated to learn. Massachusetts schools should be reformed around new, more scientific, pedagogical principles that demanded professional training for all educators. (It probably did not help Mann's cause that he was advocating Prussian pedagogy at a time when he was being accused of heading a board that aimed to replicate Prussian despotism.)

Mann's pedagogical arguments became implicated in sectarian controversy. Mann believed that children were born inherently good. Enlightened pedagogues since Locke and Rousseau had argued that young children are not born evil and that their character depends on the influences to which they are exposed. A bad education could destroy a child's moral potential in the same way that a good education might cultivate it. Mann concluded that the pedagogy practiced in most schools was detrimental to creating virtuous autonomous adults. He condemned corporal punishment for encouraging obedience instead of curiosity. He also condemned "emulation," which taught children to copy their superiors in order to win their praise. Mann believed that a virtuous adult must be capable of self-government, and thus must do right because of an internal commitment to the right principles.[59]

Mann's pedagogical innovations were challenged by many practitioners. Antebellum educators agreed that schools must inculcate moral virtues but they disagreed on how. By entering the fray from his bully pulpit as secretary, Mann raised the stakes. In 1844 thirty-one Boston grammar school masters published a critique of Mann's seventh *Annual Report.* They argued that by emphasizing a child's innate interest, Mann's pedagogy would not teach children self-mastery but instead would weaken their wills as children became "accustomed to act only through the force of that excitement which is supplied by the teacher." The Boston masters turned the tables on Mann, suggesting that virtuous self-government requires a more disciplined pedagogy than Mann advocated. The core of the disagreement was sectarian, Michael Katz argues. Many teachers remained bound by an orthodox worldview in which children had to be trained and disciplined because humanity's natural state is fallen. The masters argued that educators must take "human nature as it really exists." To Mann, science helped us understand human psychology and should therefore be the foundation of all pedagogy. To the masters, however, science was wrong because human nature simply could not be without sin. Teachers should not teach children to follow their internal instincts but "obedience to rightful authority." In a diverse society full of temptations, obedience was a more valuable skill than internal self-guidance. Mann's utopian hopes had little basis in human or social reality.[60]

Mann could not resist responding to the attacks, and a pamphlet war ensued. Mann condemned the partisan and sectarian nature of the attacks and again defended his professional autonomy.[61] Mann opposed the selfish, factional interests of his critics to his own scientific, disinterested ones. A number of Boston's teachers responded that Mann ignored original sin. Philanthropic reformers like Mann imagined the innate goodness of humanity, but in the real world children must obey their parents and their god. There can be no doubt that "there is in the nature of man an innate element of evil, prompting him to rebellion." The Boston masters rejected enlightened science and embraced the religious doctrines of New Divinity Calvinism. The fall of Adam and Eve could not be denied by true-believing Christians.[62]

Despite the above disagreements, Massachusetts teachers supported professionalization. Teachers realized that they were underpaid and lacked the status of the other learned professions. In 1847 they established the Massachusetts Teachers Association, which started publishing a new journal, *Massachusetts Teacher*, the following year. Like other professionals, a writer proclaimed in the journal's first issue, teachers were now "taking the reins in their own hands," and "driving on, by motive powers entirely their own,—*Association* and the *Press*." Another writer asked, "Ought not teaching to be raising to the rank of a liberal profession, distinctly recognized as such?" Individuals motivated by "caprice" or pecuniary gain should not become teachers. Teachers, like all professionals, were moved by a higher calling. To protect their calling, teachers must establish professional standards of excellence and morality, including a "professional faculty, or appropriate body, of whatever name, competent and empowered to grant professional certificates, licenses, or diplomas." In the 1850s teachers joined forces with the normal schools to enter the exclusive realm of professional occupations. An 1851 writer argued that teaching, like medicine, was a science that could only be learned through proper academic training. Although teachers were not as successful as lawyers and doctors, their salaries rose significantly between 1840 and 1853, thanks in large part to Mann's and their own efforts to transform the occupation into a profession.[63]

Whigs' desire to insulate the professions—and science and culture—from politics was so intense that they even influenced one of America's most radical critics of capitalism, Massachusetts writer Edward Bellamy. In his utopian novel *Looking Backward* (1888) Bellamy argued for the unification of the people's interests through the ongoing rationalization of production until the nation (i.e., the people) becomes the sole capitalist. Politics is reduced to administration. The president is put in charge of an industrial army, and his primary job is to ensure efficiency. In Bellamy's work one can sense the culmination of the Whigs' desire to transcend conflict, yet even Bellamy's utopian state does not take control of the professions. Unlike other occupations, doctors, teachers, writers, intellectuals, and other members of the "liberal professions" are governed not by the state but by "by boards or regents of their own."[64] Even in utopia there remains a belief that professionals should govern themselves in order to resist political pressure and to serve the common good.

~ THE FINAL PRONG of Whig reform was to extend their principles of institutional and professional autonomy to the state through the establishment of regulatory boards composed of publicly appointed but independent administrators. Regulatory boards, like nonprofit institutions, would ideally be insulated from the give-and-take of partisan politics. Independent administrators, like professionals, would examine problems based on their expert knowledge and superior virtue rather than their political loyalties. At the national level, Whigs condemned President Jackson's spoils system for appointing partisans instead of virtuous public servants.[65] Massachusetts Whigs offered an alternative to Jackson's approach.

Whigs first relied on boards for economic regulation. By the 1830s most business corporations were considered private institutions and their affairs were regulated by the state's general police powers. To ensure that corporations obeyed the terms of their charters and other laws, Whigs set up commissions. The legislature had previously appointed ad hoc commissions on a case-by-case basis. One of the first areas to employ the permanent commission was banking. Following the Panic of 1837, many Massachusetts banks, including Democrat David Henshaw's Commonwealth Bank, failed. Many bankers suspected that banks had been too loose with credit. In 1838 Governor Edward Everett and his fellow Whigs established a three-person banking commission with the authority to examine banks' affairs. If banks were suspected of being unsound or of engaging in foul play, the commissioners were authorized to bring them to court. The commission was extremely controversial because it seemed to target rural and Democratic institutions.[66]

Whigs assailed Democrats for the failure and the supposed corrupt practices of Henshaw's bank. When Marcus Morton became governor in 1840 he therefore urged legislators to abolish the commission as part of his larger program of government retrenchment. Although Democrats were hostile to powerful and corrupt corporations, they opposed permanent commissions for the same reason they opposed professionalization and corporations: commissions placed control over important economic and political matters in the hands of a powerful elite not subject to direct popular oversight. The commission was abolished (although it was reestablished in 1851 by a coalition government of Democrats and Free-Soilers, many of whom were once Whigs. When Whigs regained control in 1852, they retained the commission).

No board was more controversial than the Board of Education, also established under Governor Everett. The governor believed that the state's schools were in dire straits and he proposed a "board of commissioners" to examine them. The General Court assigned the Board of Education the task of assessing the condition of the state's schools and suggesting ways to improve them.[67] The Board served solely an advisory role. Whigs envisioned it as an autonomous governmental agency whose expert members would promote educational improvement without partisan or sectarian bias. Yet, although the legislature sought to appoint a diverse group, nine of the Board's ten members were Whigs and seven were Unitarians.[68] Horace Mann, the new Board's secretary, was attacked not just by orthodox Congregationalists but by Democrats who believed, as Orestes Brownson suggested, that the Board was a state-run monopoly through which Unitarian-Whigs would sustain their power just as they relied on Harvard and other corporations. In his 1839 essay, Brownson accused the Board of giving "Whiggism a self-perpetuating power."[69]

In response to these attacks from his religious and political opponents, Mann argued that the sectarian and political agenda of his accusers was proof that the Board must be insulated from public opinion, invoking the standard Whig fear of allowing the common good to become hostage to the fickle sway of the electorate. Mann accused his orthodox critics of promoting sectarianism instead of working, as he did, "for mankind."[70] No less than autonomous nonprofit institutions and professionals, independent regulatory boards allowed virtuous patriots like Mann to serve the common good without caving in to partisan or sectarian interests:

> To the patriot, then, who desires the well-being of his nation; to
> the philanthropist, who labors for the happiness of his race; to the

Christian, who includes both worlds in his comprehensive survey,—is not the path of duty clear and radiant? Is it not the duty of the wise and good of all parties to forget their personal animosities and contentions; to strike the banners of party; to unfurl a flag of truce; to come together, and unite in rearing new institutions, or giving new efficiency to old ones, for the diffusion of useful knowledge, for the creation of intellectual ability, for the cultivation of the spirit of concord; for giving to those who are to come after us better means of discovering truth, higher powers of advocating it, stronger resolutions of obedience to it, than we have ever enjoyed, possessed, or felt?

Since society was carved up into "institutions, associations, combinations, amongst men, whose tendency is to alienation and discord, to whet the angry feelings of individuals against each other, to transmit the contentions of the old to the young, and to make the enmities of the dead survive to the living," it was imperative that schools and their administrators abdicate "the spirit of party."[71]

Mann expressed the ideals of Whig reformers, dodging any accusations of partisanship or self-interest by emphasizing his own disinterestedness and enlightened expertise. From another perspective, however, Mann was a sectarian. Like other educated Unitarians, Mann was committed to scientific knowledge and professionalism. While he served what he considered the common good, he believed his critics suffered from "that limitation of the faculties which orthodoxy imposes." That they could not transcend their parochialism was no reason for Mann and the state of Massachusetts to succumb to it.[72]

The Board of Education was a model for subsequent independent boards. In 1852 Whigs established a Board of Agriculture to teach the public about improved farming methods. In 1855 Massachusetts Know-Nothings established an independent liquor agency. In 1863 the state established a Board of State Charities to oversee its various public charitable institutions and, in 1869, a Board of Health.[73] Temporary boards to regulate the railroad industry were granted rate-setting and investigatory powers. Permanent regulatory boards were established to regulate the insurance industry in 1855 and the railroad industry in 1869.[74] Independent boards justified elite political power in a pluralistic partisan environment. By defending the role of expertise and virtue, these early boards laid a foundation for subsequent changes in American governance. While no American, including Whigs, argued that regulatory boards should be entirely independent of public control, they encouraged greater autonomy for public officials. In later decades, political reformers would promote civil service reform to replace, at least in theory, party with expertise as the basis for holding nonelective government positions.

~ OVER SEVERAL DECADES, elite Whigs had developed new ideas connecting nonprofit institutions to civic ends. Private institutions, and the virtuous experts who ran them, would promote the common good without giving in to selfish interests. In 1840 Governor John Davis commented with pride that "works of Christian charity and voluntary benevolence every where abound . . . bearing testimony to the disinterested philanthropy of our citizens."[75] Whigs extended these principles to the state by forming independent regulatory boards. In a state divided by parties, class, and religion, when political leaders were forced to pander to voters, Whigs hoped that private institutions and well-trained professionals would better serve the common good than did the corporatist state that Federalists had earlier sought to establish. Some even hoped that private philanthropy would re-create the harmonious society envisioned by Revolutionary leaders. Unlike the partisan state, private institutions forged bonds of "sympathy" between their members as well as between elite philanthropists and the beneficiaries of their charity, linking citizens together "by feelings and interests intertwining in every direction."[76] Perhaps the Revolutionary goal of a community united by the ties of affection could be produced in civil society by the voluntary actions of individuals.

Whigs consciously articulated a vision distinct from the logic of political popularity and market-based self-interest. In civil society Whigs established boundaries to protect and to nurture civic life, while arguing that citizenship requires specific virtues for both individuals and institutions.[77] Whigs sustained the worthy idea that citizenship is premised on devotion to the common good. They endowed the private space of civil society with public value. Their arguments set the foundation for our current assumption that private charitable institutions serve the public good and deserve tax exemption. In 1874 Harvard's president convinced the Massachusetts legislature to extend tax exemption to any "educational, charitable, benevolent, or religious" institution, including "any antiquarian, historical, literary, scientific, medical, artistic, monumental, or musical" organization as well as "any missionary enterprise," associations for athletics and yachting, libraries and reading rooms, and fraternal societies. Massachusetts's law became a model for other states.[78] Because they could resist public opinion, and thus pressure from the state and from the grassroots public sphere, elite nonprofit institutions had been reimagined as serving rather than subverting the common good.

# ～ 6

## *Democrats Strike Back*

THE PARTY THAT ORGANIZED around Andrew Jackson proclaimed that democracies are governments run by the people and that there should be no mediating institutions or associations that perverted the people's true will. Inheriting the Jeffersonian faith in a virtuous people and the Jeffersonian fear of concentrated private power, Democrats challenged the legitimacy of both the evangelicals' grassroots public sphere and the Whigs' elite counterpart. Thomas Jefferson and his allies in the 1790s had assumed that the people's voice could be heard directly in civil society, but by the 1830s American civil society had been thoroughly transformed by middle-class joiners and Whig philanthropists. American civil society was now filled with what Democrats considered to be dangerous special interests. Unlike Federalists, Democrats could not turn to the state, which they believed ought to be the people's servant, not their master. The only place where the unmediated uncorrupted voice of the people could still be heard, they concluded, was within the Democratic Party itself. The Democratic Party would have to act as the people's agent in a world composed of competing interests, each organizing in civil society to trump the people's will. It would have to be, in Sean Wilentz's words, "the constitutional party of the sovereign people," the unorganized many against the associated power of the few.[1]

Few Americans expressed the Democrats' position as eloquently as Massachusetts intellectual George Bancroft. To Bancroft, "the best government rests on the people and not on the few." "The public happiness," Bancroft continued, would be achieved "by the masses of mankind themselves awakening to the knowledge and the care of their own interests." Progress did not come from a government that served only "the happy few," but from the individual efforts of ordinary people. No particular individual, or interest, could embody the absolute truth, the common good.[2] New York journalist John L. O'Sullivan echoed Bancroft's celebration of the people. Democrats, O'Sullivan wrote in 1837, believe "in the principle of *democratic republicanism*." They "have an abiding confidence in the virtue, intelligence, and full capacity for self-government of the great mass of our people." The greatest threat to popular self-government came from an organized minority that would "abuse power for promotion of its own special interests, at the expense of the majority."[3] Only the Democratic Party could protect the majority from well-organized minorities.

Andrew Jackson sought to reduce the public influence of what Jackson and his followers considered to be untrustworthy minorities. His rotation in office plan, in which he replaced many existing bureaucrats with Democrats, was billed as an expression of the principle that ordinary people were equally capable of running the government as educated elites.[4] Jackson, like other Democrats, was also hostile to powerful corporations that might put their interests ahead of the people's interest. When, in 1832, National Republicans decided to test his commitment by seeking an early renewal of the Bank of the United States's charter, Jackson expressed his own anger against elite efforts to use corporations to trump the popular will by vetoing the renewal bill.

The bank received all federal deposits and it used its financial power to regulate the nation's currency and credit, but it was governed largely by private trustees, which, to Jackson, was corruption of the worst kind. National Republicans and then Whigs argued that independent trustees were most likely to serve the common good. Daniel Webster proclaimed that "banks are safest under private management" because they would not be beholden to changing public opinion, echoing a position he had taken before the Supreme Court during the Dartmouth College controversy.[5] Jackson reached the opposite conclusion. Using corporations, Jackson argued, "the rich and powerful too often bend the acts of government to their selfish purposes." Inequalities of wealth, talent, and power will always exist, Jackson acknowledged, but the goal of government was to minimize unjust inequalities in the broader interest of democracy. Thus,

> when the laws undertake to add to these natural and just advantages artificial distinctions, to grant titles, gratuities, and exclusive privileges, to make the rich richer and the potent more powerful, the humble members of society—the farmers, mechanics, and laborers—who have neither the time nor the means of securing like favors to themselves, have a right to complain of the injustice of their Government.[6]

Jackson's bank veto expresses the skepticism with which Democrats approached private institutions claiming to serve the common good but that Democrats believed served minority interests. To Democrats, democracy took place locally, where ordinary citizens could exert direct control over their affairs. Centralized government—whether at the state or national level—placed power in the hands of the few instead of the many. Corporations and voluntary associations in civil society, by the same token, allowed the few to exercise power over the many by manipulating public opinion or influencing elected leaders. By keeping democracy local, limiting state power, and weakening civil society, Democrats hoped to expand popular self-government. In doing so, they pitted themselves against evangelicals and Whig philanthropists who had constructed alternative conceptions of democracy and the public sphere.[7]

DEMOCRATS FEARED voluntary associations and corporations because they exhibited what Adam Smith called "the corporation spirit," the tendency of all private groups to promote their interests at the public's expense. Private corporations concentrated power in the hands of a few who would then ruthlessly serve themselves while the unorganized majority was left behind. Following Adam Smith's advice, Democrats concluded that the best antidote to the corporation spirit was competition. Thanks to the *Dartmouth* decision, Democrats could not invalidate existing charters but they could minimize the influence of any particular corporation by exposing it to competition. Whether in the market or in civil society, competition would ensure that no particular corporation, and thus no particular group of men, held a monopoly on the provision of a public good. Ideally, competition would reduce the influence of any particular institution in public life. Competition was the means toward a larger end: equality and majority control of government.[8]

The meaning Democrats ascribed to competition was given clear expression in a conflict over the Charles River Bridge, culminating in an 1837 U.S. Supreme Court decision. The Charles River Bridge (CRB) had been originally chartered in 1785 to connect Boston to Charlestown. As the Boston area expanded, so did bridge traffic, and the original investors were amply rewarded. During the 1820s many Bostonians complained about the CRB's supposedly excessive rates. A "free bridge party" led by David Henshaw argued that the CRB's high rates were a result of its monopolistic power and that the best solution was to build a competing bridge. After making up the construction costs, the proprietors of the new bridge would turn it over to the state to provide free passage. The new bridge would terminate only ninety yards from the old one.[9]

Massachusetts Democrats coalesced around this fight to incorporate a new bridge over the Charles River. Echoing the arguments of their Jeffersonian predecessors, Democrats claimed that National Republicans were handing out charters as patronage, privileging an elite few at the public's expense. They accused the state's leaders of creating a corporate aristocracy that threatened equality in the market and in politics. With presidential candidate Andrew Jackson they emphasized equality, at least for white men, as democracy's highest ideal. But to achieve equality, no group of citizens should have privileges different from any other. In 1828 Henshaw organized the state's first Jacksonian caucus.[10] The CRB conflict was perfect political fodder for the new party because it pitted moneyed interests against "the people." In their 1830 address to voters, Democrats argued that monopolies threaten the common good by serving the few instead of the many. The "great interests in the Commonwealth," Democrats proclaimed, have been sacrificed to "privileged orders."

Monopolies of various grades and characters, from exclusive privilege in banking, to an exclusive right to bridge navigable

> streams—from a compulsory support of a religious order, to
> unfair exemptions and exclusive privileges to members of the
> learned professions—from *entails* by literary and religious mort-
> mains, to private entails in life annuities and life Insurance offices,
> have been the favourite means by which the federal party has built
> up an Aristocracy, and sought to establish its permanency. Their
> banking monopoly crumbled beneath the democratic power in
> 1811: and by the wisdom of that measure which brought life into
> the State Bank, and established the principle that all were alike
> entitled to bank Corporations . . . At the same period and by the
> same party, the link which in some degree bound together Church
> and State, was broken assunder.

Democrats linked Massachusetts's leadership to the discredited Federalists while portraying themselves as inheritors of the Jeffersonian
tradition. State leaders "entrench themselves behind ever varying and
ever increasing monopolies" that served their interests, not those of the
common people. Jacksonians, in contrast, would fight the corporation
spirit by attacking monopolies and ensuring that no corporation or
association could threaten the will or the interests of the majority. Just
as Republicans had broken the Federalists' banking monopoly in 1811
and then passed the Religious Freedom Act to grant dissenters corporate privileges that same year, so Democrats would fight any effort to
use corporations to protect minority interests. Since they could not
abolish corporations, they turned to an alternative public rationale:
"free competition of all."[10]

The General Court granted Henshaw's group a charter in 1827, but
National Republican governor Levi Lincoln vetoed it. Invoking the
Supreme Court's *Fletcher v. Peck* and *Dartmouth* decisions, Lincoln
reminded legislators that charters were contracts that could not be violated. The proprietors of the CRB had anticipated a monopoly and fair
returns on their investments; a new free bridge would effectively strip
them of what had been promised in their charter. If the state did not
respect contracts, investors would no longer be willing to support public works.[11] In 1828 the legislature again chartered the new bridge and
this time Governor Lincoln signed it, his earlier veto having exacted
a political toll.[12]

Having lost the political battle, CRB proprietors turned to the
courts. They argued that by incorporating a rival bridge the legislature

had effectively taken property from them in violation of their charter. Daniel Webster was hired to plead their case. As in *Dartmouth* and his defense of the Bank of the United States, Webster believed that the law should protect corporations from a fickle public. "Public necessity is apt to be public feeling," he remarked, "and on this rock we are in danger of making shipwreck of the bill of rights."[13] The state supreme court divided evenly. The two Democratic justices, Marcus Morton and Samuel Wilde, supported the new bridge. While charters must be respected, they argued, the original charter did not explicitly grant a monopoly. To protect the public interest from corporations, no corporation should be afforded rights or privileges not expressly given. Monopolies stalled progress by protecting vested interests and eroded the present generation's control over their affairs. In other words, monopolies threatened a democratic majority's ability to promote the common good. Competition would both check the corporation spirit and promote economic improvement. The two National justices disagreed. Chief Justice Isaac Parker stated simply that the new bridge violated the property rights of the older bridge. Justice Samuel Putnam added that bridges were public, not private, corporations that received monopoly privileges in return for their public service. The CRB proprietors were agents of the state. They had to provide safe passage to all citizens at reasonable rates. If the legislature stripped them of their charter privileges and exposed them to competition, future investors would lose faith in the state and the state could no longer rely on private investment to fund public improvements.[14]

The CRB proprietors appealed to the U.S. Supreme Court. The case was heard originally by the Marshall court, which could not reach judgment and ordered the case continued. In *Providence Bank v. Billings* (1830), Marshall had rejected the Providence Bank's assertion that a Rhode Island state tax violated its charter since, the Court proclaimed, the right to tax was fundamental to sovereignty. One can imagine Marshall struggling to balance *Providence Bank* against *Dartmouth*. Over the next six years, however, the Marshall court gave way to a new court. Two justices, including Marshall, died and a third retired, allowing President Jackson to make his imprint on the Court. His most important appointment was new Chief Justice Roger B. Taney of Maryland, who would later go down in historical infamy for his *Dred Scott* opinion denying citizenship to black Americans. Although Taney, as a former Federalist, agreed with Daniel Webster that the state must promote the common good, he and Webster disagreed on the best way for the state to do so.[15]

Taney ruled against the bridge. In language as communitarian as the Whigs', Taney argued that "the object and end of all government is to promote the happiness and prosperity of the community," but the question was how. Corporate rights must be balanced against the public interest. There were two aspects to Taney's opinion. First, if the CRB could file a claim against any competing interest, progress would come to a halt as turnpikes and canals shut down competing railroads. Competition, Taney believed, giving expression to J. Willard Hurst's argument, promoted innovation over stasis.[16] Equally important, democratic citizens should not be beholden to the past. Monopolies protected the vested interests of the few from the present interest of the many. In a democracy the people themselves should rule, not an incorporated minority with special privileges.[17]

The ideal of competition gave Democrats a rationale to take apart the old Federalist and National Republican policy of favoring certain institutions in civil society over others. In other words, competition promoted the common good while weakening the power of any particular group in civil society. According to New York's Democratic leader and future president Martin Van Buren, all corporations and voluntary associations opposed the people's will. It was their "law of nature," Van Buren believed, since they "ally themselves with the dynasty of associated wealth" to make "the few masters over the many."[18] The fundamental political question for Democrats was how to separate the people's government from corporate interests.

⌒ BUILDING ON the rhetoric of the Charles River Bridge controversy, Massachusetts Democrats opened the 1830s with a strong platform condemning the power of organized corporate monopolies in the "learned professions" and denouncing state support for such private institutions as the Whig-dominated Massachusetts General Hospital.[19] All corporations must "be controlled in the exercise of power and checked in their operations when the public good requires it," Democrats averred.[20] "All combinations, whether open or secret, favored by special acts of legislation, for the purpose of enjoying some advantages over the rest of the community, are *in the nature of monopolies*, and subversive of the equal rights of man," Democratic legislators proclaimed.[21] They were not opposed "to *corporations*," but asked that all citizens have an equal right to associate and that no institution has special privileges: "EQUAL LAWS TO SECURE EQUAL RIGHTS."[22]

A commitment to antimonopolism and free competition united most Democrats, but a few Democrats wished to return to the older idea that corporations were public franchises and that charters should be granted only to institutions that serve a clear public purpose.[23] Robert Rantoul Jr., following his election to the General Court in 1835, challenged the routine incorporation of a manufacturing company, asking why his colleagues did not spend more time figuring out whether the corporation would serve the common good. He reminded legislators about Article Six, adding that "he had noticed a sneer upon the faces of some gentlemen, when this article was alluded to." Rantoul admitted that if the legislature was not willing to limit charters, it then must do the opposite and make them accessible to all citizens so that the many enjoy the same rights and privileges as the few.[24]

Democrats explicitly challenged Whig claims that virtuous educated elites should retain public influence because of their professional expertise. To Democrats, elite control of the learned professions was no different from any other monopoly; professionals misused their power to serve themselves at the public's expense. Rantoul argued that any person "of good moral character" should be permitted to practice law and attacked the bar as "a close corporation" that granted its "members the exclusive power to admit or reject candidates for the profession."[25] In 1835 Democrats supported a bill to abolish the bar's control over who could practice law.[26] While county courts had generally admitted attorneys, an 1836 Whig law required all new attorneys to either complete a three-year apprenticeship or pass an examination. Democrats condemned the "law monopoly" for erecting barriers that favored the few, in this case lawyers, over the rights of the many.[27]

No "close corporation" received more scrutiny than the Massachusetts Medical Society (MMS). Despite the MMS's claim that it protected the public by ensuring qualified doctors, Republicans since 1810 had condemned the association for using its power for partisan purposes.[28] When the MMS expelled Marblehead doctor John S. Bartlett in 1836 for consulting with an English oculist with a Parisian degree, Democrats jumped at the opportunity to convince the public that monopolistic corporations threaten the public welfare. To

the MMS's members, Bartlett's interest in alternative medicine challenged the scientific foundation of the medical profession. But Democrats pointed to a case where another Marblehead doctor had refused
to call Dr. Bartlett for aid, sending for a doctor two hours away, leading to a patient's death. Whether true or not, the story raised concerns
about whether the MMS's monopoly could "consist with humanity
and the general good of mankind, or is it for the special good of the
members" alone?[29]

Democrats established a legislative committee to investigate the
MMS's abuse of power, leading the MMS to respond that their organization's members did not seek "personal benefit or emolument" but
"the promotion of medical knowledge . . . for the general benefit of
the public." Yet like the proprietors of Harvard, Dartmouth, and the
Charles River Bridge, when push came to shove they defended their
charter rights and argued that the legislature could not take away their
privileges without judicial determination.[30] The committee met any-
way and, despite Whigs' best efforts, did not absolve the MMS. Nonetheless, the MMS retained its ability to determine who could practice
medicine until the 1850s, when statutes granting it exclusive privileges
were removed from the books.[31]

In the 1839 elections voters elected a Democratic governor for the
first time. Marcus Morton won in part because of voter anger toward
a Whig-backed law prohibiting the sale of liquor in amounts less than
fifteen gallons and because many Massachusetts citizens, like those
around the nation, embraced the Democrats' hard-money policies in
the wake of the Panic of 1837 and the Bank of the United States's seem-
ingly callous response.[32] In his inaugural address Governor Morton
outlined his ambitious goal to transform the relationship between the
state and corporations. Speaking of banks in particular, Morton condemned monopoly as "the worst feature of unequal legislation" because
"it creates separate interests, eager for its preservation and defence."
Rather than permit a few corporate interests to have their way, Morton
urged the passage of general incorporation laws. General laws would
ensure civic equality by granting all citizens the same opportunity to
form a corporation and would stimulate the competition necessary to
reduce the dangers of monopoly.[33]

Morton also attacked Whig efforts to build up nonprofit corporate
endowments. Morton admitted that "municipal, parochial, literary,

benevolent and charitable incorporations, are sometimes necessary and useful," but he questioned Whig intentions. Whigs seemed to use nonprofit institutions "for the purpose of holding and managing property" rather than for serving the public good. While Whigs argued that corporate endowments and equity were necessary to ensure nonprofits institutional autonomy from politics and the market, Morton responded that since trusts and corporations are immortal, their wealth creates "a kind of mortmain inconsistent with the spirit of our laws and the genius of our government." If corporate wealth was not limited or broken up, immortal institutions like Harvard would amass increasing riches and power over generations, the basis of aristocracy. "Reestablish entails and the right of primogeniture and I should despair of the continuance of our government," Morton warned his fellow citizens. Morton urged legislators to grant special charters "only for public purposes, beyond the ability of individual efforts, and when the public exigencies require that private property should be taken for public uses." Presumably these institutions would be closely regulated by the state. Private civic institutions, just like businesses, should form under general laws "accessible to all." Powerful and immortal private institutions, protected in law by their charters and gaining the political power that comes with wealth, would undermine the people's ability to govern themselves. The past would then dominate the present, destroying democratic self-government.[34]

While Morton lacked legal authority to abrogate existing charters, he hoped that general incorporation laws would encourage competition and minimize the corrupting influence of corporations in public life, a position he had staked out in the *Charles River Bridge* case. Morton's legislative program proved a failure, however, since Whigs retained control in the legislature and successfully resisted his reforms.[35] Other states were meanwhile moving to limit the influence of monopolistic corporations. Southern states followed the "Virginia doctrine's" limitations on charitable trusts and corporate charters. Charleston, South Carolina's, elites tended to give their fortunes to the city and to municipal institutions instead of private charities. In the 1820s New York Democrats passed legislation to regulate the amount of property voluntary associations could hold, placed the activities of associations under the oversight of the Regents of the State of New York, limited how much of their estate testators could leave to charity, and prohibited charitable bequests to organizations not incorporated—and thus sanctioned—by the legislature. New York's 1846 constitution mandated general incorporation laws, and New York legislators soon passed such laws for medical colleges, churches, academies and high schools, libraries, charities, and other nonprofit corporations.[36] Pennsylvania made similar changes.[37] Although general incorporation laws encouraged the spread of corporations, by equalizing access to corporate privileges they ensured that no particular corporation held a monopoly. Competition and limits on the wealth of any particular institution would correct for the dangerous power claimed by a few organizations, undermining the Whigs' elite public sphere.

In the late 1840s, as Whigs fractured over slavery, Massachusetts Democrats gained another chance to implement their program. Massachusetts Whigs split between economic conservatives tied to the South's Cotton Kingdom and "conscience" Whigs who opposed slavery's expansion. By the late 1840s Whigs could not achieve electoral majorities in many state senate elections and retained control only by using their legislative plurality to appoint their co-partisans to fill contested seats. Following the Compromise of 1850, many angry Whigs moved toward the Free Soil Party. By teaming up with Free Soilers in the elections of 1850 and 1851, Democrats elected a Coalition government.[38] Democrats were given one more antebellum opportunity to reform the state's relationship to civil society.

The Coalition government passed a general incorporation law for banks, and legislation altering Harvard's Board of Overseers. They removed the General Court and ministers from the Overseers and replaced them with laypersons appointed by the legislature. Acknowledging their limited authority, the law required Harvard's consent. Coalition Governor George Boutwell, a Democrat, had proposed more radical changes, so Harvard's proprietors were relieved by the more moderate legislation and agreed to accept the changes even if it meant greater state oversight.[39]

The Coalition also called for a constitutional convention, which voters overwhelmingly approved, to address such popular reforms as changing how representation was apportioned, permitting the popular election of judges, and limiting special privileges for corporations. Delegates debated a clause mandating general incorporation. Democrats argued that corporate privileges "should belong to the whole people as a right, and not be dealt out to a few individuals as a privilege." Most delegates agreed that nonprofit institutions should not be included and could continue to form under special charters, although others argued that all corporations—whether for business or civic purposes—should form under general laws. A compromise amendment passed stating that it was "inexpedient" to grant special charters where general laws existed but left it to future legislatures to pass such laws.[40]

Not surprisingly, Harvard's official relationship to the state was once again debated. A committee suggested deleting any reference to Harvard in the constitution since Harvard had effectively become a private college. George Boutwell disagreed that Harvard should be made "a private institution."[41] If Harvard was to remain public, however, the state should have clear authority over it. Another resolution therefore proposed giving the legislature the authority to alter Harvard's charter, provided that the legislature did not violate the federal constitution's protection of contracts. Former Whig governor George Briggs responded that the state should just "cut her adrift" and "let the college stand, as the other colleges do, upon her own foundation, and be left to her own conduct and management." Since state control over the institution was the source of all its problems, why not finally remove any ties between college and state?[42] Other Whigs could not yet accept this reality and refused to sever the connection between college and state even as they denounced the Democrats' efforts to impose greater state control. Whigs maintained the paradoxical position of defending Harvard's charter (invoking *Dartmouth*) while refusing to call it private, leading delegate Henry Wilson to conclude:

> There is a class of men in, and about the city of Boston, who seem to think that they were born to guard, guide, govern, direct and control, Harvard College. With the cry of "No Party! No sect!" upon their lips, they have evinced the spirit of partisan and sectarian bigotry, intolerance, and exclusiveness.[43]

The convention did not remove Harvard from the constitution but it passed an amendment granting the General Court greater oversight authority. The convention also proposed altering how representation was apportioned, establishing an elected judiciary, adopting secret ballots, and barring public support for sectarian (Catholic) schools. The amendments failed because Democrats and Free Soilers divided over various provisions while Whigs united against them.[44]

Despite their continued disappointments, Massachusetts Democrats had articulated an alternative public philosophy that sought to expand the freedom of association, break up monopolies, and unleash the benefits of competition. These three themes united Democrats' hope that if the new civil society could be weakened, there was a greater chance that citizens could govern themselves.

⁓ IN ORDER FOR the people to govern themselves, they had to have control over their government. Local control was another Democratic strategy to minimize civil society's influence. Local governance, Democrats believed, would enhance direct popular control without the interference of special interests. Democrats therefore challenged Whig efforts to establish independent state regulatory agencies, especially the Board of Education. They argued that these supposedly independent government boards, no less than corporations, reflected Whigs' desire to use state authority to maintain elite control of the people's government. In time, they argued, teaching, like medicine and law, would become a Whig monopoly.

Marcus Morton invoked these themes in his 1840 inaugural address. In a democracy, Morton agreed with Horace Mann, education "cannot be too highly appreciated," but the best guarantee of school quality was local control, which would "arouse that strong and universal interest in them, which is so necessary to their utility and success." If schools were to fall into the hands of a state-level monopoly, Morton argued, schools would lose popular support.[45] Other Democrats joined the fight against independent boards not subject to popular oversight. Although a few prominent Democrats, notably Rantoul, supported Mann's Board, most did not. When the 1840 house committee on Morton's retrenchment program issued its report it accused the Board of Education of endangering liberty by creating an educational monopoly: "District schools, in a republican government, need no police regulation, no systems of state censorship, no checks or moral, religious, or political conservatism," the committee argued, continuing:

> Instead of consolidating the education interest of the Commonwealth in one grand central head, and that head the government,

let us rather hold on to the good old principles of our ancestors, and diffuse and scatter this interest far and wide, divided and sub-divided, not only into towns and districts, but even into families and individuals. The moment this interest is surrendered to the government, and all responsibility is thrown upon civil power, farewell to the usefulness of common schools, the just pride, honor and ornament of New England; farewell to religious liberty, for there would be but one church; farewell to political freedom, for nothing but the name of a republic would survive such a catastrophe.

The report recommended eliminating Secretary Mann's salary but turned the question of whether to eliminate the Board over to the committee on education.[46]

Horace Mann considered the attack on his Board to be the work of "some partisan men" who placed party above the common good.[47] The Board's usefulness, Mann believed, depended on its autonomy from partisan politics, but Governor Morton insisted on placing "selfish interests" over "great principles."[48] The vote on retrenchment proved, however, that even as Mann portrayed the Board of Education as above party politics it was supported by partisanship. Ninety-five percent of Democrats supported retrenchment but it failed because 92 percent of Whigs did not.[49]

In March 1840 the committee on education, chaired by orthodox Whig Allen Dodge, took up the issue. The committee had four Whigs and three Democrats on it. Their allegiances were mixed. One Democrat voted against abolishing the Board without supporting the minority's report, whereas two Whigs joined two Democrats to support abolition. Dodge considered the Board to be a Unitarian stronghold that threatened orthodoxy. The majority report noted that although the Board had no official coercive power, its stature grants it "an equivalent power." The state had created a "monopoly of power in a few hands, contrary, in respect, to the true spirit of our democratical institutions." Localities should retain control over school curriculum, the committee concluded. Local governance would ensure democratic equality and promote school quality as local teachers' associations competed against each other.[50]

The Whig minority report, drafted in consultation with Mann, pointed out that the committee provided no "single instance" where

the Board violated the legal privileges of local districts. More important, they argued, if every board that might do wrong is abolished, the
state would be left incapable of promoting the common good: "Take
away the power of doing wrong, and the power of doing right will be
destroyed at the same time." The bill to abolish the Board failed, again
on party lines, although one-third of Democrats supported the Board
while one-fifth of Whigs did not.[51]

The debate over the Board of Education exemplifies why Democrats
feared centralized government. Just as Whigs used private nonprofit
institutions in civil society to carry out their minority aims, so too
they relied on supposedly independent regulatory boards to maintain
public power against the majority's wishes. Government should be
directly responsible to, and responsive to, citizens. If control over such
vital matters as educating the next generation of children were submitted to elite professionals, democracy itself would be next.

~ DEMOCRATS WERE committed to breaking down all monopolies in order to encourage equality, to challenge power, and to enhance
the people's control over their government. Their fear of monopolistic
corporations extended to the pubic religious system, which they considered little different from other Whig-supported institutions. While
they were also hostile to evangelicals' reliance on grassroots voluntary
associations, Democrats forged a marriage of convenience with Massachusetts evangelicals to separate church from state.

Orthodox Congregationalists remained frustrated with the public
religious system, especially after two 1830 state supreme court cases
upheld the *Sandwich* and *Dedham* decisions, leading one orthodox
writer to proclaim that orthodox citizens were being reduced to "legal
dependence and vassalage."[52] While orthodox evangelicals were turning to voluntary associations as an alternative to the state, Democrats,
who considered religious liberty a fundamental right, attacked the public church as another corporate monopoly using its special privileges
to threaten the people's liberties. In a democracy, Democrats argued,
"there would be no monopolies or exclusive privileges. For his standing and wealth, each man would rely on his own integrity and industry.
Each would enjoy his freedom of religion unmolested, content that his
neighbor, whether Christian, Jew, Mahometan, or Pagan, should do
the same."[53]

Unitarian minister and future Whig governor Edward Everett told the state senate that "society falls into a state of dissolution" without a public church.[54] By the 1830s, however, most voters agreed with the Democrats. Orthodoxy had already abandoned the public system, and the growing number of dissenters had long sought to separate church and state. In 1830 petitions favoring disestablishment flooded the legislature. Whether orthodox or liberal, Baptist or Universalist, Massachusetts voters seemed to favor disestablishment. In 1831 a legislature composed of about sixty to seventy Democrats, a few Antimasons, and a majority of Nationals approved disestablishment, but the National-dominated senate voted it down.[55] Disestablishment then became a central issue in that fall's elections. Petitions to the legislature from congregations throughout the state demonstrated that most citizens favored amending Article Three. Nationals, who were reorganizing themselves into the Whig Party and seeking Antimasonic voters' support, thought it better to rid themselves of the issue than push voters into their rivals' camps. The senate thus confirmed an amendment for disestablishment in March 1833, and voters overwhelmingly ratified it 32,234 to 3,273.[56] In April 1834, in accord with the amendment, the legislature passed a law granting voluntary churches corporate privileges.[57] The last bulwark of the Revolutionary Commonwealth had fallen.

There was a tension in disestablishment that would haunt Democrats, however. Democrats sought equality before law, and thus hoped that removing the public religious monopoly would grant all citizens equal rights in civil society. To many orthodox voters, however, the essence of disestablishment was not just equal rights but also their hope that a voluntary system would prove more effective at promoting public religiosity than the older state-supported one. Therefore, although Democrats joined forces with evangelicals to disestablish the church, they also turned their sights against evangelical efforts to create a grassroots public sphere.

AMERICAN LEADERS first felt the force of the grassroots public sphere during the sabbatarian controversy. It was during this controversy that William Ellery Channing penned his essay condemning public opinion as fickle and dangerous. The best leaders, Channing wrote, must be willing to stand up against public opinion; they must promote the common good even when it means going against the majority's will. Democrats were never convinced that the evangelicals represented public opinion, however. Confident in the virtue of the people, they believed that evangelicals, like their elite Whig counterparts, were nothing more than a dangerous minority whose influence was enhanced by successful organizing. Evangelical voluntary associations were no more legitimate than Whig corporations, and Democrats were no less committed to limiting their power.

In his 1829 report for the U.S. Senate committee on the post office, Kentucky Democrat Richard M. Johnson condemned the sabbatarians' efforts to impose their minority vision on all Americans. Sabbatarians represented a mass but minority movement whose disproportionate influence stemmed from their organized power. They threatened the separation of church and state and thus the liberty of the vast majority. The Democracy must stand strong against these efforts to trump the people's will, Johnson asserted.[58] When the House offered a more moderate response, noting that the sabbatarians' request was not so outrageous given that Congress and the courts closed on Sundays, Senator Johnson reiterated Democratic hostility. The strong Democratic critique convinced many evangelicals that public opinion was not on the sabbatarians' side and, in 1832, the movement disbanded.[59]

Not coincidentally, the sabbatarian movement overlapped with evangelicals' protests of Jacksonian Indian policy. President Andrew Jackson had built a reputation as an Indian fighter, and southern Democrats sought Jackson's aid in pushing Indians off their land and giving it to white farmers and planters. When Jackson and his Democratic allies initiated legislation to remove the Creek and Cherokee Indians from their tribal lands, reformers mobilized to turn public opinion against the Democrats' cruel policies. Evangelical women were particularly involved in this effort. Relying on the organizational networks created by the Benevolent Empire, especially the auxiliaries of the American Board of Commissioners for Foreign Missions, men and women drafted and signed petitions to Congress and held public meetings to shape public opinion. Again, Jacksonians attacked reformers for seeking to interfere with politics and (southern) local control. Although they had the support of many northern National Republicans, the reformers proved unsuccessful in stopping an American tragedy.[60] Despite the limited success of the sabbatarian and Indian humanitarian movements, however, they redefined the relationship between individual citizens and the national government by empowering individual citizens to appeal directly to their legislators.[61]

The temperance movement proved more successful in shaping public policy at the state, and later at the national, level. The organized temperance movement in Massachusetts began with the 1813 formation of the Massachusetts Society for the Suppression of Intemperance (MSSI). The MSSI's original members were elite politicians and ministers, both orthodox and liberal Congregationalists.[62] The MSSI was organized as a parent society and it actively encouraged the formation of local auxiliaries. As religious tensions between orthodox Congregationalists and Unitarians increased, orthodox ministers responded by forming the rival American Temperance Society (ATS) in 1826.

The ATS's leadership was committed to grassroots organizing. By 1829 the ATS had one thousand auxiliaries with about a hundred thousand members nationwide; by 1835 it had five thousand auxiliaries. ATS leaders believed that their success depended on changing public opinion, and Lyman Beecher was at the fore. In a series of sermons in 1825, Beecher laid out why Christians should support temperance. Calling liquor "the sin of our land," Beecher argued that intemperance led men to sin, harmed one's health, and produced such negative social outcomes as poverty and crime.[63] ATS leaders argued that by permitting liquor sales the state condoned sin.

Democrats responded that the state should abandon all liquor laws and leave liquor sales to the market. Liquor licenses were like any other monopoly, Democrats argued, granting some citizens greater privileges than others.[64] Although many Democrats supported the temperance movement, they did not support reformers' efforts to influence public policy. Marcus Morton was the ATS's first president, but he resigned in 1829 when they began pushing for political change. Temperance reformers could rely on persuasion, but by lobbying for new laws they interfered with democratic processes.

National Republicans and Whigs were more amenable to the temperance movement. They supported the MSSI and believed that alcohol had negative effects on society. Temperance thus provided Whigs an opportunity to appeal to the growing evangelical movement. In 1831 Whigs passed a law limiting the ability of common victuallers to participate in the retail alcohol business, raising licensing fees, and requiring local officials to take an oath to uphold all licensing laws. Vendors condemned the new law so soundly, however, that it was repealed the following year.[65] Reformers did not give up but instead redoubled their efforts. Responding to this grassroots pressure, Whigs in 1835 passed legislation permitting local elections for county commissioners, who controlled liquor licensing. By 1838 seven counties had gone dry. Reformers then launched a major petition campaign to prohibit liquor sales. Whigs responded this time with the 1838 "15-gallon law," which prohibited liquor sales in quantities under fifteen gallons.[66]

Democrats attacked reformers for interfering with popular self-government. They accused temperance activists of "subjecting masses of men to their control" and told reformers to "let the law alone."[67] Reformers, they argued, were a "sect" (or a minority) of "*Simon Pures*" who sought "despotic power" to "make their own crude notions of morality the *measure of rights and duties of others.*" Reformers "called in the arm of a most obnoxious law to aid them in the conversion of men to their peculiar faith." The law was "*anti-democratic* in its nature."[68] Temperance advocates, like sabbatarians, proved how dangerous voluntary associations could be to the people's civil liberties.

Democrats judged public opinion correctly. In 1839 voters elected Marcus Morton governor and Democrats gained control of almost half the legislature while members of a breakaway "liberal" party, committed to the rights of liquor vendors, further weakened Whig control.[69] Morton celebrated temperance when accomplished by "moral suasion" but argued that no citizens have the right to interfere with "individual rights, personal habits, or private business."[70] In other words, Morton expressed the Democratic belief that reformers should not try to affect public policy by grassroots organizing. In the face of their losses, Whigs too responded with their standard objection to the grassroots public sphere. They blamed their electoral loss on party leaders who caved to public opinion, becoming "subservient to a moral and religious fanaticism."[71]

Whigs distrusted social movements but they believed the state had the responsibility to regulate liquor. As early as 1831, when liquor sellers complained that new license laws violated their rights in the market, Whigs countered that the same could be said for "three fourths of our general laws," including those regulating gambling houses, brothels, lotteries, and quarantines. Whigs believed that the state must use its police power to regulate businesses that aim for "the destruction instead of the promotion of the general good."[72] The most important defense of licensing laws came from Chief Justice Lemuel Shaw in two 1837 cases. In the first, Democrat Robert Rantoul argued that licensing laws were unconstitutional because they legislated inequality between citizens. Shaw countered that the General Court's job was to "judge what the welfare of the community may require." The licenses were not intended to create inequality but to promote the common good. In the second case, Shaw rejected Rantoul's claim that licensing laws violated the federal constitution's prohibition on regulating interstate commerce. The states, Shaw argued, retained the ability to pass laws for "the peace, safety, health, morals and general welfare of the community."[73] Whig defenses of temperance and licensing had a different emphasis than the reformers', however. They relied primarily on the common good, not public opinion.

Democrats worried about evangelicals' growing influence. In 1839 the Democrats' national journal praised their opponent William Ellery Channing, agreeing with him that evangelical voluntary associations posed "a greater danger to the freedom of our political institutions than standing armies." They threatened "independence of thought and action" and enabled "designing men" to control public opinion.[74] Orestes Brownson accused reformers of "ultraism." Reformers went too far: "Matters have come to such a pass, that a peaceable man can hardly venture to eat or drink, to go to bed or to get up, to correct his children or kiss his wife, without obtaining the permission of some moral or other reform society." In civil society, associations had become so powerful that a person "has nothing to call his own, not even his will. There is left him no spot, no sanctum, into which some association committee cannot penetrate."[75] To Democrats, "the spirit of propagandism, when it becomes overzealous, is next to kin to the spirit of persecution" and "extravagant ultraism is mistaken for moral courage."[76]

⁓ DEMOCRATS' HOSTILITY to the corporation spirit was directed largely against elite Whig institutions and middle-class evangelical reform associations. But many Democrats also opposed labor unions, which, they believed, were as likely to promote their own special interests as other private associations. Democrats were labor's natural allies, joining with them in opposition to the powerful commercial and manufacturing corporations Whigs controlled.[77] But Democrats denounced labor monopolies (or closed shops) when they threatened equal rights for all citizens in the market. Laborers therefore lacked clear allies in the early national era.

As older artisanal traditions gave way to large-scale industry, journeymen artisans were becoming permanent wage earners. Laborers recognized that their interests were no longer the same as their employers. To protect themselves from exploitation they formed voluntary associations to raise wages, to reduce working hours, and to improve working conditions.[78] Laborers in Philadelphia and New York formed unions and organized strikes in the first decade of the nineteenth century. The first major strike in Massachusetts took place in 1825 when almost all Boston's journeymen carpenters demanded reducing the workday to ten hours. The strike lasted three weeks but failed. There is no evidence that a formal organization was behind the strike but employers accused laborers of forming a "combination" that threatened "the public at large."[79]

The national labor movement became more outspoken during the 1830s. In 1832, lacking support from either major party, they formed the short-lived Workingmen's Party that ran candidates in 1833 and 1834.[80] More important was the founding of the New England Association of Farmers, Mechanics and Other Workingmen in February 1832 and the General Trades Union in 1833.[81] Also in 1832 shipyard workers, house carpenters, and other artisans struck under the leadership of the Society of Journeymen Shipwrights and Caulkers of Boston and Charlestown.[82] Laborers argued that they had "a right" to decide how many hours they worked each day.[83] In response, ship owners and merchants argued that labor markets should be free and they would never negotiate with a "combination" that interfered with individual liberty.[84]

Soon after the strike began, Chief Justice Lemuel Shaw echoed Channing's fear of "the general tendency of society in our times, to combine men into bodies and associations, having some object of deep interest common to themselves, but distinct from those of the rest of the community."[85] Another old Federalist judge, Peter Oxenbridge Thacher, agreed. Following a series of strikes organized by the Boston Trades Union in 1834, Thacher worried that the Commonwealth would descend into class warfare. If citizens formed associations to promote their interests instead of the common good, "a frightful despotism would soon be erected on the ruins of this free and happy commonwealth."[86]

Democrats sought laborers' votes, and some prominent Democrats supported their right to organize. Seth Luther proclaimed it intolerable that elites were allowed to associate but when workers did the same they were accused of forming "a most HORRIBLE COMBINATION."[87] In a Fourth of July oration, radical Democrat Frederick Robinson accused Judge Thacher of hypocrisy since judges were members of the bar, one of the most powerful combinations.[88] Luther and Robinson argued that that if elites could organize, laborers should have the same privileges. On the whole, however, Democrats proved unsupportive. In 1836 David Henshaw linked corporate monopolies to "the Trades union, the Bar, or of the Physicians," suggesting that labor unions posed the same problems as any other monopoly.[89] Robert Rantoul believed that the ten-hour movement would limit individual freedom in the market.[90] Democratic gubernatorial candidate Marcus Morton refused to endorse ten-hour legislation because "each laborer is a freeman."[91] To Henshaw, Rantoul, and Morton, labor unions were no different from other associations. When they sought to use their organized power to impose their will on others they expressed the corporation spirit.

These tensions came to a head in the famous case of *Commonwealth v. Hunt*, decided by the Boston municipal court in 1840 and on appeal by the state supreme court in 1842. The Boston court was headed by an unsympathetic Judge Thacher. The case concerned the Boston Journeymen Bootmakers' Society's effort to fine one of their members, Jeremiah Horne, for doing extra work without pay. Horne refused to pay his fine and the union insisted that he be fired since the union's constitution pledged all its members not to work for any employer who hired laborers that did not abide by union regulations.[92] Thacher told jurors that they must decide whether the union, by creating a monopoly in order to raise wages and thus consumer prices, was usurping the state's authority. By forming an association and compelling others to obey its terms, the union not only was acting coercively but was effectively taking upon itself the right to tax. He concluded ominously that labor unions were "a new power in the state, unknown to its constitution and laws, and subversive of their equal spirit." Unions promoted class antagonism and would erect a "despotism" of "private voluntary associations."[93] The journeymen lost.

Robert Rantoul represented the journeymen and he appealed to the state supreme court. Rantoul made two claims. First, he argued that the common law crime of conspiracy was not in force in Massachusetts. This argument reflected Rantoul's desire to simplify the legal code by removing English common laws he considered incompatible with democracy. Chief Justice Shaw dismissed this argument. Rantoul's second argument proved more convincing. Rantoul claimed that the journeymen's indictments were "fatally flawed" because they did not explicitly state "any unlawful acts or means" undertaken by the journeymen. In essence, other than forming a voluntary association, the bootmakers were not accused of any particular crimes. The "mere combination is nowhere said to be unlawful," Rantoul concluded. Essentially, Rantoul defended the laborers by arguing that their indictments did not accuse them of doing what they had hoped to do, establish a closed shop. This was lukewarm support for the laborers at best.

Perhaps not surprisingly, then, Shaw agreed with Rantoul. Two people from opposing parties, neither of whom were particularly sympathetic to labor unions, united around the laborers' freedom to associate. Shaw argued that an indictment for conspiracy must accuse a group of specific acts that were unlawful or harmed the common good. One could not assume the bootmakers' guilt because they formed an association. Nor was their effort to persuade all bootmakers to join their association a crime.

Why did Shaw and Rantoul defend the laborers' freedom to associate? The answer is uncertain, but it may have to do with the changed context in which Rantoul made his argument. Had he made a similar argument in the first decades of the nineteenth century he would have lost, as laborers did in similar cases in Pennsylvania and New York. By the 1840s, however, the number of voluntary associations had expanded dramatically. To prevent laborers the right to form a voluntary association when everyone else was doing so would be indefensible. Moreover, to find the laborers guilty would mean finding almost every voluntary association guilty of conspiracy.

Neither Rantoul nor Shaw abandoned their core commitments. Rantoul never defended closed shops or monopolies, but he denied the right of employers to organize while employees could not. Shaw also did not claim that laborers could form closed shops that fostered class antagonism and violated market freedom. Rantoul and Shaw never denied that laborers—or others—could be indicted for specific acts if they used their organized power for coercive purposes. This placed laborers at a disadvantage in the new civil society and market economy. Like that of the farmers in the Whiskey Rebellion, laborers' freedom of association was premised on limiting traditional forms of collective action that relied on force over persuasion. Laborers could associate, however they could not act as a class but simply as a voluntary association of free individuals. In future cases laborers would be convicted for actions similar to those at issue in *Commonwealth v. Hunt*.[94] By treating unions like other voluntary associations, both Rantoul and Shaw expanded the laborers' freedom of association but did not protect the objects of their association. Not until the New Deal would unions' status change. But even then unions required a special status. Since they sought to create closed shops, they had to agree to greater governmental oversight and regulation than other voluntary associations. They had to become not merely private voluntary associations but quasi-public agencies.[95]

The real significance of *Commonwealth v. Hunt* is its articulation of a new consensus. Despite their disagreements, Rantoul and Shaw defended the freedom of association. Even as Americans continued to disagree on what associations could or could not do, the state would no longer condemn citizens for organizing without the state's sanction. The debate would now be over the actions of associations rather than their mere existence. Rejecting much of the intellectual and legal implications of Article Six in 1780, the state supreme court in 1842 extended legal protection to ordinary citizens associating.

∽ THE CONFLICTS OVER sabbatarianism, Indian removal, temperance, and labor—as well as Antimasonry—were prelude to debates over the most divisive issue in American politics: slavery. When William Lloyd Garrison and members of Boston's black community formed the New England Anti-Slavery Society (NEAS) in 1832, they built on the foundation of other movements, but now aimed their sights at the immediate abolition of American slavery, threatening the ability of both parties to maintain their national coalitions. Not surprisingly, then, both the Whig and Democratic parties condemned what they considered the fanaticism of the new movement. But abolitionists had successfully mastered the grassroots organizing techniques pioneered by evangelical ministers, and they were determined to bypass political leaders and appeal to public opinion. The debate over slavery thus brought to a head the tensions between the Whigs' elite public sphere and the evangelicals' grassroots public sphere, and the Democrats' hostility to both.

The movement to end slavery began with the American Revolution. By 1800 all northern states had abolished slavery, although gradual emancipation laws kept slavery alive in some places into the antebellum era. In 1783 the Massachusetts supreme court ruled slavery unconstitutional. Although many northerners agreed that slavery was wrong, they did not agree on what to do about it. The American Colonization Society was established in 1816 to build consensus between northerners and progressive southerners. It was part of an older civic ecology in which elite public trustees advocated the common good.[96]

Garrison's new association by contrast was not started by genteel leaders but rather by citizens who had cut their teeth in various other reform movements. Its members were largely middle class and came from diverse denominations, with large numbers of Quakers and Unitarians. It included women and sought to treat African Americans as equals. It was a radical association committed to the equality of all American citizens. In 1833, Garrisonians would join forces with mid-Atlantic antislavery activists to form the American Anti-Slavery Society (AASS).[97]

The abolitionists exhibit the culmination of two ideas. Although relying on distinct theologies, both evangelical and Unitarian ministers had argued that each citizen must behave according to a higher law. Simultaneously, evangelical ministers had taught citizens that the best way to promote social change was to organize to convert public opinion.[98] Combined, these two ideas convinced many citizens that it was their moral obligation to organize to fight slavery and gave them the organizational repertoire to do it. In essence, evangelical ministers had unwittingly taught a new cadre of radicals how to organize a cause that risked subverting the social order those ministers were trying to create.

Abolitionists relied on the same methods as other associations but they used these methods to engage in what Richard S. Newman calls a "mass action strategy."[99] Both the AASS and the NEAS (soon renamed the Massachusetts Anti-Slavery Society [MASS]) hired agents to organize auxiliary societies. By 1838, the AASS claimed more than thirteen hundred auxiliaries.[100] Abolitionists formed their own press and reached out to existing newspapers. They encouraged the women and men who joined their associations to sign petitions, to attend lectures, and to preach to their neighbors the horrors of slavery. Like other reformers, abolitionists believed that the best way to eliminate slavery was to change public opinion and the only way to change public opinion was by organizing. According to the MASS, "Our speeches, our publications, our Societies, our Conventions and our prayers are kindling up a sacred fire that shall cause the public mind to glow . . . and our public servants to feel its warming influence."[101]

Many ministers responded with hostility to the new movement. Evangelicals worried that abolitionists would destabilize the social order that the sabbatarian and temperance movements sought to institute. Ministers were appalled that their own followers turned the tools they had developed—voluntary associations—against them. They considered the abolitionists radicals who riled up popular passion. But they could not stop citizens from organizing. The most famous example of how orthodox leaders were losing control to a new generation of middle-class reformers is the controversy between the Rev. Lyman Beecher and his students at Lane Theological Seminary in Cincinnati. Lane had been established to spread evangelicalism in the west. In 1832 Beecher moved out to become its president. Although Beecher opposed slavery, he disagreed with the abolitionists' fanaticism and tactics. When several of his students formed an abolitionist society and started socializing with Cincinnati's black community, white citizens in the community protested. Beecher responded to the pressure of Lane's trustees by cracking down on his students. Unwilling to yield, fifty-one of Beecher's students withdrew to Oberlin. The Lane controversy exposed not only the unwillingness of abolitionists to compromise, but also how Beecher, one of the founders and leaders of the moral reform movement, had lost control of it. Beecher had taught all citizens how to turn their individual moral commitments into a social movement and now he could not halt the consequences.[102]

Whigs once again worried that radical demagogues would mobilize public opinion and endanger the common good. They labeled

abolitionists "ardent, but mistaken Philanthropists."[103] Harrison Gray
Otis called the American Anti-Slavery Society a "dangerous association" that was allied with "auxiliary and *ancillary* societies, in every
state and community."[104] Whigs hoped to silence them before they
threatened the intersectional unity necessary for national parties.
Democrats agreed. Although many Democrats, including Marcus
Morton, opposed slavery, they upheld their party's commitment to
states' rights. Democrats accused abolitionists of using "inflamma-
tory harangues" and "armies of women and children" to force their
values on the majority.[105] But as part of a national party whose pro-
slavery platform was unpopular in the North, Massachusetts Democrats preferred to avoid the issue.

Neither party could stop the spread of antislavery sentiment. Whigs
hoped to "abstain altogether from the discussion" of slavery but "the
over heated and indiscreet zeal of the abolitionists" kept the issue
alive in the public sphere.[106] Although only a handful of voters were
radicals, both Garrisonians and their more moderate allies used their
organizations to stoke antislavery opinion throughout the state.[107]
Whigs worried that abolitionists would split the party and, while they
did not want to "stifle free discussion," they pressured abolitionists to
be more discreet.[108]

In 1835 the AASS decided to flood the public sphere with abolitionist literature. Through print, abolitionists hoped to spread their
message to white and black readers in every state. By the end of 1837,
the AASS had sent more than one million pieces of mail. Southern
Democrats responded in anger. In July 1835 the Charleston, South
Carolina, postmaster wrote to ask the incoming Democratic Postmaster General Amos Kendall whether the mailings fell under South
Carolina's prohibition of "incendiary" publications. In the meantime
he locked up all AASS material in the post office. Learning about the
mailings, a small group of elite slaveholders broke into the post office
and publicly burned the AASS material in violation of federal law. In
response, Kendall decided to obey state and local laws even if it meant
that the postal office would refuse to deliver certain material. In his
annual message, President Jackson went one step further and asked
Congress to pass a law banning abolitionist material from the mail.
Jackson's request is shocking since the Democrats considered themselves heirs to the Jeffersonians who opposed the 1798 Sedition Act,

but it illustrates how, when push came to shove, Democrats were willing to limit the political influence of civil society when it threatened Democrats' conception of direct and local democracy.[109]

Southerners also asked northerners to silence abolitionists. Connecticut responded in 1836 with a law prohibiting traveling abolitionist speakers. Massachusetts Whigs refused to do the same, commenting that the "mere suggestion" of using "*the strong arm of the law*" to silence debate "would be the signal for revolution."[110] Despite these statements of principle, however, in 1836 Whig Governor Edward Everett asked the legislature to pass a bill outlawing abolitionist meetings because they threatened "the peace of this Commonwealth." The General Court formed a committee before which abolitionists from the MASS vehemently defended their freedoms of speech, press, and association and denounced any effort to silence their voices in the public sphere. The committee criticized abolitionist tactics but did not recommend legislating against them.[111]

Another tool employed by abolitionists was the petition. Petitions had a long tradition in Anglo-American constitutional history. The right to petition one's leaders, like the right of assembly, had originally been a communal right. For example, during the movement for American independence the people of the colonies petitioned the King for redress, but they did so as a community. For this reason, the federal constitution and Article Nineteen of the Declaration of Rights in the 1780 Massachusetts constitution protected the right to petition.[112] Orthodox ministers in the 1820s had transformed petitioning from an act undertaken by the civic community to one undertaken by voluntarily organized advocacy groups—namely sabbatarians and temperance reformers. Once again, abolitionists built on the tools of civic engagement pioneered by elite ministers. Petitions built grassroots support because they required the members of local auxiliaries to recruit signatures within their communities. And, by signing a petition, an individual citizen cemented his or her commitment to a cause in a binding and public manner. Thus, petitioning was an extremely effective way to shape public opinion.[113] Petitioning also connected organizational activities in civil society to the state. If public opinion is the source of authority, by sending petitions citizens let their elected leaders know where public opinion was headed.

The American Anti-Slavery Society's 1835 petition drive focused on pressuring Congress to abolish slavery in the District of Columbia, where none could deny the federal government's jurisdiction. Their effort was not unprecedented. In the immediate post-Revolutionary era, the Pennsylvania Abolition Society (PAS) had petitioned Congress to abolish slavery, setting off a debate within Congress about the legitimacy of petitioning. The PAS, however, was an elite institution composed of public trustees. The AASS, by contrast, organized thousands of citizens across the nation. Their efforts were more abrasive, more adamant, and more popular than anything the PAS ever undertook. By 1836 petitions representing more than thirty thousand signatories had been received by Congress. In May 1837 the AASS announced that it would intensify its efforts and asked local auxiliaries to recruit signatures in their communities. By December 1838 petitions signed by more than 414,000 Americans reached Congress. Women were particularly active in this process, and their efforts demonstrated how they had acquired new civic skills that could be used to influence public opinion. In turn, many congressmen questioned whether women should be allowed to petition, leading antislavery women—and former president John Quincy Adams, now a member of Congress—to defend the civic activity of female citizens.[114] Congress refused to debate the petitions. Two years earlier, it had passed its infamous gag rule mandating that abolitionist petitions were to be received without debate or referral to a committee.

Whigs criticized the abolitionists' "extremely ill-advised" petition campaign but the gag rule gave them an opportunity to contrast Democratic tyranny with Whig liberty without taking a stand on slavery itself.[115] Whigs lashed out at both the gag rule and, in 1842, Congress's effort to censure Representative John Quincy Adams for continuing to introduce petitions concerning slavery in Congress. Although they were "against the Abolitionists," Whigs criticized the South's effort "to deny all right of discussion" about slavery when doing so would "deprive the people of this country of rights most sacredly guaranteed by the Constitution."[116] Massachusetts Democrats said less about it, but in one important statement they suggested that the public sphere, like the government, should reflect American federalism. Since Congress could not alter slavery in the South, Northern citizens could not agitate against it. Sovereignty resides with the states, Democrats averred, and abolitionists' efforts to affect politics in the South "must violate the compact" of 1787.[117] These comments reflected the words of President Jackson's 1837 Farewell Address, in which Jackson argued that "the citizens of every State should . . . frown upon any proceedings within their borders likely to disturb the tranquillity of their political brethren in other portions of the Union," continuing that "every State must be the sole judge of the measures proper to secure the safety of its citizens and promote their happiness."[118] Defending the gag rule, John C. Calhoun argued that slavery "is beyond the jurisdiction of Congress; they have no right to touch it in any shape or form, or to make it the subject of deliberation or discussion. In opposition to this view, it is urged that Congress is bound by the Constitution to receive petitions in every case and on every subject, whether it is within its Constitutional competency or not. I hold this doctrine to be absurd."[119]

These were not just idle words. Under Jackson, the U.S. postal service, which had long been one of the major institutions holding the nation together, implemented a policy of censoring the mails to protect the Southern states' public spheres from abolitionist literature.[120] By invoking federalism, Democrats managed to turn the gag rule—which greatly limited the freedoms of civil society—into something that could be seen as protecting it. Just as states' rights protected the people of the states from an overbearing government so the gag rule ensured that the people of each state did not interfere with the affairs of the people of other states. As Northern sentiment turned against the expansion of slavery, thanks in part to the efforts of antislavery activists, some Northern antislavery Democrats would conclude that the Southern Slave Power posed an even more serious threat to democratic equality than abolitionists. Because they sought to dominate the party, Southern Democrats came to be seen by some of their Northern counterparts as just another minority using its organized power to trump the majority's values and interests. These Democrats, including Marcus Morton, would join Martin Van Buren and a coalition of Whig and Democratic antislavery leaders in the Free Soil Party. The Democracy's equalitarian ideals could lead both toward and away from defending slavery.[121]

Abolitionists countered all efforts to silence them. They argued that they had the right to use every constitutional tool at their disposal—

associations, the press, petitions—to influence public opinion and to spur their elected leaders to act. Like Antimasons, they proclaimed it the duty of each citizen to decide which issues were important. Abolitionists pointed out that since the Constitution could be amended Northern citizens had as much a right to discuss slavery as anyone else. In addition, the federal government had jurisdiction over slavery in the District of Columbia. Finally, the Constitution protected the freedoms of assembly, speech, and petition. Abolitionists condemned any efforts to limit what they said or how many people they organized to say it. They were in favor of a free public sphere in which associations in civil society could both appeal to public opinion and pressure lawmakers.[122]

When all else failed to silence abolitionism, political leaders from both parties turned to violence. In the South, vigilantism was encouraged as a way of protecting the Southern social order from Northern meddling. In the North, antiabolitionist mobs often attacked abolitionists when they tried to form an association in a new town. In the 1830s hostility to abolitionism was as strong or stronger in many communities than support for antislavery. Like mobs in the Revolutionary era, many of these mobs were led by local elites, from both the Whig and Democratic parties. In October 1835 a Boston mob led by respectable gentlemen, many of them Whigs, led Garrison out of a public meeting with a rope around his neck.[123] No party officially condoned mob activity—Democrats admitted they opposed mobs even more than "the madness of the abolitionists"—but mobs were an effective way to silence abolitionism when neither law nor politics could.[124]

Abolitionists pushed the new civil society and public sphere to its limits. They forced American voters and leaders to address an issue that many would have rather avoided and that proved explosive in American politics. That they did so even when faced with violence is a testament to their bravery and to their determination that in the United States all citizens have the right and the obligation to take part in democratic deliberation. As Garrison wrote in the first edition of his newspaper *The Liberator,* "I WILL BE HEARD," and in being heard he blazed a path for subsequent American activists. And he knew it. In 1873 he wrote Theodore Weld that "battles yet to be fought for the right" will rely on "the means and methods used in the Anti-Slavery movement."[125]

Whatever Garrison may have thought about his methods, Democrats could not reconcile the new civil society, with both its elite and grassroots public spheres, with the Jeffersonian tradition. In their rhetoric and when possible through public policy, they sought to minimize civil society's influence in politics. They kept alive the Jeffersonian dream of a nation of equal citizens and a government controlled by them. Democrats ensured that Americans would continue to debate the new civil society, comparing the gains made for citizens to participate in deliberation with the cost of permitting well-organized minorities disproportionate influence.

# Conclusion

AMERICANS CONSIDER an independent civil society essential to a functioning democracy. We assume therefore that it was a natural and celebrated outcome of the American Revolution. This study has argued the opposite. America's founding elites, whether Federalist or Jeffersonian Republican, did not imagine, much less desire, a civil society composed of self-created associations and private nonprofit institutions. The development of American civil society by the 1830s represents the eclipse of a more robust ideal of republican self-government shared by leaders of the founding generation, and the fruition of a more pluralistic and deliberative conception of democracy. When Alexis de Tocqueville visited the United States in 1831, the jury was still out on whether the new civil society completed or undermined the Revolution's core ideals.

To America's largest political party in the 1830s, the proliferation of private associations and corporations posed a clear threat to democracy. Democrats, remaining true to their Jeffersonian heritage, argued that organized groups inevitably have more power and influence than the unorganized many. The new civil society and its public sphere was not a deliberative space but a site for the best-organized interests to influence politicians. Democrats concluded that civil society's public influence must be limited to protect the common good. Local control combined with the protection of individual rights would ensure that the people, not groups, retained power. This skeptical appraisal of American civil society was countered by new ideas about civil society's positive contribution to democratic public life. Rejecting the Democrats' critique, middle-class reformers suggested that by enhancing the influence of ordinary citizens, civil society completed rather than undermined the promise of the American Revolution. Individual citizens were powerless unless they organized. Voluntary associations allowed motivated citizens to promote their values and interests by appealing to public opinion. Since public opinion was malleable, the freedom of association ensured that democratic deliberation was not limited to political officeholders. Challenging both the Jacksonians and reformers, elite Whigs concluded that public opinion was a dangerous king. Some values and policies were worth promoting because they were good, not popular. A democracy that forced all persons to bow to the will of the majority was not a free society. Private institutions and government agencies staffed by virtuous educated citizens would better promote the common good because they did not rely on the shifting sands of democratic politics.

Alexis de Tocqueville listened to these debates while touring the new United States. Intrigued by the proliferation of voluntary associations and private corporations, Tocqueville sought to understand their origins and function. Believing that Americans distrusted government but lacked any other mediating institutions to carry out their collective lives, Tocqueville concluded that associations and corporations were vital to democracies. In the United States, individuals were separate and powerless. Only by coming together could they pursue their shared ends. But Tocqueville also suggested that voluntary associations and corporations enhanced democracy by protecting minorities and ensuring democratic deliberation. Tocqueville's *Democracy in America* synthesized arguments made by both elite Whigs and middle-class reformers.

Tocqueville shared Whigs' concern that democratic majorities might threaten the common good, including liberty itself.[1] Tocqueville's thinking was influenced by Massachusetts Whig, Unitarian, and Harvard historian Jared Sparks. Sparks alerted Tocqueville to the almost religious value Americans assigned to public opinion, aiding Tocqueville's conclusion that "in democratic societies, the public possesses a singular power, of which no aristocratic nation can even conceive. Rather than persuade people of its beliefs, it imposes them, it permeates men's souls with them through the powerful pressure that the mind of all exerts on the intelligence of each." Civil society acts as a countervailing power against this "tyranny of the majority," fulfilling the function Tocqueville assigned to the Old World nobility who "constitute natural associations that halt abuses of power." The American Revolution had wiped away all intermediary bodies, leaving "no impediment to any form of tyranny." Only by joining together could Americans limit the dangerous tendencies of majoritarian democracy.[2]

Tocqueville also concluded that civil society could enhance democratic deliberation by allowing ordinary people to help shape public opinion. If public opinion is king, in civil society's public sphere intelligent minorities might be able to influence it and, in time, transform a minority opinion into the majority opinion. When Tocqueville first observed temperance conventions he did not understand their significance. Upon reflection, however, he concluded that the temperance movement demonstrated how individuals could shape beliefs from the grass roots. The lesson he learned is that "when Americans have a feeling or idea they wish to bring to the world's attention, they will immediately seek out others who share that feeling or idea and, if successful in finding them, join forces. From that point on, they cease to be isolated individuals and become a power to be reckoned with, whose actions serve as an example; a power that speaks, and to which people listen."[3] If Democrats worried that organizing threatens egalitarian republicanism, Tocqueville responded that it might enhance it by giving powerless individuals like William Lloyd Garrison the ability to influence public affairs.

Unlike most Americans in the 1830s, Tocqueville was confident that voluntary associations and corporations, even as they promoted diverse and competing goals, also enhanced communal solidarity. In associations, Tocqueville wrote, "feelings are renewed, the heart enlarged, and the understanding developed by the reciprocal action of men one upon another."[4] Like Federalists in the 1790s, Tocqueville believed that associations foster ties between citizens that make it more likely that citizens will put the good of others ahead of their own interests. In ways that Americans were only beginning to understand, Tocqueville concluded that a pluralistic independent civil society could strengthen rather than undermine communities. Perhaps the Revolutionary generation was wrong to fear that the spread of associations would necessarily lead to social fragmentation.[5]

Throughout his discussion of voluntarism Tocqueville's primary concern was to protect minorities from majorities. He largely rejected Democrats' concerns. To Tocqueville, democratic majorities "pose so great a peril" to liberty that they had to be checked. Discussing political parties, Tocqueville wrote, "the freedom of association has become a necessary guarantee against the tyranny of the majority." A minority must be able "to bring all its moral force to bear on the material power that oppresses it." By organizing in civil society and offering alternatives, minorities "weaken the moral ascendancy of the majority" and also "promote competition among ideas in order to discover which arguments are more likely to make an impression on the majority."[6] Tocqueville barely addressed the Jeffersonian concern of whether organized groups in civil society could trump the common good to serve their own interests. Would equality, and thus republican liberty, be undermined if powerful groups dominated deliberation and corrupted the halls of power? Democrats would have been left wondering.

Americans continued to debate the merits of civil society even as they continued to build it. The Civil War provided elites an opportunity to prove their public utility. Serving on the United States Sanitary Commission and as officers in the Union Army, elites demonstrated the benefits of virtue and knowledge.[7] Following the war, Harvard's president Charles Eliot defended Harvard's tax exemption and argued that private nonprofit institutions provide both economic and civic benefits to the community, convincing Massachusetts's legislature to increase the ceiling of tax-exempt charitable property and to grant tax exemptions to a wide range of nonprofit organizations. Massachusetts's law served as a model for other states and, during the twentieth century, for the federal government.[8]

Elites justified their privileges by emphasizing the public value of their expertise. As many historians have noted, the late nineteenth and early twentieth centuries witnessed the rise of professionals with specialized knowledge.[9] Private institutions staffed by educated experts would solve America's social, political, and economic problems, these elites proclaimed. But experts need training. Relying on private gifts, Harvard transformed itself from a parochial college into a graduate research university while other wealthy donors established new research institutions, including Clark University, the University of Chicago, and the Johns Hopkins University. Philanthropists also endowed new foundations to fund social scientific research, most notably those established by Andrew Carnegie, John D. Rockefeller, and Margaret Olivia Sage. Private think tanks such as the Brookings Institution, the Russell Sage Foundation, and the Social Science Research Council funded experts seeking to understand America's problems. Universities, foundations, and think tanks together created a national elite of experts outside government, but government also changed. Civil service reform and Progressive distrust of party politics helped produce a new bureaucracy staffed by experts who, as the Whigs had hoped, were supposed to use knowledge instead of politics to serve the common good. The result was an elite public sphere composed of experts trained by and housed in private institutions who influenced government not by shaping public opinion or participating in electoral politics but by building relationships with like-minded experts in new government bureaucracies. In Peter Dobkin Hall's words, these relationships "would become the basis of a new kind of political process—one based on policy rather than partisan politics."[10]

Massachusetts's Charles Francis Adams, born in 1835, helps us understand the transition from the Whigs' world to that of the modern professional who seeks to use his or her expertise to serve the public welfare. Reflecting on the need for better public policies for railroads following the Civil War, Adams outlined

> a new system, springing out of a great necessity—a new phase of representative government. Work hitherto badly done, spasmodically done, superficially done, ignorantly done, and too often corruptly done by temporary and irresponsible legislative committees, is in future to be reduced to order and science by the labors of permanent bureaus, and placed by them before legislatures for intelligent action.

Adams helped establish Massachusetts's Board of Railroad Commissioners, building on the precedent of other boards, including Horace Mann's Board of Education. He was confident that virtuous educated elites, if given the right positions and bureaucratic autonomy, could manage the complex institutions of modern society better than elected politicians.[11]

Even as elites in the Gilded Age and Progressive era reinforced their authority and autonomy, reformers continued to expand the possibilities of the grassroots public sphere. They achieved their biggest victory with the Eighteenth Amendment to the Constitution prohibiting the manufacture and sale of alcohol. Temperance reformers refused to allow political elites to dominate public deliberation. Relying on voluntary associations and the auxiliary system, the Women's Christian Temperance Union and the Anti-Saloon League engaged in statewide and then national campaigns to change public opinion and to pressure lawmakers. To these reformers, like their antebellum counterparts, one of the largest benefits of living in a democracy was, as Tocqueville understood, the ability to mobilize in civil society to influence politics.[12]

As the elite and grassroots public spheres expanded, other Americans continued to invoke the Jeffersonian fear of private groups. Populists who formed the People's Party, and others within the Democratic fold, condemned the close alliance between parties and corporate interests that threatened the welfare and liberties of the unorganized many.[13] In order to weaken the dominance of parties, populists teamed up with some Progressives to support direct democracy—the referendum, initiative, and recall—which would return political power to the people by bypassing a public sphere corrupted by organized interests.[14] Labor unionists meanwhile argued that unions, unlike corporations, were not special interests but rather embodied the interests of all working Americans.[15] Jeffersonian critics also condemned the new philanthropies established by America's elite. They argued that elite control of American public life was sustained, in the words of Frank Walsh, a populist Democrat and chair of the U.S. Commission of Industrial Relations, an investigative commission created by Congress in 1912, "through the creation of enormous privately managed funds for indefinite purposes." Walsh argued that the Rockefeller endowments derived from "the exploitation of American workers" and that its money rightly belongs "to the American people."[16] In 1934 Congress embraced the Jeffersonian-Jacksonian call to separate private wealth from public power by limiting nonprofit philanthropic foundations' political activities. Following a series of attacks on foundations by Democratic Congressman Wright Patman of Texas, Congress again took up the issue in the 1960s. Senator Al Gore Sr. urged the liquidation of all foundations after forty years. Many argued that philanthropies did not merit their tax exemptions. Although these measures were not ultimately supported, Congress did raise the wall of separation in the 1969 tax reform act—one of the most important pieces of legislation in the history of American philanthropy—by prohibiting private foundations from engaging in any activity designed to influence legislation or political campaigns. As Jefferson and Massachusetts's Democratic governor Marcus Morton both argued, immortal wealthy private institutions could endanger democratic self-government. By seeking to limit the political influence of private philanthropy, Congress expressed the Jeffersonian hope that political power would remain in the hands of the many rather than the organized few.[17]

Democrats also actively resisted the grassroots public sphere when it threatened the Southern white majority. Just as they had responded to abolitionists, so they responded to civil rights activists in the 1950s and 1960s. Rather than protect the freedoms of association and speech for protestors, Southern Democrats relied on legal and illegal forms of coercion to scare and to silence them. Their failure is a testament to the power of civil society and the commitment of engaged citizens; their actions remind us that popular majoritarianism in the South has often been connected to white supremacy.

The issue of civil society is part of a larger discussion of American pluralism. Rejecting the Jeffersonian tradition, some political scientists in the early twentieth century defined democratic government as nothing more than the expression of competing group interests. The populist effort to reassert the republican idea of "the people" was misguided in a complex modern society, pluralists asserted. Arthur Bentley's classic *The Process of Government* (1908) concluded that every individual is composed of various interests, and thus a member of many interest groups, each of which pressures government for particular outcomes. To Bentley, "society itself is nothing other than the complex of the groups that compose it."[18] Bentley's work anticipated those of David Truman and Robert Dahl.[19] In response, Mancur Olson offered a Jeffersonian-inspired critique of interest group pluralism in *The Logic of Collective Action* (1965). Like Jefferson and Jackson before him, Olson argued that groups were factions that represent special interests. An economist, Olson applied a new theoretical perspective to the problem. The smaller and more defined, the more "special" the interest, the easier it is and the greater the incentive its members have to organize. The more diffuse common good requires the unorganized many to represent themselves, a much harder task when the opportunity costs for not participating are low. As Jefferson himself recognized, the groups most likely to organize effectively did not represent the majority. Olson's argument suggests that the common good may be the true loser in a pluralistic group-based political system.[20]

The growth and acceptance of interest group politics has altered the relationship between civil society and democracy in twentieth-century America. The expansion of government combined with professional lobbying has resulted in voluntary membership associations that are unabashedly committed to serving minority group interests. Because political success now depends on lobbying distant lawmakers and administrative agencies rather than convincing a broad electorate, many organizations have little need of an active local grassroots base other than for dues. Voluntary associations have undergone, in Theda Skocpol's formulation, a transformation "from membership to management" as profound as the shift from trustee to member discussed in this study. If nineteenth-century reformers professed that their groups represented a higher good, modern interest groups need make no such apology. Interest groups instead rely on close alliances with government agencies and legislators to ensure that their constituents are well served.[21] The acceptance of interest-based politics fundamentally demeans civic activity. Yet even if Skocpol is correct that citizens today lack the same opportunities to participate in organizations as they had in the nineteenth century, the success of the civil rights movement and the rise of popular conservatism, including once again the growing influence of evangelicals, suggests that committed citizens can still influence politics from the grass roots.[22]

Even as we rightly celebrate America's voluntary tradition, it is worth remembering its tangled and contested history. Depending on the associations and institutions, their power and influence, and their goals, civil society can both expand and limit the possibilities for democratic self-government. Tocqueville was no doubt correct that private associations and nonprofit institutions encourage new forms of civic activity, protect minorities from overbearing majorities, and enhance democratic deliberation by permitting otherwise powerless citizens a place to speak. But the Jeffersonian critique is also a vital part of America's democratic tradition. We invoke it whenever we condemn special interests' influence in government and seek to put more political power into the hands of "the people." We also invoke it whenever we seek to retain political control over policies instead of permitting better-educated and more knowledgeable experts to decide for us our fate. In many ways the Jeffersonian populist remains true to the Revolutionary faith. We may be less sanguine today about the righteousness of democratic majorities than were the Jeffersonians, but even as we recognize the democratic possibilities opened up by civil society we should heed their warnings about the dangers. Idealistic Americans following the Revolution had a different vision for the American republic, one that had little room for an independent, pluralistic civil society. America was not foreordained to be a nation of joiners. Given the forces arrayed against it in 1776, its development is a remarkable achievement.

Notes
Acknowledgments
Index

# Notes

## Introduction

1. John L. Thomas, *The Liberator: William Lloyd Garrison, a Biography* (Boston, 1963).

2. Arthur M. Schlesinger, "Biography of a Nation of Joiners," *American Historical Review* 50, no. 1 (October 1944), 1–25.

3. Alexis de Tocqueville, *Democracy in America*, trans. Arthur Goldhammer (New York, 2004), 595–599.

4. For the purposes of this study, civil society is defined as the realm of voluntary associations and nonprofit corporations that are neither part of the state nor primarily interested in profit. In the 1780s, American civil society would not meet this definition. The institutions of civil society, for reasons elaborated in the text, were much more closely tied to and dependent on the state. It was only as a result of intense debates over the relationship between civil society and the state that Americans separated the one from the other. Not until the 1820s did Americans really start talking about an independent civil society. It should also be noted that the term civil society has its own history. At first, it referred simply to the realm of law; as John Locke wrote, one moved from the state of nature to form "Political, or Civil Society." Americans in the eighteenth and early nineteenth centuries tended to use the term in this manner, which is different from our contemporary usage. For theoretical explorations of civil society, see Michael Walzer, "The Idea of Civil Society," *Dissent* (Spring 1991), 293–304; Adam B. Seligman, *The Idea of Civil Society* (Princeton, N.J., 1992); Jean L. Cohen and Andrew Arato, *Civil Society and Political Theory* (Cambridge, Mass., 1992); H. Islamoglu, "Concept and History of Civil Society," in *International Encyclopedia of the Social and Behavioral Sciences*, ed. Paul M. Baltes, 26 vols. (New York, 2001), 1891–1896. For a history of the idea of civil society, see John Keane, *Civil Society and the State: New European Perspectives* (London, 1988), 35–71; John Ehrenberg,

*Civil Society: The Critical History of an Idea* (New York, 1999); Seligman, *The Idea of Civil Society;* Cohen and Arato, *Civil Society and Political Theory,* 82–174; Stefan-Ludwig Hoffmann, *Civil Society, 1750–1914* (New York, 2006).

5. Robert A. Nisbet, *The Quest for Community: A Study in the Ethics of Order and Freedom* (New York, 1953), 232, 235. For a discussion of the Cold War context, see David Ciepley, "Why the State Was Dropped in the First Place: A Prequel to Skocpol's 'Bringing the State Back In,'" *Critical Review* 14, nos. 2–3 (2000 [2001]), 157–213.; Karen Orren and Stephen Skowronek, *The Search for American Political Development* (New York, 2004), 2.

6. Galbriel Almond and Sidney Verba, *The Civic Culture: Political Attitudes and Democracy in Five Nations, an Analytic Study* (Boston, 1965), 245. See also Gabriel Almond, "The Intellectual History of the Civic Culture Concept," in *The Civic Culture Revisited,* ed. Gabriel Almond and Sidney Verba (Newbury Park, Calif., 1989), 1–36.

7. Schlesinger, "Biography of a Nation of Joiners"; Oscar Handlin and Mary Handlin, *The Dimensions of Liberty* (Cambridge, Mass., 1961), 89–112.

8. Theda Skocpol, "Bringing the State Back In: Strategies of Analysis in Current Research," in *Bringing the State Back In,* ed. Peter B. Evans, Dietrich Rueschemeyer, and Theda Skocpol (Cambridge, 1985), 3–37; Theda Skocpol, *Diminished Democracy: From Membership to Management in American Civic Life* (Norman, Okla., 2003), 20–73; Theda Skocpol, Marshall Ganz, and Ziad Munson, "A Nation of Organizers: The Institutional Origins of Civic Voluntarism in the United States," *American Political Science Review* 94, no. 3 (September 2000), 527–546; Michael Schudson, "The 'Public Sphere' and Its Problems: Bringing the State (Back) In," *Notre Dame Journal of Law, Ethics, and Public Policy* 8 (1994), 529–546; Richard R. John, "Governmental Institutions as Agents of Change: Rethinking American Political Development in the Early Republic, 1787–1835," *Studies in American Political Development* 11, no. 2 (1997), 347–380, and *Spreading the News: The American Postal System from Franklin to Morse* (Cambridge, Mass., 1995); William J. Novak, "The American Law of Association: The Legal-Political Construction of Civil Society," *Studies in American Political Development* 15 (Fall 2001), 163–188; Keith Whittington, "Revisiting Tocqueville's America: Society, Politics, and Association in the Nineteenth Century," in *Beyond Tocqueville: Civil Society and the Social Capital Debate in Comparative Perspective,* ed. Bob Edwards, Michael W. Foley, and Mario Dani (Hanover, N.H., 2001), 21–31.

9. Kathleen D. McCarthy, *American Creed: Philanthropy and the Rise of Civil Society* (Chicago, 2003), 1–2, 13–14; Gordon S. Wood, "Thomas Jefferson, Equality, and the Creation of a Civil Society," *Fordham Law Review* 64, no. 5 (April 1996), 2133–2146; Gordon S. Wood, *Radicalism of the American Revolution* (New York, 1991), 328–329; Marc Harris, "Civil Society in Post-Revolutionary America," in *Empire and Nation: The American Revolution in the Atlantic World,* ed. Eliga H. Gould and Peter S. Onuf (Baltimore, 2005), 197–216, esp. 211. Joyce O. Appleby, *Inheriting the Revolution: The First Generation of Americans* (Cambridge, Mass., 2000), 194–238, draws a less direct connection between voluntary associations and Jeffersonianism, although she implies that associations expressed the Jeffersonian spirit: "Yet the rhetoric of free choice may have faded with the memory of Jefferson's election had democratic bombast not yielded to new cultural forms" (voluntary associations). Appleby quoted at 194.

10. Thomas Jefferson to Jedidiah Morse, March 6, 1822, in *Thomas Jefferson: Writings*, ed. Merrill D. Peterson (New York, 1984), 1454–1458.

11. Oscar Handlin and Mary Flug Handlin, *Commonwealth: A Study of the Role of Government in the American Economy: Massachusetts 1774–1861*, rev. ed. (Cambridge, Mass., 1969); Edgar W. Knight, "North Carolina's 'Dartmouth College Case,'" *Journal of Higher Education* 19, no. 3 (March 1948), 116–122; Irvin G. Wyllie, "The Search for an American Law of Charity," *Mississippi Valley Historical Review* 44, no. 2 (September 1959), 203–221; Howard S. Miller, *The Legal Foundations of American Philanthropy, 1776–1844* (Madison, Wis., 1961); Richard Hofstadter, *The Idea of a Party System: The Rise of Legitimate Opposition in the United States, 1780–1840* (Berkeley, Calif., 1969); William G. McLoughlin, *New England Dissent, 1630–1883: The Baptists and the Separation of Church and State*, 2 vols. (Cambridge, Mass., 1971); Jürgen Herbst, *From Crisis to Crisis: American College Government, 1636–1819* (Cambridge, Mass., 1982), 216–218; Henrik Hartog, *Public Property and Private Power: The Corporation of the City of New York in American Law, 1730–1870* (Ithaca, N.Y., 1983); Ralph Ketcham, *Presidents above Party: The First American Presidency, 1789–1829* (Chapel Hill, N.C., 1984); Bruce A. Campbell, "Social Federalism: The Constitutional Position of Nonprofit Corporations in Nineteenth-Century America," *Law and History Review* 8, no. 2 (Fall 1990), 149–188; Peter Dobkin Hall, *Inventing the Nonprofit Sector and Other Essays on Philanthropy, Voluntarism, and Nonprofit Organizations* (Baltimore, 1992); Hall, "A Historical Overview of Philanthropy, Voluntary Associations, and Nonprofit Organizations in the United States, 1600–2000," in *The Nonprofit Sector: A Research Handbook*, ed. Walter W. Powell and Richard Steinberg, 2nd ed. (New Haven, Conn., 2006), 32–65; Stanley Elkins and Eric McKitrick, *The Age of Federalism: The Early American Republic, 1788–1800* (New York, 1993), 451–461; Pauline Maier, "The Revolutionary Origins of the American Corporation," *William and Mary Quarterly* 50, no. 1 (January 1993), 51–84; John L. Brooke, "Ancient Lodges and Self-Created Societies: Voluntary Association and the Public Sphere in the Early Republic," in *Launching the Extended Republic: The Federalist Era*, ed. Ronald Hoffman and Peter J. Albert (Charlottesville, Va., 1996), 273–377; Thomas E. Buckley, S.J., "The Use and Abuse of Jefferson's Statute: Separating Church and State in Nineteenth-Century Virginia," in *Religion and the New Republic: Faith in the Founding of America*, ed. James H. Hutson (Lanham, Md., 2000), 41–63, esp. 45–49; Albrecht Koschnik, "The Democratic Societies of Philadelphia and the Limits of the American Public Sphere, circa 1793–1795," *William and Mary Quarterly* 68, no. 3 (July 2001), 615–636, and *"Let a Common Interest Bind Us Together": Associations, Partisanship, and Culture in Philadelphia, 1775–1840* (Charlottesville, Va., 2007), chs. 1–3; Johann N. Neem, "Freedom of Association in the Early Republic: The Republican Party, the Whiskey Rebellion, and the Philadelphia and New York Cordwainers' Cases," *Pennsylvania Magazine of History and Biography* 127, no. 3 (July 2003), 259–290, and "Politics and the Origins of the Nonprofit Corporation in Massachusetts and New Hampshire, 1780–1820," *Nonprofit and Voluntary Sector Quarterly* 32, no. 3 (September 2003), 344–365; Mark D. McGarvie, *One Nation Under Law: America's Early National Struggles to Separate Church and State* (DeKalb, Ill., 2004); Harris, "Civil Society in Post-Revolutionary America"; Scott Gregory Lien, "Contested Solidarities: Philanthropy, Justice, and the Reconstitution of Public Authority in the United States, 1790–1860" (Ph.D. diss., University of Chicago, 2006).

12. The case is *Currie's Administrators v. Mutual Assurance Society* (1809), as quoted and discussed in Margaret E. Horsnell, *Spencer Roane: Judicial Advocate of Jeffersonian Principles* (New York, 1986), 96–119.

13. Massachusetts Constitution of 1780, reprinted in Oscar Handlin and Mary Handlin, eds., *Popular Sources of Political Authority: Documents on the Massachusetts Constitution of 1780* (Cambridge, Mass., 1966), 441–472.

14. Fisher Ames to Thomas Dwight, September 11, 1794, in *Works of Fisher Ames*, ed. Seth Ames (Boston, 1854), 150.

15. *Thomas Barnes v. The Inhabitants of the First Parish of Falmouth* (6 Tyng 334 [1810]). To understand the development of an independent civil society we must take an approach similar to historians of religion who have written about the disestablishment of the church. We must find out why the state was hostile to the proliferation of self-created groups, figure out which constituencies challenged the state's monopoly in civil society, and determine what arguments they made to justify their claims. In other words, we must think about the separation of civil society from the state as a process similar to that which led to the separation of church from state.

16. On this point see most recently Koschnik, *"Let a Common Interest Bind Us Together."*

17. Jürgen Habermas, *The Structural Transformation of the Public Sphere: An Inquiry into a Category of Bourgeois Society*, trans. Thomas Burger (Cambridge, Mass., 1989). My understanding of Habermas relies on James Van Horn Melton, *The Rise of the Public in Enlightenment Europe* (New York, 2001), 1–15; Ehrenberg, *Civil Society*, 219–224; Charles Taylor, "Liberal Politics and the Public Sphere" in *New Communitarian Thinking: Persons, Virtues, Institutions, and Communities*, ed. Amitai Etzioni (Charlottesville, Va., 1995), 183–217; Anthony J. La Vopa, "Conceiving a Public: Ideas and Society in Eighteenth-Century Europe," *Journal of Modern History* 64, no. 1 (March 1992), 76–116; Craig Calhoun, ed., *Habermas and the Public Sphere* (Cambridge, Mass., 1992).

18. For a good discussion of the literature on the public sphere, see John L. Brooke, "Consent, Civil Society, and the Public Sphere in the Age of Revolution and the Early American Republic," in *Beyond the Founders: New Approaches to the Political History of the Early American Republic*, ed. Jeffrey L. Pasley, Andrew W. Robertson, and David Waldstreicher (Chapel Hill, N.C., 2004), 207–250; Brooke, "Reason and Passion in the Public Sphere: Habermas and the Cultural Historians," *Journal of Interdisciplinary History* 29 (Summer 1998), 43–67. Representative works include Michael Warner, *The Letters of the Republic: Publication and the Public Sphere in Eighteenth-Century America* (Cambridge, Mass., 1990); Mary P. Ryan, *Women in Public: Between Banners and Ballots, 1825–1880* (Baltimore, 1990), esp. 130–171, *Civic Wars: Democracy and Public Life in the American City during the Nineteenth Century* (Berkeley, Calif., 1997), and "Gender and Public Access: Women's Politics in Nineteenth-Century America," in *Habermas and the Public Sphere*, ed. Craig Calhoun, 259–288; David Waldstreicher, *In the Midst of Perpetual Fetes: The Making of American Nationalism* (Chapel Hill, N.C., 1997); Simon P. Newman, *Parades and Politics of the Street: Festive Culture in the Early American Republic* (Philadelphia, 1997); Nancy Isenberg, *Sex and Citizenship in Antebellum America* (Chapel Hill, N.C., 1998); Christopher Grasso, *A Speaking Aristocracy: Transforming Public Discourse in Eighteenth-Century Connecticut* (Chapel Hill, N.C., 1999); Saul Cornell, *The Other Founders: Anti-Federalism and the Dissenting Tradition in*

*America, 1788–1828* (Chapel Hill, N.C., 1999), 195–218; John L. Brooke, "To Be 'Read by the Whole People': Press, Party, and Public Sphere in the United States, 1789–1840," *Proceedings of the American Antiquarian Society* 110, no. 11 (2002), 41–118; Koschnik, *"Let a Common Interest Bind Us Together".*

19. Albrecht Koschnik, John L. Brooke, Stanley Elkins, Eric McKitrick, and Saul Cornell have all examined how Americans conceptualized the public sphere in relation to political parties and partisan politics. I build on their approach but broaden the discussion to include more types of associations and other social groups involved in reconceptualizing American civil society and its public sphere. See Koschnik, *"Let a Common Interest Bind Us Together";* Brooke, "To Be 'Read by the Whole People'"; Elkins and McKitrick, *The Age of Federalism,* 451–461; Cornell, *The Other Founders,* 195–218.

20. For the rise of the public sphere in eighteenth-century Europe and Britain, in addition to the formulation of Habermas, *Structural Transformation,* see Van Horn Melton, *The Rise of the Public;* Dorinda Outram, *The Enlightenment* (Cambridge, 1995), 14–30; Reinhart Koselleck, *Critique and Crisis: Enlightenment and the Pathogenesis of Modern Society* (Cambridge, 1988).

21. On this point, see Brooke, "Consent, Civil Society, and the Public Sphere" and "To Be 'Read by the Whole People.'" See also Harris, "Civil Society in Post-Revolutionary America."

## 1. The Revolutionary Commonwealth

1. Stanley Elkins and Eric McKitrick, *The Age of Federalism* (New York, 1993); Peter Onuf and Nicholas Onuf, *Federal Union, Modern World: The Law of Nations in an Age of Revolutions, 1776–1814* (Madison, Wis., 1993).

2. Gordon S. Wood, "Alexander Hamilton and the Making of a Fiscal-Military State," in *Revolutionary Characters: What Made the Founders Different* (New York, 2006), 121–140; Stephen Minicucci, "The 'Cement of Interest': Interest-Based Models of Nation-Building in the Early Republic," *Social Science History* 25, no. 2 (Summer 2001), 247–274; Rogers Smith, "Constructing American National Identity: Strategies of the Federalists," in *Federalists Reconsidered,* ed. Doron Ben-Atar and Barbara Oberg (Charlottesville, Va., 1998), 19–40; Johann N. Neem, "Civil Society and American Nationalism, 1776–1865," in *Politics and Partnerships: Nonprofit Organizations and American Governance,* ed. Elisabeth Clemens and Douglas Guthrie (forthcoming, University of Chicago Press).

3. Benedict Anderson, *Imagined Communities: Reflections on the Origin and Spread of Nationalism* (London, 1983).

4. Thomas Jefferson, "A Declaration by the Representatives of the United States of America, in General Congress Assembled" (July 4, 1776), in *Thomas Jefferson: Writings,* ed. Merrill D. Peterson (New York, 1984), 19–24. On the idea of "the people" generally, see Edmund S. Morgan, *Inventing the People: The Rise of Popular Sovereignty in England and America* (New York, 1988).

5. Edmund S. Morgan, *The Puritan Dilemma: The Story of John Winthrop* (Boston, 1958); Richard L. Bushman, *King and People in Provincial Massachusetts* (Chapel Hill, N.C., 1985).

6. Richard D. Brown, *Revolutionary Politics in Massachusetts: The Boston Committee of Correspondence and the Towns, 1772–1774* (Cambridge, Mass., 1970); John L. Brooke, *The Heart of the Commonwealth: Society and Political Culture in Worcester*

*County, Massachusetts, 1713–1861* (New York, 1989); William Pencak, *War, Politics, and Revolution in Provincial Massachusetts* (Boston, 1981). As François Furet has observed about the French Revolution, when a group of leaders seek to speak on behalf of the population they are also likely to conflate their own ideas and goals with those of "the people." See Furet, "The French Revolution Is Over," in *Interpreting the French Revolution* (trans. 1978; Cambridge, 1981), 1–79. See also Reinhart Koselleck, *Critique and Crisis: Enlightenment and the Pathogenesis of Modern Society* (trans. 1959; Cambridge, 1988); Keith Michael Baker, "Representation Redefined," in *Inventing the French Revolution: Essays on French Political Culture in the Eighteenth Century* (Cambridge, 1990), 224–251; James Van Horn Melton, *The Rise of the Public in Enlightenment Europe* (New York, 2001); Pierre Rosanvallon, *The Demands of Liberty: Civil Society in France since the Revolution* (Cambridge, Mass., 2007). A similar process took place during the 1989 revolution in Poland, in which the organization Solidarity claimed to speak for "the people" against the communist regime but, following the demise of the regime, lacked the language to differentiate between itself and the people. See Krishan Kumar, "Civil Society: An Inquiry into the Usefulness of a Historical Term," in *1989: Revolutionary Ideas and Ideals* (Minneapolis, Minn., 2001), 142–170, esp. 155–157.

7. For a discussion of these divisions, see Stephen E. Patterson, *Political Parties in Revolutionary Massachusetts* (Madison, Wis., 1973).

8. *Journal of the Convention for Framing a Constitution of Government for the State of Massachusetts Bay* (Boston, 1832), 192. The constitution is reprinted in Oscar Handlin and Mary Handlin, eds., *Popular Sources of Political Authority: Documents on the Massachusetts Constitution of 1780* (Cambridge, Mass., 1966), 441–472. Many historians have commented on the communitarian character of the Massachusetts constitution. See Oscar Handlin and Mary Flug Handlin, *Commonwealth: A Study of the Role of Government in the American Economy: Massachusetts 1774–1861* (Cambridge, Mass., 1969), 3–31; Ronald Peters Jr., *The Massachusetts Constitution of 1780: A Social Compact* (Amherst, Mass., 1978); Willi Paul Adams, *The First American Constitutions: Republican Ideology and the Making of the State Constitutions in the Revolutionary Era* (trans. 1973; Chapel Hill, N.C., 1980); Donald S. Lutz, *The Origins of American Constitutionalism* (Baton Rouge, La., 1988). In general, see also Quentin Skinner, *Liberty before Liberalism* (Cambridge, 1998); Gordon S. Wood, *Creation of the American Republic, 1776–1787* (New York, 1969).

9. Henry Cumings, "A Sermon preached before His Honor Thomas Cushing . . ." (Boston, 1783).

10. *Journal of the Convention*, 216–217.

11. Among many books, see Amy Gutmann and Dennis Thompson, *Democracy and Disagreement* (Cambridge, Mass., 1996); Michael Walzer, *Thick and Thin: Moral Argument at Home and Abroad* (Notre Dame, Ind., 1994); John Rawls, *Political Liberalism* (New York, 1993); William A. Galston, *Liberal Purposes: Goods, Virtues, and Diversity in the Liberal State* (Cambridge, 1991); Stephen Macedo, *Liberal Virtues: Citizenship, Virtue and Community in Liberal Constitutionalism* (New York, 1990). For a discussion of these distinctions in early America, see Lutz, *Origins of American Constitutionalism*; Wood, *Creation of the American Republic*.

12. Nathanael Niles, *Two Discourses on Liberty . . .* (Newburyport, Mass., 1774).

13. John Adams to Mercy Warren, April 16, 1776, quoted in John R. Howe Jr., *The Changing Political Thought of John Adams* (Princeton, N.J., 1966), 31–32.

14. Samuel Adams, "Determinatus" (January 8, 1770), in *The Writings of Samuel Adams*, 4 vols., ed. Harry Alonzo Cushing (New York, 1904–1908), 2:05. See also Adams to Caleb Davis (April 3, 1781) in Ibid., 4:255; Adams, "Extract of a Letter from the *Southward*" (April 12, 1781), in Ibid., 4:25–55; Adams to the Legislature of Massachusetts (January 16, 1795), in Ibid., 4:370. On Samuel Adams's conception of virtue, see Pauline Maier, *The Old Revolutionaries: Political Lives in the Age of Samuel Adams* (New York, 1980), 3–50.

15. Samuel Adams to Caleb Davis, April 3, 1781, in *Writings of Samuel Adams*, 4:255.

16. [Theophilus Parsons] "Essex Result" (1778), in *Popular Sources*, 330.

17. Robert Taylor, *Western Massachusetts in the Revolution* (Providence, R.I., 1954); Gregory H. Nobles, *Divisions Throughout the Whole: Politics and Society in Hampshire County, Massachusetts, 1740–1775* (New York, 1983); John L. Brooke, "To the Quiet of the People: Revolutionary Settlements and Civil Unrest in Western Massachusetts, 1774–1789," *William and Mary Quarterly* 46, no. 3 (July 1989), 425–462, and *The Heart of the Commonwealth*; Barry Alain Shain, *Myth of American Individualism: The Protestant Origins of American Political Thought* (Princeton, N.J., 1994); Woody Holton, "An 'Excess of Democracy'—Or a Shortage? The Federalists' Earliest Adversaries," *Journal of the Early Republic* 25, no. 3 (Fall 2005), 339–382.

18. "Return of Sandisfield" (1779), in *Popular Sources*, 420.

19. "Return of Sunderland" (1780), in Ibid., 610.

20. *Journal of the Convention*, 216–217.

21. "Return of Ward, Worcester County" (1780), in *Popular Sources*, 888. For others, see Ibid., 478, 483, 503, 519, 524, 565, 566, 567, 590–591, 604, 607, 610, 623, 639, 644, 654, 663–664, 695, 735–738, 742–743, 792, 810–812, 849–850, 869, 887, 888, 889, 893, 895, 896, 898, 905, 917, 923. For opposing perspectives, see Ibid., 539, 575, 793, 840.

22. John Adams, "Thoughts on Government" (1776), in *The Works of John Adams*, ed. Charles Francis Adams (Boston, 1851), 4:195.

23. [Parsons], "Essex Result," 341.

24. *Journal of the Convention*, 219. See Patterson, *Political Parties*, 143–170.

25. Massachusetts Constitution of 1780 Declaration of Rights, Art. 7.

26. For Adams's political thought, see C. Bradley Thompson, *John Adams and the Spirit of Liberty* (Lawrence, Kans., 1998); Richard Adam Samuelson, "The Adams Family and the American Experiment" (Ph.D. diss., University of Virginia, 2000).

27. For the debate over the ratification of the constitution, see Samuel Eliot Morison, "The Struggle over the Ratification of the Constitution of 1780," *Proceedings of the Massachusetts Historical Society* 50 (1917), 353–411; Samuel Eliot Morison, *The Formation of the Massachusetts Constitution. An Address on the Occasion of the 175th Anniversary of the Constitution* (Boston, 1955); Patterson, *Political Parties*, 234–235, 244–246; Peter S. Field, *The Crisis of the Standing Order: Clerical Intellectuals and Cultural Authority in Massachusetts, 1780–1833* (Amherst, Mass., 1998), 30–46.

28. In her dissertation on the evolution of the freedom of assembly in American constitutional law, Betty Barnes argues that the right of assembly was intended to protect the interests of the whole community from corrupt governments and

"was not originally aimed at protecting small segments of the community who were opposed to the values and interests which the majority believed to be necessary for the common good." See Barnes, "The Origins and Development of Freedom of Assembly" (Ph.D. diss., University of Houston, 1990), 34–35. See also Susan Zaeske, *Signatures of Citizenship: Petitioning, Antislavery, and Women's Political Identity* (Chapel Hill, N.C., 2003), 11–28; Don L. Smith, "The Right to Petition for Redress of Grievances: Constitutional Development and Interpretations" (Ph.D. diss., Texas Tech University, 1971). For an overview of the development of the freedom of association in the United States, see Johann N. Neem, "Freedom of Association," in *The Encyclopedia of American Civil Liberties*, 4 vols., ed. Paul Finkelman (New York, 2006), 1:634–636

29. Massachusetts Constitution of 1780. As radical as Article Six might be, it did not go as far as legislators in Virginia, who repealed the Elizabethan statute for charitable uses and were generally hostile to corporations, nor France, where the republican revolution sought to destroy all corporate privileges, especially those of the Old Regime. See H. Miller, *The Legal Foundations of American Philanthropy, 1776–1844* (Madison, Wis., 1961); Rosanvallon, *The Demands of Liberty*; Edith Archambault, "Historical Roots of the Nonprofit Sector in France," *Nonprofit and Voluntary Sector Quarterly* 30, no. 2 (2001), 204–220. On corporations in early America, see Lawrence M. Friedman, *A History of American Law* (New York, 1973), 177–201; Handlin and Handlin, *Commonwealth*, 51–105; Albrecht Koschnik, "Voluntary Associations, Political Culture, and the Public Sphere in Philadelphia, 1780–1830" (Ph.D. diss., University of Virginia, 2000), 25–78. For the development of English corporate law, see Jeffrey Steven Kahana, "Regulating Labor: Tradition and Change in American Law, 1790–1850" (Ph.D. diss., Brandeis University, 2002), 74–82.

30. On this question, see Mark D. McGarvie, *One Nation under Law: America's Early National Struggles to Separate Church and State* (DeKalb, Ill., 2004).

31. Thomas Hobbes, *Leviathan* (1651), Part 2, ch. 23, in Edwin A. Burtt, ed., *The English Philosophers from Bacon to Mill* (New York, 1939), 211.

32. "Cato" quoted in Ralph Ketcham, *Presidents above Party: The First American Presidency, 1789–1829* (Chapel Hill, N.C., 1984), 55.

33. Adam Smith quoted and discussed in John Dwyer, *The Age of the Passions: An Interpretation of Adam Smith and Scottish Enlightenment Culture* (East Linton, Scotland, 1998), 43, 65–66. See also James F. Becker, "The Corporation Spirit and Its Liberal Analysis," *Journal of the History of Ideas* 30, no. 1 (January–March 1969), 69–84.

34. Among many sources, see Oscar Handlin and Mary Handlin, *The Dimensions of Liberty* (Cambridge, Mass., 1961), 90–91; Anthony Black, *Guilds and Civil Society in European Political Thought from the Twelfth Century to the Present* (Ithaca, N.Y., 1984); Rosanvallon, *The Demands of Liberty*; Archambault, "Historical Roots of the Nonprofit Sector in France."

35. For example, see Jack P. Greene, *Peripheries and Center: Constitutional Development in the Extended Polities of the British Empire and the United States, 1607–1788* (Athens, Ga., 1986).

36. *Journal of the Convention*, 57–58.

37. W. C. Kessler, "Incorporation in New England: A Statistical Study, 1800–1875," *Journal of Economic History* 8, no. 1 (1948), 43–62; Pauline Maier,

"The Revolutionary Origins of the American Corporation," *William and Mary Quarterly* 50, no. 1 (January 1993), 51–84; Peter Dobkin Hall, *The Organization of American Culture, 1700–1900: Private Institutions, Elites and the Origins of American Nationality* (New York, 1982), 82. See also Edwin Merrick Dodd, *American Business Corporations until 1860, with Special Reference to Massachusetts* (Cambridge, Mass., 1954); Handlin and Handlin, *Commonwealth*, esp. 51–86. For a discussion of the role of corporations and internal improvements at the national level, see Lawrence M. Friedman, *A History of American Law* (New York, 1973), 177–201; Daniel B. Klein, "The Voluntary Provision of Public Goods? The Turnpike Companies of Early America," *Economic Inquiry* 28 (October 1990), 788–812; John Lauritz Larson, *Internal Improvement: National Public Works and the Promise of Popular Government in the Early United States* (Chapel Hill, N.C., 2001). Klein argues that investors were acting out their roles as public trustees and had little expectation of future profit. He notes that turnpike companies were consistently unprofitable and thus social obligation best explains why elites continued to buy stock in them.

38. Ch. 5, sec. 2 of the Massachusetts Constitution of 1780, in Handlin and Handlin, *Popular Sources*, 467.

39. Massachusetts Constitution of 1780, Declaration of Rights, Art. 3. John Adams did not draft this section of the Article.

40. *Journal of the Convention*, 216–217.

41. *Boston Gazette*, November 27, 1780.

42. For example, see Zabdiel Adams, "A Sermon preached before His Excellency John Hancock . . ." (Boston, 1782).

43. William G. McLoughlin, *New England Dissent, 1630–1883: The Baptists and the Separation of Church and State*, 2 vols. (Cambridge, Mass., 1971), 1:556–568.

44. Morison, "The Struggle over the Ratification of the Constitution of 1780"; Jacob C. Meyer, *Church and State in Massachusetts from 1740 to 1833: A Chapter in the History of the Development of Individual Freedom* (Cleveland, Ohio, 1930), 90–132. In *Crisis of the Standing Order*, 34–46, Peter S. Field argues that Article Three was a "compromise" that granted Congregational ministers the status and taxing power they desired while protecting religious liberty. Nonetheless, according to Field, ministers were determined to use the state to support their churches. Similarly, in his authoritative study of church-state issues, *New England Dissent*, William G. McLoughlin notes that both sides of the debate have merit and it depends on the perspective one took toward religious liberty. McLoughlin's narrative, however, emphasizes the struggle of Baptists and other dissenters to secure the freedom of conscience in the face of hostile state leaders.

45. Conrad Wright, "Piety, Morality, and the Commonwealth," in *The Unitarian Controversy: Essays on American Unitarian History* (Boston, 1994), 17–35; Charles H. Lippy, "The 1780 Constitution: Religious Establishment or Civil Religion?" *Journal of Church and State* 20, no. 3 (Autumn 1978), 533–549; John Witte Jr., "'A Most Mild and Equitable Establishment of Religion': John Adams and the Massachusetts Experiment," in *Religion and the New Republic: Faith in the Founding of America*, ed. James H. Hutson (Lanham, Md., 2000), 1–40.

46. On this subject, see J. C. D. Clark's discussion of the English polity in *The Language of Liberty, 1660–1831: Political Discourse and Social Dynamics in the Anglo-American World* (Cambridge, 1994). Clark argues that even though England had

a strong tradition of toleration, New England Congregationalists could not forget that the English constitution was tied to the Anglican Church. The same is true for religious minorities within Massachusetts, who could not ignore the fact that the major beneficiaries of Article Three were Congregationalists. On natural law, see also Knud Haakonssen, *Natural Law and Moral Philosophy from Grotius to the Scottish Enlightenment* (New York, 1996); Perry Miller, "Marrow of Puritan Divinity," in *Errand into the Wilderness* (Cambridge, Mass., 1956), 48–98.

47. Harry Stout, *The New England Soul: Preaching and Religious Culture in Colonial New England* (New York, 1986); Nathan O. Hatch, *The Sacred Cause of Liberty: Republican Thought and the Millennium in Revolutionary New England* (New Haven, Conn., 1977); Clark, *Language of Liberty*, 111–125.

48. Samuel Cooper, "A Sermon preached before His Excellency John Hancock . . . being the day of the Commencement of the Constitution and Inauguration of the new Government" (Boston, 1780), in *Political Sermons of the American Founding Era, 1730–1805*, ed. Ellis Sandoz (Indianapolis, Ind., 1991), 627–656. For the manner in which theological, republican, and Enlightenment ideas merged in American religious thought, see Mark A. Noll, *America's God: From Jonathan Edwards to Abraham Lincoln* (New York, 2002).

49. *Independent Chronicle* (Boston), December 9, 1779.

50. *Boston Gazette*, May 13, 1780. See also "Objections of the Minority of the Town of Boston," *Boston Gazette*, May 22, 1780.

51. *Independent Chronicle* (Boston), March 21, 1780.

52. *Boston Gazette*, October 23, 1780; November 27, 1780. Isaac Backus made a similar argument in *Independent Chronicle* (Boston), December 9, 1779.

53. John Adams, "Draft Constitution," in *Works of John Adams*, 4:221. For a discussion of Adams's utilitarian support for public religion, see Thompson, *John Adams and the Spirit of Liberty*, 23.

54. Phillips quoted in Field, *Crisis of the Standing Order*, 41. See also Zabdiel Adams, "A Sermon Preached before His Excellency John Hancock . . ." (Boston, 1782).

55. Aaron Bancroft, "A Sermon, Preached before His Excellency Caleb Strong . . ." (Boston, 1801).

56. Shaftesbury, "Sensus Communis, an Essay on the Freedom of Wit and Humour," in *Characteristics of Men, Manners, Opinions, Times*, ed. Lawrence Klein (Cambridge, 1999), 29–69. For a discussion of Shaftesbury, see David S. Shields, *Civil Tongues and Polite Letters in British America* (Chapel Hill, N.C., 1997), esp. xii–xxxii; Lawrence Klein, "The Third Earl of Shaftesbury and the Progress of Politeness," *Eighteenth-Century Studies* 18, no. 2 (Winter,1984–1985), 186–214.

57. Francis Hutcheson, "Morality and the Moral Sense," in *The Scottish Enlightenment: An Anthology*, ed. Alexander Brodie (Edinburgh, UK, 1997), 117–142, at 138. Gordon S. Wood, *Radicalism of the American Revolution* (New York, 1991), 215, argues that "these natural affinities, the love and benevolence that men felt toward each other, were akin to traditional classical republican virtue but not identical to it."

58. Haakonssen, *Natural Law and Moral Philosophy, passim*. See also Gordon S. Wood, "The American Love Boat," *New York Review of Books* 46, no. 15 (October 7, 1999); Marvin B. Becker, *The Emergence of Civil Society in the Eighteenth Century: A Privileged Moment in the History of England, Scotland, and France* (Bloomington,

Ind., 1994), 45–46; Charles Taylor, *Sources of the Self: The Making of the Modern Identity* (Cambridge, 1989), 248–265; J. B. Schneewind, *The Invention of Autonomy: A History of Modern Moral Philosophy* (Cambridge, 1998), 295–309, 330–353.

59. See Adam Smith, *The Theory of Moral Sentiments*, ed. D. D. Raphael and A. L. Macfie (Indianapolis, Ind., 1984), esp. Part I, sec. I. For a discussion of the idea of sympathy in Hutcheson and Smith, see John B. Radner, "The Art of Sympathy in Eighteenth-Century British Moral Thought," in *Studies in Eighteenth-Century Culture*, ed. Roseann Runte (Madison, Wis., 1979), 9:189–210; Norman S. Fiering, "Irresistible Compassion: An Aspect of Eighteenth-Century Sympathy and Humanitarianism," *Journal of the History of Ideas* 37, no. 2 (April–June 1976), 195–218. For the centrality of sympathy in American political culture, see Andrew Burstein, "The Political Character of Sympathy," *Journal of the Early Republic* 21, no. 4 (Winter 2001), 601–632, and Gordon S. Wood's review of the same, "The American Love Boat."

60. "Sympathy," *Massachusetts Magazine* 5, no. 11 (November 1793), 681–683; "The Mirror. No. 1," *Massachusetts Magazine* 5, no. 22 (February 1793). Skeptical about the goodness of human nature, John Adams told his cousin Samuel that "human appetites, passions, prejudices and self-love will never be conquered." Instead, only a good government with checks and balances could protect the common good from the self-interested machinations of powerful individuals. In response, Samuel Adams agreed that a well-balanced government was necessary, but, he countered, "without knowledge and benevolence, men would neither have been capable nor disposed to search for the principles or form of that system." Turning John against himself, Samuel declared that his cousin's own desire to seek a political system that would adequately protect the common good was proof of his benevolence. See John Adams to Samuel Adams, October 18, 1790, in *Works of John Adams*, 6:416, and Samuel Adams to John Adams, November 20, 1790, Ibid., 6:422.

61. Jonas Clark, "A Sermon preached before His Excellency John Hancock . . ." (Boston, 1781). See also Henry Cumings, "A Sermon preached before His Honor Thomas Cushing . . ." (Boston, 1783); "Irenaeus" in *Boston Gazette*, November 27, 1780.

62. Samuel West, "A Sermon, preached before His Excellency James Bowdoin . . ." (Boston, 1786). See also Samuel Parker, "A Sermon, preached before his honor the Lieutenant-Governor . . ." (Boston, 1793).

63. Jonathan French, "A Sermon, preached before His Excellency Samuel Adams . . ." (Boston, 1796). See also David Tappan, "A Sermon preached before His Excellency John Hancock . . ." (Boston, 1792).

64. Gill's speech is reprinted in *Columbian Centinel*, June 15, 1799. The House of Representatives agreed, stating in 1800 that both "the University at Cambridge, and the Religious establishments of our country" are "intimately interwoven with the essential and most important interests of society." "Answer of the House," *Independent Chronicle* (Boston), January 13–16, 1800.

65. On Jefferson and Rush, see Lawrence Cremin, *American Education: The National Experience, 1783–1876* (New York, 1980), 107–121. Jefferson's bill is also discussed in Richard Brown, *The Strength of a People: The Idea of an Informed Citizenry in America, 1650–1870* (Chapel Hill, N.C., 1996), 74–77. On education in the new republic more generally, in addition to the above, see Daniel Walker Howe,

"Church, State, and Education in the Young American Republic," *Journal of the Early Republic* 22, no. 1 (Spring 2002), 1–24; Carl F. Kaestle, *Pillars of the Republic: Common Schools and American Society, 1780–1860* (New York, 1983).

66. James Axtell, *The School upon a Hill: Education and Society in Colonial New England* (New Haven, Conn., 1974); Robert Middlekauf, *Ancients and Axioms: Secondary Education in Eighteenth-Century New England* (New Haven, Conn., 1963).

67. Brown, *Strength of a People*, 21–24; Peter Berkowitz, *Virtue and the Making of Modern Liberalism* (Princeton, N.J., 1999), 97–105.

68. "The Worcester Speculator," *Worcester Magazine* (October 1787), in *American Political Writing during the Founding Era, 1760–1805*, ed. Charles S. Hyneman and Donald S. Lutz (Indianapolis, Ind., 1983), 2 vols., 1:699–701. See also Peters, *Massachusetts Constitution of 1780*, 118–120; Brown, *Strength of a People*, 54–55; Cremin, *American Education*, 1–13.

69. Massachusetts Constitution of 1780, ch. 5, sec. 2.

70. John Adams, "A Dissertation on the Canon and Feudal Law" (1765), in *Works of John Adams*, 3:447–464. Also reprinted in C. Bradley Thompson, ed., *The Revolutionary Writings of John Adams* (Indianapolis, Ind., 2000), 21. See also John Adams, "Thoughts on Government" (1775), in *Works of John Adams*, 4:188–209. Brown, *Strength of a People*, 49–84, writes that eighteenth-century English elites argued the opposite—that an uneducated population was more likely to be orderly and thus maintain social hierarchy.

71. Adams, "A Dissertation on the Canon and Feudal Law."

72. In *Strength of a People*, 94, Richard D. Brown argues that America's leaders supported education because they were "so steeped . . . in classical models that they expressed a most un-British, indeed, positively Roman, confidence in the state, modeling their notions on citizenship on their readings of Cicero and the history of the Roman republic." In contrast, see Wood, *Radicalism*, 215–216.

73. *Columbian Centinel*, December 26, 1795.

74. "The Philanthropist. No. XX. The Importance of a Virtuous Education," *Massachusetts Magazine* 2, no. 8 (August 1790).

75. Samuel Adams's speech printed in *Columbian Centinel*, January 28, 1797.

76. "An Act to provide for the Instruction of Youth, and for the Promotion of good Education" (June 25, 1789), *Laws of the Commonwealth of Massachusetts, Passed by the General Court*, May 1789 session, ch. 19, p. 18. For a brief discussion of the 1789 act, see Middlekauf, *Ancients and Axioms*, 129–130.

77. "An Act to establish a Corporation, by the name of the Trustees of the Marblehead Academy" (November 17, 1792), *Acts and Laws, Passed by the General Court of Massachusetts*, November 1792 session, ch. 8, p. 229; "Hallowell Academy," *Massachusetts Centinel*, September 21, 1791.

78. Middlekauf, *Ancients and Axioms*, 123–124.

79. Samuel Adams to the Legislature of Massachusetts, June 3, 1795, in *Writings of Samuel Adams*, 4:375–382, esp. 378–379.

80. *Massachusetts Centinel*, March 22, 1786; March 7, 1787; *Columbian Centinel*, June 26, 1793; "On Public Education," *Massachusetts Magazine* 8, no. 3 (March 1796), 158–159.

81. *Independent Chronicle* (Boston), February 9, 1786. See also the Senate's response to Samuel Adams's speech in *Columbian Centinel*, June 13, 1795: "Academies have been considered as useful institutions to afford the means of instruction

in several branches of science, of general and obvious utility, for which Grammar Schools are not well calculated . . . it shall be our special care at all times, to patronize them in such a manner as to encourage and effectually protect the whole."

82. Linda Kerber, *Women of the Republic: Intellect and Ideology in Revolutionary America* (Chapel Hill, N.C., 1980), 199–204; Mary Beth Norton, *Liberty's Daughters: The Revolutionary Experience of American Women, 1750–1830* (Boston, 1980), 256–294; Kathryn Kish Sklar, "The Schooling of Girls and Changing Community Values in Massachusetts Towns, 1750–1820," *History of Education Quarterly* 33, no. 4 (Winter 1993), 511–542; J. M. Opal, "Exciting Emulation: Academies and the Transformation of the Rural North, 1780s–1820s," *Journal of American History* 91, no. 2 (September 2004), 445–470. For the debate over female education in the press, see *Massachusetts Centinel*, March 9, 1785; March 30, 1785; August 4, 1787; July 30, 1788; October 3, 1789; Samuel Adams to John Adams, October 4, 1790, in *Works of John Adams*, 6:413–414. For Boston's school plan, see *Massachusetts Centinel*, September 19, 1789; January 9, 1790.

83. *Independent Chronicle* (Boston), January 4, 1781.

84. Quote and discussion of the colonial effort to incorporate Williams in Jürgen Herbst, *From Crisis to Crisis: American College Government, 1636–1819* (Cambridge, Mass., 1982), 135–137.

85. David W. Robson, "College Founding in the New Republic, 1776–1800," *History of Education Quarterly* 23, no. 3 (Autumn 1983), 323–341, at 328.

86. *Independent Chronicle* (Boston), February 13, 1794; June 5, 1794.

87. "An Act to establish a College in the County of Berkshire, within this Commonwealth, by the name of William's College" (June 22, 1793), *Acts and Laws, Passed by the General Court of Massachusetts*, May 1793 session, ch. 15, p. 319; "An Act to establish a College in the Town of Brunswick, in the District of Maine, within this Commonwealth" (June 24, 1794), *Acts and Laws, Passed by the General Court of Massachusetts*, May 1794 session, ch. 16, p. 419. Between 1780 and 1800, most of Harvard's funding came from the public sector. Only after subsequent political developments in the nineteenth century did the state stop funding Harvard. See Ronald Story, *The Forging of an Aristocracy: Harvard and the Boston Upper Class, 1800–1870* (Middletown, Conn., 1980), 25.

88. For a discussion of learned societies in the post-Revolutionary era, see the essays collected in Alexandra Oleson and Sanborn C. Brown, eds., *The Pursuit of Knowledge in the Early American Republic: American Scientific and Learned Societies from Colonial Times to the Civil War* (Baltimore, 1976), esp. Walter Muir Whitehill, "Early Learned Societies in Boston and Vicinity," 151–173. Bowdoin quoted in Alexandra Oleson, "Introduction: To Build a New Intellectual Order," in Ibid., xv. For a general survey of these institutions, see Merrill Jensen, "The Betterment of Humanity," in *The New Nation: A History of the United States during the Confederation, 1781–1789* (New York, 1950), 129–153.

89. "An Act to enable the Proprietors of Social Libraries to manage the same" (March 3, 1798), *Acts and Laws, Passed by the General Court of Massachusetts*, January 1798 session, ch. 45, p. 200.

90. John L. Brooke, "Ancient Lodges and Self-Created Societies: Voluntary Association and the Public Sphere in the Early Republic," in *Launching the Extended Republic: The Federalist Era*, ed. Ronald Hoffman and Peter J. Albert (Charlottesville, Va., 1996), 273–377, at 274. Statistics in Richard D. Brown,

"Emergence of Urban Society in Rural Massachusetts, 1760–1820," *Journal of American History* 61, no. 1 (June 1974), 29–51; Brown, "The Emergence of Voluntary Associations in Massachusetts, 1760–1830," *Journal of Voluntary Action Research* 2, no. 2 (1973), 64–73. See also Randolph Roth, *The Democratic Dilemma: Religion, Reform, and the Social Order in the Connecticut River Valley of Vermont, 1791–1850* (New York, 1987).

91. Melton, *The Rise of the Public*; Koselleck, *Critique and Crisis*.

92. Steven C. Bullock, "The Revolutionary Transformation of American Freemasonry, 1752–1792," *William and Mary Quarterly* 47, no. 3 (July 1990), 347–369, and *Revolutionary Brotherhood: Freemasonry and the Transformation of the American Social Order, 1730–1840* (Chapel Hill, N.C., 1996); Wood, *Radicalism of the American Revolution*, 223–225.

93. "Social Influence of Free Masonry," *Massachusetts Magazine* 5, no. 5 (May 1793), 278–280. See also Josiah Bartlett, "An Address to the Ancient and Honourable Society of Free and Accepted Masons . . . ," *Massachusetts Magazine* 2, no. 10 (October 1790).

94. "On Friendship," *Massachusetts Magazine* 1, no. 1 (January 1789); W. Walter, "A Charge . . . delivered at Charlestown . . . ," *Massachusetts Magazine* 5, no. 9 (September 1793), 553–557.

95. Shaftesbury, "Sensus Communis," 52–53. For a discussion of how fraternal clubs promoted the social affections, see Stefan-Ludwig Hoffmann, "Democracy and Associations in the Long Nineteenth Century: Toward a Transnational Perspective," *Journal of Modern History* 75, no. 2 (June 2003), 269–299; Wood, "The American Love Boat."

96. Thaddeus Mason Harris, "A Discourse delivered at Bridgewater . . ." (Boston, 1797), quoted in Bullock, *Revolutionary Brotherhood*, 191–192. For the tension between particularity and the common good, see Ibid., 184–219. See also *Columbian Centinel*, March 24, 1792.

97. Thaddeus Harris, "Discourse delivered at Bridgewater" (1794), quoted in Bullock, *Revolutionary Brotherhood*, 197; Brooke, "Ancient Lodges and Self-Created Societies," 274–275.

98. George A. Levesque, *Black Boston: African American Life and Culture in Urban America, 1750–1860* (New York, 1994), 319–320.

99. William G. McLoughlin, *Isaac Backus and the American Pietistic Tradition* (Boston, 1967), 212–213.

100. The relationship between Morse and the Illuminati is discussed in Brooke, "Ancient Lodges and Self-Created Societies," 319–322; Wright, "Piety, Morality, and the Commonwealth," 65–67; Joseph W. Phillips, *Jedidiah Morse and New England Congregationalism* (New Brunswick, N.J., 1983), 78–89.

101. "The Gleaner. No. XIV.," *Massachusetts Magazine* 5, no. 7 (July 1793).

## 2. Fragmentation and Contestation

1. George Washington, "Farewell Address" (September 1796), reprinted in *The Founders' Constitution*, ed. Ralph Lerner, 5 vols. (Chicago, 1978), vol. 1, ch. 18, no. 29.

2. On the Jeffersonian conception of society-state relations, see Arieli Yehoshua, *Individualism and Nationalism in American Life* (Cambridge, Mass.,

1964), chs. 7–8. For the response of Republicans in Pennsylvania to Washington's address, see Albrecht Koschnik, *"Let a Common Interest Bind Us Together": Associations, Partisanship, and Culture in Philadelphia, 1775–1840* (Charlottesville, Va., 2007), ch. 1.

3. Thomas Hutchinson to Lord Dartmouth, December 22, 1772, quoted in Richard D. Brown, *Revolutionary Politics in Massachusetts: The Boston Committee of Correspondence and the Towns, 1772–1774* (Cambridge, Mass., 1970), 86.

4. Hutchinson to Richard Jackson, October 5, 1768, quoted in Brown, *Revolutionary Politics*, 31; Hutchinson to Lord Hillsborough, March 27, 1770, quoted in Ibid., 35.

5. Hutchinson quoted in Gordon S. Wood, *Creation of the American Republic, 1776–1787* (New York, 1969), 313.

6. Thomas Jefferson, *Notes on the State of Virginia*, in *The Portable Thomas Jefferson*, ed. Merrill D. Peterson (New York, 1975), 166–171. On the evolution of constitutional thought concerning conventions, see Wood, *Creation of the American Republic*, 306–343; Edmund S. Morgan, *Inventing the People: The Rise of Popular Sovereignty in England and America* (New York, 1988), 209–287; Harry A. Cushing, *History of the Transition from Provincial to Commonwealth Government in Massachusetts*, Studies in History, Economics and Public Law, ed. the faculty of political science of Columbia University (New York, 1896), no. 17; Willi Paul Adams, *The First American Constitutions: Republican Ideology and the Making of the State Constitutions in the Revolutionary Era* (trans. 1973; Chapel Hill, N.C., 1980), 63–98.

7. "Pittsfield Addresses the Committee of the General Court" (November 1778), in *Massachusetts, Colony to Commonwealth: Documents on the Formation of Its Constitution, 1775–1780*, ed. Robert J. Taylor (Chapel Hill, N.C., 1961), 98–101. See also Oscar Handlin and Mary Handlin, eds., *Popular Sources of Political Authority: Documents on the Massachusetts Constitution of 1780* (Cambridge, Mass., 1966), 374–379. For a discussion of the Berkshire constitutionalists, see Stephen E. Patterson, *Political Parties in Revolutionary Massachusetts* (Madison, Wis., 1973), 203–212; Robert J. Taylor, *Western Massachusetts in the Revolution* (Providence, R.I., 1954), 75–102. See also "Berkshire County Remonstrance" (August 26, 1778), in *Popular Sources*, 366–368; "Statement of Berkshire County Representatives" (November 17, 1778), in Ibid., 374–379; Taylor, ed., *Massachusetts, Colony to Commonwealth*, 48–111. For constitutional arguments in Worcester County, see John L. Brooke, *The Heart of the Commonwealth: Society and Political Culture in Worcester County, Massachusetts, 1713–1861* (New York, 1989), 158–188.

8. John L. Brooke, "To the Quiet of the People: Revolutionary Settlements and Civil Unrest in Western Massachusetts, 1774–1789," *William and Mary Quarterly* 46, no. 3 (July 1989), 425–462; Brooke, *Heart of the Commonwealth*, 189–229. See also Wood, *Creation of the American Republic*, 372–383.

9. On the economic difficulties faced by western farmers and Massachusetts politics, see Richard Buel Jr., "The Public Creditor Interest in Massachusetts Politics, 1780–86," and Joseph A. Ernst, "Shays's Rebellion in Long Perspective: The Merchants and the 'Money Question,'" both in *In Debt to Shays: The Bicentennial of an Agrarian Rebellion*, ed. Robert A. Gross (Charlottesville, Va., 1993), 47–80.

10. Numbers from Brooke, "To the Quiet of the People."

11. *Independent Chronicle*, March 25, 1784. See also *Independent Chronicle*, August 3, 1786; December 21, 1786.

12. "Charge to the Middlesex Grand Jury at Cambridge, Oct. 31, 1786," in *Massachusetts Centinel*, November 11, 1786.

13. James Sullivan to Samuel Adams, October 12, 1786, in *Life of James Sullivan*, ed. Thomas C. Amory, 2 vols. (Boston, 1859), 1:196–197; Samuel Adams to Noah Webster, April 30, 1784, in *Writings of Samuel Adams*, ed. Harry Alonzo Cushing, 4 vols. (New York, 1904–1908), 4:303–306.

14. "Middlesex County Convention," in *Independent Chronicle*, September 7, 1786.

15. "An Address to the Inhabitants of the County of Worcester," *Massachusetts Centinel*, October 14, 1786.

16. "A grievance," a writer in the *Independent Chronicle*, September 21, 1786, pointed out, "is a wrongful, oppressive and unconstitutional exercise of authority over the subjects of the state."

17. Peter S. Onuf, *The Origins of the Federal Republic: Jurisdictional Controversies in the United States, 1775–1787* (Philadelphia, 1983).

18. "Berkshire County Remonstrance" (August 26, 1778), in *Popular Sources*, 366–368.

19. "Maine Convention," in *Massachusetts Centinel*, September 20, 1786.

20. Incident described and quoted in Brooke, *Heart of the Commonwealth*, 189.

21. Richard D. Brown, "Shays's Rebellion and Its Aftermath: A View from Springfield, Massachusetts, 1787," *William and Mary Quarterly* 40, no. 4 (October 1983), 598–615. William Pencak counters Brown's interpretation, arguing instead that the Shaysites "went well beyond the practices of Revolutionary crowds." For Pencak, the Shaysites behaved less like a crowd than an army, and their goals struck at the heart of the new constitution. See William Pencak, "'The Fine Theoretic Government of Massachusetts Is Prostrated to the Earth': The Response to Shays's Rebellion Reconsidered," in *In Debt to Shays*, 121–143.

22. James Bowdoin, "A Proclamation" [dated September 2, 1786] (Boston, 1786); "Address to the General Court, Sept. 28, 1786," reprinted in *Independent Chronicle*, October 5, 1786, and *Massachusetts Centinel*, September 30, 1786; "An Address, To the good people of the Commonwealth" [dated January 12, 1787] (Boston, 1787), also reprinted in *Massachusetts Centinel*, January 17, 1787; Massachusetts General Court, "An Address from the General Court to the People of the Commonwealth of Massachusetts" (Boston, 1786).

23. [Alexander Hamilton], *Federalist 21* in *The Federalist Papers*, ed. Isaac Kramnick (New York, 1987), 174.

24. *Columbian Centinel*, May 4, 1796; May 7, 1796. See also Brooke, *Heart of the Commonwealth*, 199.

25. Following the suppression of Shays's Rebellion, a convention meeting in Worcester condemned violence and accepted that "the only constitutional way of seeking redress" was to petition the General Court. Refusing to accept the illegitimacy of conventions themselves, the Worcester convention instead sought to carve out a space for legitimate political opposition. *Massachusetts Centinel*, January 20, 1787.

26. *Independent Chronicle*, January 29, 1784. The essay was a reprint of Judge Aedenus Burke's of South Carolina, *Considerations on the Order or Society of the Cincinnati* (1783). See Minor Myers Jr., *Liberty without Anarchy: A History of the Society of the Cincinnati* (Charlottesville, Va., 1983), 48–69; Marc L. Harris, "'Cement to

the Union': The Society of the Cincinnati and the Limits of Fraternal Sociability," *Proceedings of the Massachusetts Historical Society* 10 (1995), 115–140; Wallace Evan Davies, "The Society of the Cincinnati in New England 1783–1800," *William and Mary Quarterly* 5, no. 1 (January 1948), 3–25.

27. Myers, *Liberty without Anarchy*, 98–99; Max Farrand, ed., *The Records of the Federal Convention*, 3 vols. (New Haven, Conn., 1966), 2:114. It is worth noting that Gerry's speech was sure to ruffle some feathers; according to Myers, 38 percent of the delegates to the Constitutional Convention were also members of the Cincinnati. John Adams also worried about the influence of Masons in political life. See John Quincy Adams to John Adams, June 30, 1787, in *Writings of John Quincy Adams*, ed. Worthington C. Ford, 7 vols. (New York, 1913–1917), 1:33.

28. *Independent Chronicle*, January 29, 1784. See Harris, "'Cement to the Union.'" Theda Skocpol, "How the United States Became A Civic Nation," in *Diminished Democracy: From Membership to Management in American Civic Life* (Norman, Okla., 2003), 20–73, argues that the federal government's structure provided a model for voluntary associations to copy, thus encouraging their formation. This may be true but in the early and uncertain days after the Revolution, many Americans thought such a structure to be threatening.

29. Washington's letter of May 15, 1784, is reprinted in *Independent Chronicle*, June 3, 1784, and *Columbian Centinel*, June 2, 1784. See also the Massachusetts Society of Cincinnati's reply to Washington, *Columbian Centinel*, October 31, 1789.

30. "The Committee of both Houses of the General Court, appointed to enquire into the Existence, Nature, Object, and probable Tendency or Effect of an Order or Society called the CINCINNATI . . . ," *Independent Chronicle*, March 25, 1784. Reprinted in *Independent Chronicle*, September 9, 1790.

31. On the prohibition of guilds in colonial Massachusetts, see Stephen Innes, *Creating the Commonwealth: The Economic Culture of Puritan New England* (New York, 1992), 220–227; Lisa Beth Lubow, "Artisans in Transition: Early Capitalist Development and the Carpenters of Boston, 1787–1837" (Ph.D. diss., University of California, Los Angeles, 1987), 310–391.

32. On Adam Smith, see Emma Rothschild, *Economic Sentiments: Adam Smith, Condorcet, and the Enlightenment* (Cambridge, Mass., 2001), 7–51, 87–115; James F. Becker, "The Corporation Spirit and Its Liberal Analysis," *Journal of the History of Ideas* 30 (1969), 69–84.

33. Gary John Kornblith, "From Artisans to Businessmen: Master Mechanics in New England, 1789–1850" (Ph.D. diss., Princeton University, 1983); Sean Wilentz, *Chants Democratic: New York City and the Rise of the American Working Class, 1788–1850* (New York, 1984); Ronald Schultz, *The Republic of Labor: Philadelphia Artisans and the Politics of Class, 1720–1830* (New York, 1993).

34. On the organization of Boston's artisans following American independence, see Kornblith, "From Artisans to Businessmen," 49–130; Lubow, "Artisans in Transition," esp. 310–391.

35. Benjamin Russell, *An Address Delivered before the Massachusetts Charitable Mechanic Association, December 21, 1809* (Boston, 1810), as quoted in Kornblith, "From Artisans to Businessmen," 110–111. See also Joseph T. Buckingham's comments in the *Annals of the Massachusetts Charitable Mechanic Association, 1795–1802* (Boston, 1892).

36. *Monthly Anthology and Boston Review* 3 (1806), as quoted in Christopher L. Tomlins, *Law, Labor, and Ideology in the Early American Republic* (Cambridge, Mass., 1993), 102–103. Philadelphia's Federalists shared these attitudes. See Johann N. Neem, "Freedom of Association in the Early Republic: The Republican Party, the Whiskey Rebellion, and the Philadelphia and New York Cordwainers' Cases," *Pennsylvania Magazine of History and Biography* 127, no. 3 (July 2003), 259–290.

37. On the formation of the Republican Party, see Lance Banning, *The Jeffersonian Persuasion: Evolution of a Party Ideology* (Ithaca, N.Y., 1978); Stanley Elkins and Eric McKitrick, *The Age of Federalism* (New York, 1993); Saul Cornell, *The Other Founders: Anti-Federalism and the Dissenting Tradition in America, 1788–1828* (Chapel Hill, N.C., 1999).

38. For the origins of the democratic societies and their relationship to questions of sovereignty, see Albrecht Koschnik, "The Democratic Societies of Philadelphia and the Limits of the American Public Sphere, circa 1793–1795," *William and Mary Quarterly*, 3rd ser., 68, no. 3 (July 2001), 615–636; Elkins and McKitrick, *Age of Federalism*, 451–461; Cornell, *The Other Founders*, 195–218; Neem, "Freedom of Association in the Early Republic"; Marc Harris, "Civil Society in Post-Revolutionary America," in *Empire and Nation: The American Revolution in the Atlantic World*, ed. Eliga H. Gould and Peter S. Onuf (Baltimore, 2005), 197–216. See also Seth Cotlar, "Reading the Foreign News, Imagining an American Public Sphere: Radical and Conservative Visions of 'the Public' in Mid-1790s Newspapers," in *Periodical Literature in Eighteenth-Century America*, ed. Mark L. Kamrath and Sharon M. Harris (Knoxville, Tenn., 2005), 307–338.

39. On the emergence of the Republican Party in Massachusetts, see Paul Goodman, *The Democratic-Republicans of Massachusetts: Politics in the New Republic* (Cambridge, Mass., 1964); Brooke, *Heart of the Commonwealth*, 233–268.

40. *Independent Chronicle*, January 16, 1794; "Circular Letter from the Massachusetts Constitutional Society," *Independent Chronicle*, September 8, 1794. Also reprinted in *The Democratic-Republican Societies, 1790–1800: A Documentary Sourcebook of Constitutions, Declarations, Addresses, Resolutions, and Toasts*, ed. Philip S. Foner (Westport, Conn., 1976), 255–260.

41. *Independent Chronicle*, September 8, 1794, italics added. This argument is made by Koschnik, "The Democratic Societies of Philadelphia."

42. *Columbian Centinel*, August 7, 1793.

43. Ibid.

44. "To the Democratic Society of Philadelphia," *Columbian Centinel*, February 5, 1794.

45. *Columbian Centinel*, September 27, 1794.

46. "A Watchman," *Columbian Centinel*, December 27, 1794.

47. David Osgood quoted in Nathan O. Hatch, *The Sacred Cause of Liberty: Republican Thought and the Millennium in Revolutionary New England* (New Haven, Conn., 1977), 127.

48. On the Whiskey Rebellion, see Thomas Slaughter, *The Whiskey Rebellion: Frontier Epilogue to the American Revolution* (New York, 1986). For accounts of the relationship between the rebellion and the democratic societies in the Federalists' minds, see Neem, "Freedom of Association in the Early Republic"; Elkins and

McKitrick, *Age of Federalism*, 461–488; Michael Schudson, *The Good Citizen: A History of American Civic Life* (New York, 1998), 55–64.

49. Washington's Proclamation was reprinted in the *Columbian Centinel,* October 4, 1794, and *Independent Chronicle*, October 6, 1794. By employing the word *combination*, the president expressed his belief that the clubs met the terms necessitated by the federal Militia Act of 1792 for the chief executive to call out troops. According to the Militia Act, a federal judge had to certify the existence of "combinations too powerful to be suppressed by the ordinary course of judicial proceedings." See Elkins and McKitrick, *Age of Federalism*, 478.

50. Thomas Hart Benton, ed., *Abridgement of the Debates of Congress, From 1789 to 1856* (New York, 1857), 1:520–522, 531–542.

51. Benton, *Abridgement of the Debates of Congress*, 1:533–534.

52. Fisher Ames to Thomas Dwight, September 11, 1794, in *Works of Fisher Ames*, ed. Seth Ames (Boston, 1854), 150; Ames as quoted in Elkins and McKitrick, *Age of Federalism*, 486. Ames's correspondence during this period makes clear that he believed the democratic societies went well beyond the boundaries of legitimate political opposition.

53. Neem, "Freedom of Association in the Early Republic."

54. "Address to the Citizens of the United States, Dec. 18, 1794," in *The Democratic-Republican Societies, 1790–1800*, ed. Philip S. Foner, 98–102.

55. *Independent Chronicle*, December 8, 1794.

56. "Self-Created Societies," *Independent Chronicle*, December 8, 1794.

57. *Independent Chronicle*, December 8, 1794. See also *Independent Chronicle,* March 16, 1795.

58. Pauline Maier, "Popular Uprisings and Civil Authority in Eighteenth-Century America," *William and Mary Quarterly* 27, no. 1 (January 1970), 3–35, at 5, 24; Paul A. Gilje, *The Road to Mobocracy: Popular Disorder in New York City, 1763–1834* (Chapel Hill, N.C., 1987), 3–65, and *Rioting in America* (Bloomington, Ind., 1996) 12–51; Gordon S. Wood, "A Note on Mobs in the American Revolution," *William and Mary Quarterly* 34, no. 4 (October 1966), 635–642; Alfred F. Young, "English Plebeian Culture and Eighteenth-Century American Radicalism," in *The Origins of Anglo-American Radicalism*, ed. Margaret Jacob and James Jacob (London, 1984), 185–214. Young examines various traditional rituals and explores their English origins and emergence in the colonies. For England, see E. P. Thompson, "The Moral Economy of the English Crowd in the Eighteenth Century," in *Customs in Common: Studies in Traditional Popular Culture* (New York, 1993), 185–258; Tim Harris, *London Crowds in the Reign of Charles II: Propaganda and Politics from the Restoration until the Exclusion Crisis* (Cambridge, 1987). For the role of mob activity during the Stamp Act crisis, see Pauline Maier, *From Resistance to Revolution: Colonial Radicals and the Development of American Opposition to Britain, 1765–1776* (New York, 1972), 3–27; Edmund S. Morgan and Helen M. Morgan, *The Stamp Act Crisis: Prologue to Revolution* (Chapel Hill, N.C., 1953).

59. Neem, "Freedom of Association in the Early Republic"; Cornell, *The Other Founders*, 195–218.

60. Richard Hofstadter, *The Idea of a Party System: The Rise of Legitimate Opposition in the United States, 1780–1840* (Berkeley, Calif., 1969).

61. Bolingbroke, *The Idea of a Patriot King* (1749), quoted in Hofstadter, *Idea of a Party System*, 21.

62. James Sullivan to William Eustis, January 13, 1802, as quoted in Ronald P. Formisano, *The Transformation of Political Culture: Massachusetts Parties, 1790s–1840s* (New York, 1983), 70–71.

63. Thomas Jefferson, "First Inaugural Address" (March 4, 1801), in *The Portable Thomas Jefferson*, ed. Merrill D. Peterson (New York, 1975), 290–295. For a discussion of why Jefferson conflated his opinions with those of "the people," see Peter S. Onuf, *Jefferson's Empire: The Language of American Nationhood* (Charlottesville, Va., 2000), 80–108.

64. Adams to Benjamin Rush, September 3, 1808, in *The Works of John Adams*, ed. Charles Francis Adams (Boston, 1851), 9:602; Adams to Rush, September 27, 1808, in Ibid., 9:603.

65. This is the central argument of David Hackett Fischer, *The Revolution in American Conservatism: The Federalist Party in the Era of Jeffersonian Democracy* (New York, 1965). See also Noble E. Cunningham Jr., *The Jeffersonian Republicans in Power: Party Operations, 1801–1809* (Chapel Hill, N.C., 1963), 133–142; Hofstadter, *Idea of a Party System*, 212–271; Gordon S. Wood, *The Radicalism of the American Revolution* (New York, 1991), 287–305; Koschnik, *"Let a Common Interest Bind Us Together"*, ch. 2.

66. Formisano, *Transformation of Political Culture*, 10.

67. Although the First Amendment applied only to the federal government, state constitutions also protected citizens' freedom of conscience.

68. Gary B. Nash, "The American Clergy and the French Revolution," *William and Mary Quarterly* 22, no. 3 (July 1965), 392–412; Joseph W. Phillips, *Jedidiah Morse and New England Congregationalism* (New Brunswick, N.J., 1983); Jonathan D. Sassi, "The First Party Competition and Southern New England's Public Christianity," *Journal of the Early Republic* 21, no. 2 (Summer 2001), 261–299.

69. William G. McLoughlin, "The Balkcom Case (1782) and the Pietistic Theory of Separation of Church and State," *William and Mary Quarterly* 24, no. 2 (April 1967), 267–283. For an earlier example, see Isaac Backus's essay in the *Independent Chronicle*, April 20, 1780.

70. Backus quoted in William G. McLoughlin, *New England Dissent: 1630–1833: The Baptists and the Separation of Church and State*, 2 vols. (Cambridge, Mass., 1971), 1:639.

71. John D. Cushing, "Notes on Disestablishment in Massachusetts, 1780–1833," *William and Mary Quarterly* 26, no. 2 (April 1964), 169–190; McLoughlin, *New England Dissent*, 1:642–648.

72. Isaac Backus, *The Diary of Isaac Backus*, ed. William G. McLoughlin, 3 vols. (Providence, R.I., 1979), 3:1173, 1326.

73. James Sullivan to Rufus King, June 1785, in *Life of James Sullivan*, 1:184. See also "An Appeal to the Impartial Public by the Society of Christian Independents" (Boston, 1785); *Independent Chronicle*, January 1, 1789; January 29, 1789. It is important to remember that despite the court's defense of the civic function of religious corporations, the separation of the spiritual church from its earthly body was fundamental to Congregationalism. Thus the court could not legitimately interfere in theological issues but could use its authority to protect public churches from the challenge of self-created voluntary associations.

74. "An Act for the Better Securing, and Rendering More Effectual, Grants and Donations to charitable Uses," an exact reenactment of 1755's "An Act Regulating Parishes and Precincts, and the Officers Thereof." See Kirk Gilbert

Alliman, "The Incorporation of Massachusetts Congregational Churches, 1692–1833: The Preservation of Religious Autonomy" (Ph.D. diss., University of Iowa, 1970), 187.

75. Cushing, "Notes on Disestablishment," 183.

76. *Diary of Isaac Backus*, 3:1395. It is clear that this was not an isolated incident from the petitions Baptists sent to the General Court when seeking incorporation. See Massachusetts Acts, ch. 31 (1790), ch. 32 (1790), both in Massachusetts State Archives, Boston.

77. "An Act to Regulate Parishes and Precincts, and the Officers thereof" (1786), discussed in Alliman, "The Incorporation of Massachusetts Congregational Churches," 187.

78. "An Act providing for the Public Worship of God, and other purposes therein mentioned, and for repealing Laws heretofore made, relating to this subject" (March 4, 1800), *Acts and Laws Passed by the General Court of Massachusetts*, January 1800 session, ch. 52, p. 405. See Cushing, "Disestablishment in Massachusetts," 183.

79. This paragraph relies on William G. McLoughlin's discussion of Sullivan's term in *New England Dissent*, 2:1065–1083. See also Cushing, "Disestablishment in Massachusetts," 183–184. Despite their hostility to corporations, Kirk Gilbert Alliman has demonstrated that Congregational churches increasingly sought charters for ministerial funds in order to insulate their endowments from the public will of the parish. See Alliman, "Incorporation of Massachusetts Congregational Churches," 139–170.

80. William Bentley quoted in Goodman, *Democratic-Republicans*, 164.

81. *Thomas Barnes v. The Inhabitants of the First Parish of Falmouth* (6 Tyng 334 [1810]).

82. For the growth of the Baptist population in Massachusetts, see McLoughlin, *New England Dissent*, 2:698–699, 1113.

83. *Independent Chronicle*, May 20, 1811. See also *Independent Chronicle*, May 15, 1811; May 27, 1811; June 13, 1811; July 4, 1811.

84. *Independent Chronicle*, May 15, 1811. There exists some proof that the framers explicitly chose not to include dissenting churches under Article Three. A 1780 writer who claimed to have been a delegate to the constitutional convention denied that the convention ever debated whether to incorporate voluntary churches. The fact that the discussion took place in the press suggests the issue of incorporation was on the table in 1780. See *Boston Gazette*, July 3, 1780.

85. *Columbian Centinel*, June 8, 1811.

## 3. The Political Transformation of Civil Society

1. Theda Skocpol, "Bringing the State Back In: Strategies of Analysis in Current Research," in *Bringing the State Back In*, ed. Peter B. Evans, Dietrich Rueschemeyer, and Theda Skocpol (Cambridge and New York, 1985), 3–37, at 21. See also Richard R. John, "Governmental Institutions as Agents of Change: Rethinking American Political Development in the Early Republic, 1787–1835," *Studies in American Political Development* 11, no. 2 (1997), 347–380.

2. Nancy F. Cott, *Public Vows: A History of Marriage and the Nation* (Cambridge, Mass., 2000); Michael Grossberg, *Governing the Hearth: Law and the Family in Nineteenth-Century America* (Chapel Hill, N.C., 1985).

3. Lawrence Cremin, *American Education: The National Experience, 1783–1876* (New York, 1980), 270–271. Lorraine Smith Pangle and Thomas L. Pangle, *The Learning of Liberty: The Educational Ideas of the American Founders* (Lawrence, Kans., 1993), 146–184, discuss the tension between Jefferson's proposed "modern" curriculum for the University of Virginia and the classical curriculum. See also Linda K. Kerber, *Federalists in Dissent: Imagery and Ideology in Jeffersonian America* (Ithaca, N.Y., 1970), 95–134, on partisan divisions over curriculum.

4. Conrad Wright, *The Unitarian Controversy: Essays on American Unitarian History* (Boston, 1994); Peter S. Field, *The Crisis of the Standing Order: Clerical Intellectuals and Cultural Authority in Massachusetts, 1780–1833* (Amherst, Mass., 1998); Joseph W. Phillips, *Jedidiah Morse and New England Congregationalism* (New Brunswick, N.J., 1983).

5. "An act to alter and amend the constitution of the Board of Overseers of Harvard College" (March 6, 1810), *Acts and Laws of Massachusetts*, January 1810 session, ch. 113, p. 200. See also Josiah Quincy, *The History of Harvard University*, 2 vols. (1840; reprint, New York, 1977), 2:295; Peter Dobkin Hall, *The Organization of American Culture, 1700–1900: Private Institutions, Elites and the Origins of American Nationality* (New York, 1982), 107–108.

6. John Quincy Adams to Abigail Adams, November 16/28, 1810, in *Writings of John Quincy Adams*, ed. Worthington C. Ford, 7 vols. (New York, 1913–1917), 3:539–540.

7. *Boston Patriot*, March 19, 1810.

8. *Independent Chronicle*, February 26, 1810.

9. Ibid., September 17, 1810; Ibid., November 22, 1810. See also Ibid., September 9, 1810.

10. "An Act to repeal 'an act to alter and amend the Constitution of the Board of Overseers of Harvard College, and to regulate certain meetings of that Board'" (February 29, 1812), *Laws of the Commonwealth of Massachusetts*, January 1812 session, ch. 157, p. 593.

11. Oscar Handlin and Mary Flug Handlin, *Commonwealth: A Study of the Role of Government in the American Economy: Massachusetts 1774–1861* (1947; reprint, Cambridge, 1969), 51–133; Bray Hammond, *Banks and Politics in America, from the Revolution to the Civil War* (Princeton, N.J., 1957).

12. Bruce A. Campbell, "Law and Experience in the Early Republic: The Evolution of the *Dartmouth College* Doctrine, 1780–1819" (Ph.D. diss., Michigan State University, 1973), 76–86; Gareth Jones, *History of the Law of Charity, 1532–1827* (Cambridge, 1969), 16–52.

13. For example, see *Independent Chronicle* (Boston), February 26, 1810.

14. *Independent Chronicle* (Boston), April 9, 1810; November 29, 1810; June 3, 1811.

15. *Independent Chronicle* (Boston), September 17, 1810. See also *Independent Chronicle* (Boston), February 25, 1812.

16. Quoted in Samuel Eliot Morison, *Three Centuries of Harvard, 1636–1936* (Cambridge, Mass., 1964), 212.

17. "An act to alter and amend the constitution of the Board of Overseers of Harvard College" (March 6, 1810), *Acts and Laws of Massachusetts*, January 1810 session, ch. 113, p. 200.

18. *Wales v. Stetson* (2 Tyng 143 [1806]). Parsons quoted in Campbell, "Law and Experience," 213–215.

19. Reprinted in *Concord* (N.H.) *Gazette*, August 16, 1816. See also Quincy, *History of Harvard University*, 303.

20. Joseph F. Kett, *The Formation of the American Medical Profession: The Role of Institutions, 1780–1860* (New Haven, Conn., 1968), 70–79; Hall, *Organization of American Culture*, 136–147.

21. *Boston Patriot*, October 21, 1812; November 7, 1812; December 2, 1812; December 9, 1812.

22. *Boston Patriot*, October 21, 1812.

23. *Boston Patriot*, November 7, 1812.

24. Quoted in Paul Goodman, *The Democratic-Republicans of Massachusetts: Politics in the New Republic* (Cambridge, Mass., 1964), 168. See also *Independent Chronicle* (Boston), December 30, 1811; January 16, 1812; February 3, 1812; February 15, 1812.

25. Quoted in Kett, *Formation of the American Medical Profession*, 75.

26. *Boston Patriot*, January 11, 1812.

27. Quoted in Kett, *Formation of the American Medical Profession*, 75–77.

28. John S. Whitehead, *The Separation of College and State: Columbia, Dartmouth, Harvard, and Yale, 1776–1876* (New Haven, Conn., 1973), 19–20.

29. This is Peter Dobkin Hall's speculation, *Organization of American Culture*, 142.

30. "An Act to restore the Board of Overseers of Harvard College, and to make an addition thereto" (February 28, 1814), *Laws of the Commonwealth of Massachusetts*, January 1814 session, ch. 194, p. 469.

31. "An Act for the encouragement of Literature, Piety and Morality, and the useful Arts and Sciences" (February 24, 1814), *Laws of the Commonwealth of Massachusetts*, January 1814 session, ch. 150, p. 407, and "An Act in addition to an act, entitled, 'An act for the encouragement of Literature, Piety and Morality, and the Useful Arts and Sciences'" (February 26, 1814), Ibid., ch. 168, p. 428.

32. Goodman, *Democratic-Republicans*, 168–169; Peter Dobkin Hall, "What the Merchants Did with Their Money: Charitable and Testamentary Trusts in Massachusetts, 1780–1880," in *Entrepreneurs: The Boston Business Community, 1700–1850*, ed. Conrad Edick Wright and Katheryn P. Viens (Boston, 1997), 365–421, esp. 401–403.

33. *Laws of the Commonwealth of Massachusetts*, 1809–1814 sessions. See William G. McLoughlin, *New England Dissent: 1630–1833: The Baptists and the Separation of Church and State*, 2 vols. (Cambridge, Mass., 1971), 2:1088, footnote 5, for average.

34. "An Act Respecting Public Worship and Religious Freedom" (June 18, 1811), *Laws of the Commonwealth of Massachusetts, Passed by the General Court*, May 1800 session, ch. 6, p. 387. See McLoughlin, *New England Dissent*, 2:1099–1103.

35. See Wright, *The Unitarian Controversy*; Field, *Crisis of the Standing Order*.

36. McLoughlin, *New England Dissent*, 2:1207–1229.

37. Conrad Wright, "The Dedham Case Revisited," in *The Unitarian Controversy*, 111–135; Kirk Gilbert Alliman, "The Incorporation of Massachusetts Congregational Churches, 1692–1833: The Preservation of Religious Autonomy" (Ph.D. diss., University of Iowa, 1970).

38. *Kendall Boutell v. Thomas Cowden, Administrator* (9 Tyng 254 [1812]).

39. *Jonathan Burr v. First Parish in Sandwich* (9 Tyng 277 [1812]).

40. *Inhabitants of the First Parish in Shapleigh v. Zebulon Gilman* (13 Tyng 190 [1816]); *Jewett v. Burroughs* (15 Tyng 464 [1819]); *Edward Sparrow v. Wilkes Wood* (16 Tyng 457 [1820]); *Eliphalet Baker and Another v. Samuel Fales* (16 Tyng 147 [1820]; 16 Tyng 488 [1820]).

41. *Journal of the Debates and Proceedings of the Convention of Delegates Chosen to Revise the Constitution of Massachusetts* (Boston, 1853; reprint, New York, 1970), 448–449.

42. Ibid., 457–458.

43. Ibid., 613–614, 633.

44. Lyman Beecher, *Autobiography of Lyman Beecher,* ed. Barbara Cross, 2 vols. (Cambridge, 1961), 1:252–253. Italics in original.

45. Lyman Beecher, *A Sermon Delivered at the Installation of the Rev. Elias Cornelius as Associate Pastor of the Tabernacle Church in Salem, July 21, 1819* (Andover, Mass., 1819).

46. "The Congregational Churches of Massachusetts," *Spirit of the Pilgrims* (February 1828), 57–74; "Examination of Some Laws and Judicial Decisions in Relation to the Churches of Massachusetts," *Spirit of the Pilgrims* (March 1829), 128–146. See also the "Result" issued by an ecclesiastical council in 1826, republished in Mark DeWolfe Howe, ed., *Cases on Church and State in the United States* (Cambridge, Mass., 1952), 47–51. Since the distinction between the voluntary church as a spiritual institution and its corporate manifestation had always been unclear before the American Revolution, both the orthodox argument and that of such jurists as Parsons and Parker had legitimate historical roots. In delving into colonial precedents, *The Spirit of the Pilgrims* reinterpreted colonial civil society to meet orthodoxy's present needs. The magazine argued that colonial and post-Revolutionary statutes consistently upheld the rights of churches as independent voluntary associations. The truth, however, was that they did so only in the context of relatively homogenous small communities. In addition, the claim that Article Three intended to reinforce the autonomy of churches simply does not stand up to what we know about the framers of the 1780 constitution. For the founding of *The Spirit of the Pilgrims,* see Cross, *Autobiography of Lyman Beecher,* 91–92.

47. Beecher, *A Sermon Delivered at the Installation of the Rev. Elias Cornelius;* "The Congregational Churches of Massachusetts," *Spirit of the Pilgrims* (February 1828), 57–74.

48. "The Congregational Churches of Massachusetts (continued)," *Spirit of the Pilgrims* (March 1828), 113–140.

49. *Holbrook v. Holbrook et al.* (1 Pickering 248 [1822]). During the 1820–1821 convention, Justice Samuel Wilde had supported extending the Religious Freedom Act to orthodox Congregationalists, and now did so from his position on the bench. See *Journal of the Debates and Proceedings,* 372–375, 450, 584.

50. "Constitution of Massachusetts," *North American Review* 11, no. 29 (October 1820), 359–384. See also *Columbian Centinel* (1820), quoted in McLoughlin, *New England Dissent,* 2:1151–1152.

51. *Journal of the Debates and Proceedings,* 69–72.

52. Ibid., 78–80.

53. Ibid., 545.

54. Ibid., 85–86.

55. Daniel Walker Howe, "Church, State, and Education in the Young American Republic," *Journal of the Early Republic* 22, no. 1 (Spring 2002), 1–24, esp. 2–4. For a good history of the founding of West Point, see Robert M. S. McDonald, ed., *Thomas Jefferson's Military Academy: Founding West Point* (Charlottesville, Va., 2004).

56. John Lauritz Larson, *Internal Improvement: National Public Works and the Promise of Popular Government in the Early United States* (Chapel Hill, N.C., 2001). See also Peter Dobkin Hall, "Organizational Values and the Origins of the Corporation in Connecticut, 1760–1860," *Connecticut History* 29 (1988), 63–90.

57. 6 Cranch 87.

58. 9 Cranch 43.

59. See Edwin Merrick Dodd, *American Business Corporations until 1860, with Special Reference to Massachusetts* (Cambridge, Mass., 1954), 25–26; Campbell, "Law and Experience," 359–362.

60. [John Wheelock], *Sketches on the History of Dartmouth College and Moors' Charity School: with a particular account of some late remarkable proceedings of the Board of Trustees, from the year 1779 to the year 1815* ([place of publication unknown], 1815).

61. New Hampshire House of Representatives, *Journal of the House of Representatives of New Hampshire*, June 1816 session (Concord, N.H., 1816).

62. Gordon S. Wood, *Radicalism of the American Revolution* (New York, 1991), 88, observes, "Translating the personal, social, and economic power of the gentry into political authority was essentially what colonial politics was about." For a discussion of changing ideas of trusteeship in relation to the *Dartmouth* case, see Johann N. Neem, "Politics and the Origins of the Nonprofit Corporation in Massachusetts and New Hampshire, 1780–1820," *Nonprofit and Voluntary Sector Quarterly* 32, no. 3 (September 2003), 344–365.

63. Thomas Jefferson to William Plumer, July 21, 1816, in Andrew A. Lipscomb, ed., *The Writings of Thomas Jefferson* (Washington, D.C., 1903–1904), 15:46–47.

64. *Laws of New Hampshire*, June 1816 session.

65. *Concord* (N.H.) *Gazette*, July 9, 1816. Federalists were aware of the radicalism of their claim. They thus also proposed a compromise in which the Trustees would accept the creation of a Board of Overseers composed of the Counsellors, Senators, and Speaker of the House that would have the power to concur or reject any of the Trustees' actions. The Trustees were clearly uncomfortable making private rights claims to what they had long seen as a public office.

66. *New Hampshire Patriot*, September 5, 1816; *Concord* (N.H.) *Gazette*, September 12, 1816. See also John M. Shirley, *The Dartmouth College Causes and the Supreme Court of the United States* (Chicago, 1895; reprint, New York, 1971), 112–118; Francis Stites, *Private Interest and Public Gain: The Dartmouth College Case, 1819* (Amherst, Mass., 1972), 35–38.

67. *Concord* (N.H.) *Gazette*, March 6, 1817; *New Hampshire Patriot*, March 18, 1817; Stites, *Private Interest and Public Gain*, 38–41.

68. *Opinion of the Superior Court of the State of New-Hampshire, in the case of the Trustees of Dartmouth College, versus William H. Woodward, Esq. Pronounced*

*at Plymouth, in the County of Grafton, at the November term, 1817* . . . (Concord, N.H., 1818), 8. For an elaboration of the arguments made before the New Hampshire Superior Court, see Neem, "Politics and the Origins of the Non-profit Corporation."

69. *Opinion,* 22.

70. 17 Wheaton 518. Also in *Report of the Case of the Trustees of Dartmouth College against William H. Woodward. Argued and Determined in the Superior Court of Judicature of the State of New-Hampshire, November, 1817. And on Error in the Supreme Court of the United States, February, 1819,* ed. Timothy Farrar (Ports-mouth, N.H., 1819). Business historians have long emphasized the importance of the *Dartmouth* decision to protecting the legal privileges of commercial cor-porations. For some, like Albert Beveridge, the decision was to be celebrated for encouraging the growth of capitalist enterprise by protecting the right of property (Albert J. Beveridge, *The Life of John Marshall,* 4 vols. (Boston, 1919), 4:276–277). For others, the decision was condemned for the exact same reasons. I acknowledge that the decision holds a different place when discussing businesses and civil society. In business, *Dartmouth* limited the role of the state in regulating the market, hampering many liberal reforms. On the other hand, recent histo-rians interested in civil society and the nonprofit sector have reinterpreted the decision in light of new concerns. *Dartmouth* extended legal protections to private nonbusiness associations, a right fundamental to the freedom of association in civil society. Moreover, business corporations could rely on the property rights of shareholders to defend their charters from the state whereas the proprietors of charitable corporations had no property interest in the institutions they ran. Contemporaries acknowledged that the Dartmouth controversy revolved around the charters of nonprofit charitable and eleemosynary corporations. See Mark D. McGarvie, "The *Dartmouth College* Case and the Legal Design of Civil Society," in *Charity, Philanthropy, and Civility in American History,* ed. Lawrence J. Fried-man and Mark D. McGarvie (Cambridge, 2003), 91–105; Campbell, "Law and Experience"; Neem, "Politics and the Origins of the Nonprofit Corporation." See also David C. Hammack, ed., *Making the Nonprofit Sector: A Reader* (Bloom-ington, Ind., 1998).

71. Webster quoted in Hall, *Organization of American Culture,* 111.

72. To be fair, Marshall acknowledged that only the state could grant acts of incorporation. Yet once a charter had been issued, the state relinquished its direct control over a corporation, suggesting that many, if not all, corporations could violate Article Six with impunity. It was "the manner in which [corporations] are formed and the objects for which they are created" that determined whether they were public or private. Endowed by private money and governed by a largely self-perpetuating Board of Trustees, Dartmouth's charter established an autono-mous corporation that was not an agent of the state nor, by extension, the people of New Hampshire. If this was the case, any corporation could become a special interest promoting its own ends over the common good. Having separated the institutional office of corporate trustee from political office, and also extending federal protection to civic corporations, Article Six was no longer determinative once a charter had been issued. There was no way to ensure that a corporation did not promote interests distinct from the public's, a point made by Republicans in both states. The only caveat was in Story's opinion, in which he stated that the

legislature could insert a clause in each charter permitting them to make future amendments, but such a clause was not part of Dartmouth's charter. The corporation and its trustees were entitled to the rights and privileges in the charter, and these rights could not be materially altered by future legislatures.

73. Both articles are quoted and discussed in Whitehead, *The Separation of College and State*, 83–84.

74. *Boston Patriot,* January 11, 1812.

75. Kett, *Formation of the American Medical Profession*, 77–78; "Medical Societies. [A Review of] Medical Dissertations, read before the Massachusetts Medical Society . . . Boston. 1827. [and] Proceedings of a Convention of Medical Delegates at Northampton . . . Boston. 1827," *North American Review* 27, no. 60 (July 1828), 43–67.

76. "Petition for the Incorporation of Amherst College," *Daily Advertiser,* June 13, 1823.

77. *Daily Advertiser,* June 13, 1823.

78. *Daily Advertiser,* March 16, 1824.

79. *Daily Advertiser,* June 24, 1824.

80. *Daily Advertiser,* August 13, 1824; *Boston Courier,* August 14, 1824.

81. "An Act to establish a College in the town of Amherst" (February 22, 1825), *Laws of the Commonwealth of Massachusetts, Passed by the General Court,* January 1825 session, ch. 84, p. 535.

82. Whitehead, *The Separation of College and State*, 92–93; Ronald Story, *The Forging of an Aristocracy: Harvard and the Boston Upper Class, 1800–1870* (Middletown, Conn., 1980), 25–34.

83. "An Act for the encouragement of Medical Science" (February 21, 1824), *Laws of the Commonwealth of Massachusetts, Passed by the General Court,* January 1824 session, ch. 137, p. 392.

84. Quoted in McLoughlin, *New England Dissent*, 2:1202–1203.

85. "An Act in addition to an Act entitled 'An Act respecting Public Worship and Religious Freedom'" (February 16, 1824), *Laws of the Commonwealth of Massachusetts,* January 1824 session, ch. 106, p. 347. For a discussion of this act, see Ronald P. Formisano, *The Transformation of Political Culture: Massachusetts Parties, 1790s–1840s* (New York, 1983), 79–81; McLoughlin, *New England Dissent,* 2:1196–1197. Despite their willingness to extend corporate privileges to new groups, Republicans did not abandon their commitment to public oversight. Having learned from *Dartmouth* that the state could lose control of its institutions, Republicans reserved in Amherst's charter the right to appoint five trustees. In newly independent Maine, Republicans also hoped to gain better oversight of Bowdoin. Because of the *Dartmouth* ruling, they could not alter or annul Bowdoin's charter. Instead they passed a bill linking state aid to Bowdoin's acceptance of legislative supremacy. Bowdoin's trustees agreed, assuring Republicans that Bowdoin could be the state's primary public college. Equally committed to protecting religious freedom, however, Republicans incorporated the Baptist Waterville College (now Colby). Republicans in New Hampshire tried a similar tactic to that of their Maine counterparts. Daniel Webster opposed the proposal, worrying that "all would be political, nothing literary. My impression is that if the college must die, it is better it should die a natural death." (By the late 1820s, Democrats in New Hampshire would propose incorporating a

new college to break the Congregationalist-dominated Dartmouth's monopoly.) Webster believed that while the state should support civic institutions, in places dominated by Republicans like Maine or New Hampshire the state could be a greater threat than ally. In Massachusetts the goal was to ensure that the state remained an ally of the common good. See Jürgen Herbst, *From Crisis to Crisis: American College Government, 1636–1819* (Cambridge, Mass., 1982), 216–218; Whitehead, *Separation of College and State,* 76–81; Paul Goodman, *Towards a Christian Republic: Antimasonry and the Great Transition in New England, 1826–1836* (New York, 1988), 112–113.

86. On the formation of the National Republican Party, see Arthur B. Darling, *Political Changes in Massachusetts, 1824–1848: A Study of Liberal Movements in Politics* (New Haven, Conn., 1925), 40–43; Formisano, *Transformation of Political Culture,* 190; Robert J. Haws, "Massachusetts Whigs, 1833–1854" (Ph.D. diss., University of Nebraska, 1973), 9–34.

87. "An act defining the general powers and duties of Manufacturing Corporations" (March 3, 1809), *Laws of the Commonwealth of Massachusetts,* January 1809 session, ch. 65, p. 464; Dodd, *American Business Corporations,* 228–229.

88. W. C. Kessler, "Incorporation in New England: A Statistical Study, 1800–1875," *Journal of Economic History* 8, no. 1, (1948), 43–62; Dodd, *American Business Corporations,* 271; George Herberton Evans Jr., *Business Incorporations in the United States, 1800–1943* (New York: National Bureau of Economic Research, 1948).

89. Handlin and Handlin, *Commonwealth,* 161–181.

90. On Levi Lincoln, see Pauline Maier, "The Revolutionary Origins of the American Corporation," *William and Mary Quarterly* 50, no. 1 (January 1993), 69–71; Emory Washburn, *Memoir of Hon. Levi Lincoln, Prepared Agreeably to a Resolution of the Massachusetts Historical Society* (Cambridge, Mass., 1869).

91. Robert Rantoul Jr., *Memoirs, Speeches, and Writings by Robert Rantoul, Jr.,* ed. Luther Hamilton (Boston, 1854), 313–317.

92. Lincoln quoted and discussed in Maier, "Revolutionary Origins of the American Corporation," 70–72; Washburn, *Memoir of Hon. Levi Lincoln,* 20–23. On the Jeffersonian fear of corporations locking up wealth, see Hall, *Organization of American Culture,* 95–124; Irvin G. Wyllie, "The Search for an American Law of Charity," *Mississippi Valley Historical Review* 44, no. 2 (September 1959), 203–221; Howard S. Miller, *The Legal Foundations of American Philanthropy, 1776–1844* (Madison, Wis., 1961). There is no major study of Levi Lincoln Jr.'s political theory.

93. On the Charles River Bridge controversy, see Chapter 6 below.

94. The debates in the House of Representatives are reprinted in *Daily Advertiser,* March 27, 1830, and March 30, 1830. See also Robert L. Hampel, *Temperance and Prohibition in Massachusetts, 1813–1852* (Ann Arbor, Mich., 1982), 31–32.

95. "An Act Concerning Corporations" (March 11, 1831), *Laws of the Commonwealth of Massachusetts, Passed by the General Court,* January 1831 session, ch. 81, p. 613. It is possible that the act was passed as a compromise. Massachusetts banks' charters were set to expire in 1831, and most state bank charters were renewed either by an act of special legislation or by a general act during the same session ("An Act to continue the Banking Corporations therein named, and for other purposes" [February 28, 1831], *Laws of the Commonwealth of Massachusetts, Passed by the General Court,* January 1831 session, ch. 58, p. 577). National Repub-

lican legislators may have sought to balance this pro-corporation action with one that limited corporate privileges, although the act concerning corporations would not have applied to banks whose charters were renewed prior to the passage of the act, even if only by a few days. On the banking issue, see Dodd, *American Business Corporations*, 273–276.

## 4. Forging a Grassroots Public Sphere

1. On modernization, see Richard D. Brown, *Modernization: The Transformation of American Life, 1600–1865* (New York, 1976); Brown, "Emergence of Urban Society in Rural Massachusetts, 1760–1820," *Journal of American History* 61, no. 1 (June 1974), 29–51; Brown, "The Emergence of Voluntary Associations in Massachusetts, 1760–1830," *Journal of Voluntary Action Research* 2, no. 2 (1973), 64–73; Ronald G. Walters, *American Reformers, 1815–1860* (New York, 1978), 3–19; Oscar Handlin and Mary Handlin, *The Dimensions of Liberty* (Cambridge, Mass., 1961), 89–112; Stanley Elkins and Eric McKitrick, *The Age of Federalism: The Early American Republic, 1788–1800* (New York, 1993), 454–455. A critical appraisal of modernization is provided by Thomas Bender, *Community and Social Change in America* (New Brunswick, N.J., 1978).

2. On democratization, see Arthur M. Schlesinger, "Biography of a Nation of Joiners," *American Historical Review* 50, no. 1 (October 1944), 1–25; Gordon S. Wood, *Radicalism of the American Revolution* (New York, 1991), 328–329; Joyce O. Appleby, *Inheriting the Revolution: The First Generation of Americans* (Cambridge, Mass., 2000), 194–238.

3. Among many books on the role of voluntary associations in creating middle-class identity, see Stuart M. Blumin, *The Emergence of the Middle Class: Social Experience in the American City, 1760–1900* (New York, 1989), 192–229; John S. Gilkeson, *Middle-Class Providence, 1820–1940* (Princeton, N.J., 1986); Mary P. Ryan, *Cradle of the Middle Class: The Family in Oneida County, New York, 1790–1865* (New York, 1981).

4. Elisabeth S. Clemens, *The People's Lobby: Organizational Innovation and the Rise of Interest Group Politics in the United States, 1880–1925* (Chicago, 1997), 48–50.

5. Examples include Noble E. Cunningham Jr., *The Jeffersonian Republicans in Power: Party Operations, 1801–1809* (Chapel Hill, N.C., 1963); David Hackett Fischer, *The Revolution in American Conservatism: The Federalist Party in the Era of Jeffersonian Democracy* (New York, 1965); Richard P. McCormick, *The Second American Party System: Party Formation in the Jacksonian Era* (New York, 1966); Jean H. Baker, *Affairs of Party: The Political Culture of Northern Democrats in the Mid-Nineteenth Century* (Ithaca, N.Y., 1983); Joel H. Silbey, "'The Salt of the Nation': Political Parties in Antebellum America," in *The Partisan Imperative: The Dynamics of American Politics before the Civil War* (New York, 1985), 50–68; Alan Taylor, "'The Art of Hook & Snivey': Political Culture in Upstate New York during the 1790s," *Journal of American History* 79, no. 4 (March 1993), 1371–1396; David Waldstreicher, *In the Midst of Perpetual Fetes: The Making of American Nationalism, 1776–1820* (Chapel Hill, N.C., 1997); Jeffrey L. Pasley, *"The Tyranny of Printers": Newspaper Politics in the Early American Republic* (Charlottesville, Va., 2001); Theda Skocpol, *Diminished Democracy: From Membership to Management in American Civic Life* (Norman, Okla., 2003), 36–38.

6. Joan Shelley Rubin, "What Is the History of the History of Books?" *Journal of American History* 90, no. 2 (September 2003), 555–575; David D. Hall, *Cultures of Print: Essays in the History of the Book* (Amherst, Mass., 1996); David Paul Nord, "Religious Reading and Readers in Antebellum America," *Journal of the Early Republic* 15, no. 2 (Summer 1995), 241–272; Michael Warner, *The Letters of the Republic: Publication and the Public Sphere in Eighteenth-Century America* (Cambridge, Mass., 1990); Richard D. Brown, *Knowledge Is Power: The Diffusion of Information in Early America, 1700–1865* (New York, 1989). See also John L. Brooke, "To Be 'Read by the Whole People': Press, Party, and Public Sphere in the United States, 1789–1840," *Proceedings of the American Antiquarian Society* 110, no. 11 (2002), 41–118.

7. My understanding of this process was aided greatly by conversations with Conrad Edick Wright. See Wright, *The Transformation of Charity in Postrevolutionary New England* (Boston, 1992). Alexis de Tocqueville referred to the "art" or "science" of association. See Alexis de Tocqueville, *Democracy in America*, trans. Arthur Goldhammer (New York: Library of America, 2004), 596, 606. See also Thomas Haskell, "Capitalism and the Origins of the Humanitarian Sensibility, Part One," *American Historical Review* 90, no. 2 (April 1985), 339–361, esp. 356–357; William A. Galston, "Civil Society and the 'Art of Association,'" *Journal of Democracy* 11, no. 1 (January 2000), 64–70. For an elaboration of the idea of civic skills and the role of associations in fostering them, see Sidney Verba, Kay Lehman Schlozman, and Henry E. Brady, *Voice and Equality: Civic Voluntarism in American Politics* (Cambridge, Mass., 1995); Louis J. Ayala, "Trained for Democracy: The Differing Effects of Voluntary and Involuntary Organizations on Political Participation," *Political Research Quarterly* 53, no. 1 (March 2000), 99–115.

8. Historians have long argued that the piety of the Second Great Awakening was channeled into benevolent associations. Religious belief is of the utmost importance to understanding evangelicals' reform activity, but belief alone is not a sufficient explanation. We still need to know how evangelicals learned to use voluntary associations to express their religious ideals.

9. Sean Wilentz, *The Rise of American Democracy: Jefferson to Lincoln* (New York, 2005), 516–517; Silbey, "'The Salt of the Nation,'" 50–68; Joel H. Silbey, Allan G. Bogue, and William H. Flanigan, eds., *The History of American Electoral Behavior* (Princeton, N.J., 1978); Michael F. Holt, *The Political Crisis of the 1850s* (New York, 1978).

10. Tocqueville, *Democracy in America*, 584.

11. On the organizing role of parties and their relation to public opinion in American politics, see Richard J. Carwardine, *Lincoln* (Harlow, UK, 2003), 43–134; Silbey, "'The Salt of the Nation'"; Joel H. Silbey, *The American Political Nation, 1838–1893* (Stanford, Calif., 1991); Holt, *The Political Crisis of the 1850s*. On how the structure of the American polity encouraged the development of political parties, see Skocpol, *Diminished Democracy*, 36–37; Michael Schudson, "The 'Public Sphere' and Its Problems: Bringing the State (Back) In," *Notre Dame Journal of Law, Ethics, and Public Policy* 8 (1994), 529–546.

12. For a discussion of the relationship between the Federalist Party and orthodox clergy, see James M. Banner Jr., *To the Hartford Convention: The Federalists and the Origins of Party Politics in Massachusetts, 1789–1815* (New York, 1970), 152–167; Ronald P. Formisano, *The Transformation of Political Culture:*

*Massachusetts Parties, 1790s–1840s* (New York, 1983), 149–170, 197–221; John L. Brooke, *The Heart of the Commonwealth: Society and Political Culture in Worcester County, Massachusetts, 1713–1861* (New York, 1989), 238–247, 324–327. See also Peter S. Field, *The Crisis of the Standing Order: Clerical Intellectuals and Cultural Authority in Massachusetts, 1780–1833* (Amherst, Mass., 1998).

13. Jonathan D. Sassi, *A Republic of Righteousness: The Public Christianity of the Post-revolutionary New England Clergy* (New York, 2001); Mark Y. Hanley, *Beyond a Christian Commonwealth: The Protestant Quarrel with the American Republic, 1830–1860* (Chapel Hill, N.C., 1994); Steven Mintz, *Moralists and Modernizers: America's Pre-Civil War Reformers* (Baltimore, 1995).

14. This paragraph pulls from many sources, including Debra Gold Hansen, *Strained Sisterhood: Gender and Class in the Boston Female Anti-Slavery Society* (Amherst, Mass., 1993), 59–61, 64–92; Wright, *The Transformation of Charity*, 77–95; Paul G. Faler, *Mechanics and Manufacturers in the Early Industrial Revolution: Lynn, Massachusetts 1780–1860* (Albany, N.Y., 1981), 100–108, 109–163; Carol Buchalter Stapp, *Afro-Americans in Antebellum Boston: An Analysis of Probate Records* (New York, 1993), 225–228; George A. Levesque, *Black Boston: African American Life and Culture in Urban America, 1750–1860* (New York, 1994), and "Inherent Reformers- Inherited Orthodoxy: Black Baptists in Boston, 1800–1873," *Journal of Negro History* 60, no. 4 (October 1975), 491–525; Adelaide M. Cromwell, *The Other Brahmins: Boston's Black Upper Class, 1750–1950* (Fayetteville, Ark., 1994), 37–44. I am particularly thankful to Edward Kilsdonk at the University of Virginia for sharing a chapter of his dissertation in progress, entitled "Organizations, Amalgamation, and Common Christianity" (in author's possession). Conrad Edick Wright, *Transformation of Charity*, 77–95, argues, "In the early 19th century, the simultaneous development of organized evangelism and the organization of orthodox Congregationalism resulted in a religious revival more intense than either could have produced alone."

15. Paul DiMaggio and Walter W. Powell, "The Iron Cage Revisited: Institutional Isomorphism and Collective Rationality in Organizational Fields," *American Sociological Review* 48, no. 2 (April 1983), 147–160.

16. On the religious cosmology of reformers, see Robert H. Abzug, *Cosmos Crumbling: American Reform and the Religious Imagination* (New York, 1994); John L. Thomas, "Romantic Reform in America, 1815–1865," *American Quarterly* 17, no. 4 (Winter 1965), 656–681.

17. Lyman Beecher, *Autobiography of Lyman Beecher*, ed. Barbara Cross, 2 vols. (Cambridge, Mass., 1961), 1:253.

18. Ebenezer Porter, "Great Effects from Little Causes. A Sermon, delivered . . . at the Anniversary of the Moral Society in Andover" (Andover, Mass., 1815).

19. See the Rev. Noah Worcester's comments in Wright, *The Transformation of Charity*, 51. See also Wright, *Transformation of Charity*, 115-33; Samuel Worcester's 1817 comments in the fifth annual report of the Massachusetts Society for the Suppression of Intemperance, "Annual Reports," Records of the Massachusetts Temperance Society, Massachusetts Historical Society; American Society for Educating Pious Youth for the Gospel Ministry, "Fourth Report" (Andover, Mass., 1819).

20. Jesse Appleton, "A Discourse, delivered at Bath . . . before the Society for Discountenancing and Suppressing Public Vices" (Boston, 1813). See also Thomas

Appleton White, "An Address to the members of the Merrimack Humane Society, at their anniversary meeting, in Newburyport . . ." (Newburyport, Mass., 1805); "Constitution of the New-Bedford Auxiliary Society, for the Suppression of Intemperance, and Address of the Board of Counsel . . ." (New Bedford, Mass., 1815); Peter Eaton, "A Sermon, delivered at Topsfield . . . before the Moral Society of Boxford and Topsfield" (Andover, Mass., 1816); Marblehead Union Moral Society, "The Constitution and By-Laws . . ." (Salem, Mass., 1817); "Constitution of the Samaritan Female Society of Andover and Vicinity" (Andover, Mass., 1818).

21. Anne M. Boylan, *The Origins of Women's Activism: New York and Boston, 1797–1840* (Chapel Hill, N.C., 2002) 137–144, also emphasizes the importance of annual reports and other print material, but Boylan is more interested in how women accessed the public sphere of print than how the publication of reports educated citizens about voluntary associations.

22. As Warner, *The Letters of the Republic*, xiii, argues, "It becomes possible to imagine oneself, in the act of reading, becoming part of an arena of the national people that cannot be realized except through such mediating imaginings."

23. Abiel Holmes, "A Sermon, delivered before the Massachusetts Missionary Society . . ." (Cambridge, Mass., 1804).

24. For examples, see Joseph Chickering, "A Sermon, preached in Boston, before the American Society for Educating Pious Youth for the Gospel Ministry . . ." (Dedham, Mass., 1817); Thaddeus Mason Harris, "A Discourse delivered before the Humane Society . . ." (Boston, 1806), Humane Society of Massachusetts Records, Box 16, Massachusetts Historical Society.

25. For example, see "The Report of the Trustees to the HMS" in Rufus Wells, "A Sermon, preached before the Hampshire Missionary Society . . . to which is annexed, The Annual Report . . ." (Northampton, Mass., 1811).

26. Records of the Massachusetts Temperance Society, Massachusetts Historical Society.

27. Auxiliary Foreign Mission Society, in the County of Franklin, "Report of the Committee . . ." (Greenfield, Mass., 1813); "Annual Report of the Directors of the Massachusetts Society for Promoting Christian Knowledge" in David T. Kemball, "A Sermon . . ." (Cambridge, Mass., 1821).

28. New Bedford Benevolent Society, "Sixth Annual Report" (1845), New Bedford Benevolent Society Records, Massachusetts Historical Society.

29. Middlesex Bible Society, "Fifth Annual Report" (Cambridge, Mass., 1820).

30. Jeremiah Chaplin, "A Sermon, the substance of which was delivered before the Baptist Missionary Society in Massachusetts" (Boston, 1808).

31. "Fifth Annual Report," Records of the Massachusetts Temperance Society, Massachusetts Historical Society.

32. "Record Book", Records of the Massachusetts Temperance Society, Massachusetts Historical Society.

33. William E. Strong, *The Story of the American Board: An Account of the First Hundred Years of the American Board of Commissioners for Foreign Missions* (Boston, 1910), 148–149.

34. *Panoplist* 16 (1820), quoted in John A. Andrew III, *Rebuilding the Christian Commonwealth: New England Congregationalists and Foreign Missions, 1800–1830* (Lexington, Ky., 1976), 123.

35. David Paul Nord has commented on the relationship between evangelicalism and the emergence of a mass media in print. See Nord, *The Evangelical Origins of Mass Media in America, 1815–1835* (Columbia, S.C., 1984). Alexis de Tocqueville also noted the importance of newspapers in cultivating associations across space. See Tocqueville, *Democracy in America*, 600–603.

36. "Report of the Trustees, to the Hampshire Missionary Society, at their annual meeting, in Northampton . . ." (Northampton, Mass., 1803).

37. Benjamin Wadsworth, "Female Charity an Acceptable Offering. A Sermon delivered . . . at the bequest of the Charitable Female Cent Society in Danvers and Middleton . . ." (Andover, Mass., 1817). See also *Spirit of the Pilgrims* 3, no. 6 (June 1830), 301–314.

38. Thomas Snell, "Women ministering to Christ. A Discourse delivered in the West Parish of Brookfield, before the Female Bible Cent Society . . ." (Brookfield, Mass., 1815).

39. Congregational Missionary Society, "The Constitution and Address of the Congregational Missionary Society" (Stockbridge, Mass., 1798); Society for Propagating the Gospel among the Indians and Others in North America, "Brief Account of the Society for Propagating the Gospel among the Indians and Others in North-America" (Boston, 1798); Nathanael Emmons, "A Sermon, delivered before the Massachusetts Missionary Society" (Charlestown, Mass., 1800); Massachusetts Congregational Charitable Society, "Sir, on a conference . . . with the Convention of Congregational Ministers, in May last: it was agreed, that the corporation should form and issue subscription papers . . ." (Boston, 1803).

40. Morse to George Burder, October 8, 1802, in Joseph W. Phillips, *Jedidiah Morse and New England Congregationalism* (New Brunswick, N.J., 1983), 117–118.

41. For correspondence, see Washington Benevolent Society Records, Massachusetts Historical Society.

42. See, for example, "Constitution of the Samaritan Female Society of Andover and Vicinity" (Andover, Mass., 1818).

43. Evangelical Missionary Society, "The Address and Constitution of the Evangelical Missionary Society" (Cambridge, Mass., 1807).

44. "An Address of the Bible Society of Maine . . ." (Portland, Maine, 1809).

45. "A Circular Address from the Bible Society in the county of Bristol, Massachusetts, with the Constitution, List of Officers, Trustees, &c." (Taunton, Mass., 1814).

46. The auxiliary system paralleled the development of national religious denominations, and took a similar form. See Wright, *Transformation of Charity*, ch. 3; C. C. Goen, *Broken Churches, Broken Nation: Denominational Schisms and the Coming of the American Civil War* (Macon, Ga., 1985), 56–63; Sidney E. Mead, *The Lively Experiment: The Shaping of Christianity in America* (New York, 1963).

47. This is one of the major arguments of Theda Skocpol, Marshall Ganz, and Ziad Munson, "A Nation of Organizers: The Institutional Origins of Civic Voluntarism in the United States," *American Political Science Review* 94, no. 3 (September 2000), 527–546; Skocpol, *Diminished Democracy*, 40–43.

48. New England Tract Society, "Constitution . . ." (Andover, Mass., 1814).

49. American Society for Educating Pious Youth for the Gospel Ministry, "Constitution & Address . . ." (Boston, 1816).

50. Records of the Massachusetts Temperance Society, Massachusetts Historical Society. The Rev. Cotton Mather had promoted the organization of moral societies as early as the 1690s. On early moral societies, see Donald Scott, *From Office to Profession: The New England Ministry, 1750–1850* (Philadelphia, 1978), 31–35; Wright, *The Transformation of Charity*, 34–36.

51. New England Tract Society, "Constitution . . ." (Andover, Mass., 1814).

52. These associations have been described as an "evangelical united front," or more commonly the Benevolent Empire. See, for example, Charles I. Foster, *An Errand of Mercy: The Evangelical United Front, 1790–1837* (Chapel Hill, N.C., 1960). Clifford S. Griffin, *Their Brothers' Keepers: Moral Stewardship in the United States, 1800–1865* (New Brunswick, N.J., 1960), 23–43, considered the core organizations of the united front to be the Sunday School Union, the Education and the Home Missionary Societies, the Bible Society, the Tract Society, and the Temperance, Peace and Antislavery Societies.

53. See "Report of the Executive Committee of the Bible Society of Massachusetts, prepared for the anniversary of the society, June 8, 1815" (Boston, 1815). I am not sure why they resisted joining with the national institution. Perhaps liberal Unitarian members of the Massachusetts Bible Society were hesitant to form an alliance with evangelical Presbyterians from New Jersey and New York.

54. "A Citizen of New York," "A Memoir on the Subject of a General Bible Society for the United States of America" (New York, 1816).

55. American Bible Society Board of Managers, "Address to the People of the United States" (May 1816), as quoted in Peter J. Wosh, *Spreading the Word: The Bible Business in Nineteenth-Century America* (Ithaca, N.Y., 1994), 63, 65; "Report of the Executive Committee of the Bible Society of Massachusetts . . ." (Boston, 1817). On the formation of the American Bible Society, see Wosh, *Spreading the Word*; Phillips, *Jedidiah Morse*, 174–175; Griffin, *Their Brothers' Keepers*, 81–83.

56. . "Report of the Executive Committee of the Bible Society of Massachusetts" (Boston, 1817).

57. Ibid.

58. "A Circular Address, from the Berkshire Bible Society, with the Constitution . . ." (Pittsfield, Mass., 1817).

59. "Report of the Committee of the Auxiliary Bible Society in the County of Bristol, Massachusetts . . ." (Taunton, Mass., 1819).

60. Skocpol et al., "A Nation of Organizers"; Theda Skocpol, "How Americans Became Civic," in *Civic Engagement in American Democracy*, ed. Theda Skocpol and Morris P. Fiorina (Washington, D.C., 1999), 27–71; Skocpol, *Diminished Democracy*, 32, 37, 72–73, 89–98.

61. Massachusetts Society for the Suppression of Intemperance, "First Annual Report," Records of the Massachusetts Temperance Society, Massachusetts Historical Society.

62. New England Tract Society, "Constitution . . ." (Andover, Mass., 1814).

63. See the Massachusetts Peace Society's second annual report in Thomas Dawes, "An address to the Massachusetts Peace Society . . ." (Boston, 1818).

64. Numbers from Roman J. Zorn, "The New England Anti-Slavery Society: Pioneer Abolition Organization," *Journal of Negro History* 42, no. 3 (July 1957), 157–176, at 172, 175.

65. Abzug, *Cosmos Crumbling*, 90.

66. Strong, *The Story of the American Board*, 145.

67. Wosh, *Spreading the Word*, 62–71.

68. American Society for Educating Pious Youth for the Gospel Ministry, "Constitution & Address . . ." (Boston, 1816); Joseph Chickering, "A Sermon, preached in Boston, before the American Society for Educating Pious Youth for the Gospel Ministry . . . [with 2nd annual report]" (Dedham, 1817). In general, see Griffin, *Their Brothers' Keepers*, 81–98; Scott, *From Office to Profession*, 66–67.

69. Wright, *The Transformation of Charity*, 3–5.

70. Walters, *American Reformers*, 80–81.

71. American Board of Commissioners for Foreign Missions, "Report of the American Board . . . at the First Annual Meeting" (Boston, 1814).

72. American Board of Commissioners for Foreign Missions, "Report of the American Board . . . at the Eighth Annual Meeting . . ." (Boston, 1817).

73. American Society for Educating Pious Youth for the Gospel Ministry, "Constitution & Address . . ." (Boston, 1816); Joseph Chickering, "A Sermon, preached in Boston, before the American Society for Educating Pious Youth for the Gospel Ministry . . . [with 2nd annual report]" (Dedham, Mass., 1817); American Society for Educating Pious Youth for the Gospel Ministry, "Third Report of the Directors . . ." (Andover, Mass., 1818); American Society for Educating Pious Youth for the Gospel Ministry, "Fourth Report" (Andover, Mass., 1819). See also "Constitution and Circular Address of the Female Society of Boston and its Vicinity, auxiliary to the American Education Society" (Boston, 1819).

74. Religious Charitable Society in the County of Worcester, "Report of the Third Meeting" (Worcester, Mass., 1814); "Annual Report" in Joseph Field, "Prosperity Promised to the Lovers of Jerusalem. A Sermon, Delivered . . . before the Hampshire Missionary Society . . ." (Northampton, Mass., 1816).

75. Middlesex County Bible Society, "Fifth Annual Report" (Cambridge, Mass., 1820).

76. For statistics, see Griffin, *Their Brothers' Keepers*, 83; Strong, *The Story of the American Board*, 145; Wright, *The Transformation of Charity*, 5.

77. There are innumerable examples of the importance of local societies to the revenue of state and national associations, including: "Annual Report of the Directors of the Massachusetts Society for Promoting Christian Knowledge," in David T. Kemball, "A Sermon . . ." (Cambridge, Mass., 1821); "Annual Report," in Joshua Bates, "A Sermon, delivered . . . before the Massachusetts Society for Promoting Christian Knowledge . . ." (Dedham, Mass., 1816).

78. For a discussion of the organizational aspects of female benevolence, see Lori Ginzberg, *Women and the Work of Benevolence: Morality, Politics, and Class in the Nineteenth-Century United States* (New Haven, Conn., 1990), 36–66. For an examination of how female voluntary associations raised money, see Anne M. Boylan, *The Origins of Women's Activism*, ch. 5.

79. Hampshire Female Society, "A Plan for a Female Association in the County of Hampshire" (Northampton, Mass., 1803).

80. Annual report in Joseph Field, "Prosperity Promised to the Lovers of Jerusalem. A Sermon, Delivered . . . before the Hampshire Missionary Society . . ." (Northampton, Mass., 1816).

81. Elias Cornelius, "Sermon before the Salem Society for the Moral and Religious Instruction of the Poor" (Salem, Mass., 1824), quoted in Ginzberg, *Women and the Work of Benevolence*, 36.

82. Thomas Snell, "Women ministering to Christ. A Discourse delivered in the West Parish of Brookfield, before the Female Bible Cent Society . . ." (Brookfield, Mass., 1815). See also Kathleen D. McCarthy, *American Creed: Philanthropy and the Rise of Civil Society* (Chicago, 2003), 59, 81–82.

83. American Board of Commissioners for Foreign Missions, "Report of the ABCFM . . . at the First Annual Meeting" (Boston, 1814); Joshua Bates, "A Sermon, delivered . . . before the Massachusetts Society for Promoting Christian Knowledge [with annual report]" (Dedham, Mass., 1816).

84. Historians have demonstrated that middle-class men and women, including skilled craftsmen and their wives, joined many voluntary associations. Lois Banner, "The Protestant Crusade: Religious Missions, Benevolence, and Reform in the United States, 1790–1840" (Ph.D. diss., Columbia University, 1970); Gilkeson, *Middle-Class Providence*; Ginzberg; *Women and the Work of Benevolence*; Ryan, *Cradle of the Middle Class*; Christine Stansell, *City of Women: Sex and Class in New York, 1789–1860* (New York, 1986).

85. From the Appendix of Charles Augustus Goodrich, "An Address, delivered . . . before the Female Reading and Charitable Society of the First Parish in Worcester, Mass." (Worcester, Mass., 1817).

86. Ibid. See Carolyn J. Lawes, *Women and Reform in a New England Community, 1815–1860* (Lexington, Ky., 2000), 55–56; Sandra Herbert Petrulionis, "'Swelling That Great Tide of Humanity': The Concord, Massachusetts, Female Anti-Slavery Society," *New England Quarterly* (September 2001), 385–418; Ginzberg, *Women and the Work of Benevolence*, 46–47; Phillips, *Jedidiah Morse*, 121–122. More generally, see Banner, "The Protestant Crusade"; Anne M. Boylan, "Timid Girls, Venerable Widows and Dignified Patrons: Life Cycle Patterns among Organized Women in New York and Boston, 1797–1840," *American Quarterly* 38, no. 5 (Winter 1986), 779–797, and *Origins of Women's Activism*, 171–209; Ryan, *Cradle of the Middle Class*; Stansell, *City of Women*.

87. "Proceedings at the Fifteenth Anniversary of the Auxiliary Foreign Mission Society of Boston and Vicinity, June 1, 1826" (Boston, 1826).

88. Numbers from Brown, "Emergence of Urban Society." Percentages compiled in Skocpol, "How Americans Became Civic," 39.

89. These divisions are central to Gilkeson, *Middle-Class Providence*; Ginzberg, *Women and the Work of Benevolence*; Ryan, *Cradle of the Middle Class*; Boylan, *Origins of Women's Activism*.

90. The idea of a relationship between print culture and imagined communities is from Benedict Anderson, *Imagined Communities: Reflections on the Origin and Spread of Nationalism* (London, 1983). For the importance of local activity to translocal identities, see Waldstreicher, *In the Midst of Perpetual Fetes*; Brown, "Emergence of Urban Society," 42–43; Brown, *Modernization*; Donald G. Mathews, "The Second Great Awakening as an Organizing Process, 1780–1830: An Hypothesis," *American Quarterly* 21, no. 1 (Spring 1969), 23–43; Nord, "Mass Media"; Warner, *Letters of the Republic*; Skocpol, *Diminished Democracy*, 74–126.

91. Bender, *Community and Social Change in America*, 122. See also Johann N. Neem, "Civil Society and American Nationalism, 1776–1865," in *Politics and*

*Partnerships: Nonprofit Organizations in American Governance*, ed. Elisabeth S. Clemens and Douglas Guthrie (forthcoming, University of Chicago Press).

92. A similar point is made in Skocpol, *Diminished Democracy*, 77–89.

93. American Society for Educating Pious Youth for the Gospel Ministry, "Third Report of the Directors . . ." (Andover, Mass., 1818). See also Scott, *From Office to Profession*, 59–60; David F. Allmendinger Jr., *Paupers and Scholars: The Transformation of Student Life in Nineteenth-Century New England* (New York, 1975), 67–71.

94. "Report of the Executive Committee of the Bible Society of Massachusetts . . ." (Boston, 1817).

95. On the bureaucratization of the American Bible Society, see Wosh, *Spreading the Word*, 62–88, 124–129. The American Board of Commissioners for Foreign Missions also became increasingly bureaucratic over the course of the nineteenth century. See Strong, *The Story of the American Board*, 3–16, 140–162, 305–322; Andrew, *Rebuilding the Christian Commonwealth*, 70–96, 120–150.

96. Richard D. Brown lists fifty-nine missionary societies and forty-eight "needy" charitable societies in the 1810s, which declined to thirty-four and twenty-three, respectively, in the 1820s. During that same period, the number of reform associations rose from forty-three to ninety-one. See Brown, "Emergence of Urban Society in Rural Massachusetts," 40.

97. The long sweep of this transition is discussed in Theda Skocpol's recent work, *Diminished Democracy*. See also Handlin and Handlin, *The Dimensions of Liberty*, 106–107; Clemens, *The People's Lobby*, 206–234. For a thoughtful discussion of the social importance of local personal charity as opposed to organized philanthropy, see Robert A. Gross, "Giving in America: From Charity to Philanthropy," in *Charity, Philanthropy, and Civility in American History*, ed. Lawrence J. Friedman and Mark D. McGarvie (Cambridge, 2003), 29–48.

98. "The Constitution of the Salem Female Charitable Society" (Salem, Mass., 1801); Massachusetts Society for Promoting Christian Knowledge, "An Account of the Massachusetts Society for Promoting Christian Knowledge" (Cambridge, Mass., 1806). See also "Record Book," Massachusetts Congregational Charitable Society Records, Massachusetts Historical Society; Roxbury Charitable Society, "Whereas in a State of Civil Society . . ." (Boston, 1794); Congregational Missionary Society, "The Constitution and Address of the Congregational Missionary Society" (Stockbridge, Mass., 1798); "An Address of the Bible Society of Maine, established in Portland, August 30, 1809, to the Public: to which is subjoined, The Constitution & Regulations of Said Society, and the Names of its Officers" (Portland, Maine, 1809).

99. "Constitution and Address of the Religious Charitable Society in the county of Worcester, Massachusetts" (Worcester, Mass., 1812); "A Circular Address from the Bible Society in the county of Bristol . . ." (Taunton, Mass., 1814).

100. See the Massachusetts Peace Society's second annual report in Thomas Dawes, "An Address to the Massachusetts Peace Society . . ." (Boston, 1818).

101. Middlesex County Bible Society, "Fourth Annual Report" (Cambridge, Mass., 1819).

102. "Record Book," Records of the Massachusetts Temperance Society, Massachusetts Historical Society.

103. See "Doings of the Temperance Convention," printed in the *Free Press and Boston Weekly Advocate*, October 2, 1833.

104. Middlesex County Bible Society, "Fourth Annual Report" (Cambridge, Mass., 1819).

105. "Record Book," Records of the Massachusetts Temperance Society, Massachusetts Historical Society.

106. American Society for Educating Pious Youth for the Gospel Ministry, "Fourth Report" (Andover, Mass., 1819).

107. Baptist Missionary Society of Norfolk County and Vicinity, "Report of the Third Annual Meeting . . ." (Boston, 1818).

108. For example, see Salem Baptist Female Education Society, "Constitution . . ." (Salem, Mass., 1815); Hampshire Female Society, "A Plan for a Female Association in the County of Hampshire" (Northampton, Mass., 1803).

109. The impetus for the Boston Female Asylum was, however, an anonymous letter in 1800, which was later discovered to have been written by a man, reinforcing the point that men also actively promoted female benevolence. Ginzberg, *Women and the Work of Benevolence*, 38, 49–50.

110. Thomas Barnard, "A Sermon preached before the Salem Female Charitable Society [with annual report]" (Salem, Mass., 1803).

111. Quoted in Hansen, *Strained Sisterhood*, 141–142.

112. Samuel Stillman, "A Discourse delivered before the Members of the Boston Female Asylum" (Boston, 1801).

113. Daniel Dana, "Discourse delivered . . . before the members of the Female Charitable Society of Newburyport" (Newburyport, Mass., 1803).

114. Quoted in Wright, *The Transformation of Charity*, 113–114.

115. Richard D. Shiels, "The Feminization of American Congregationalism, 1730–1835," *American Quarterly* 33, no. 1 (Spring 1981), 46–62.

116. Boylan, "Timid Girls, Venerable Widows and Dignified Matrons" and *Origins of Women's Activism*, 126–159; Ginzberg, *Women and the Work of Benevolence*; Nancy A. Hewitt, *Women's Activism and Social Change: Rochester, New York, 1822–1872* (Ithaca, N.Y., 1984). For an intriguing discussion about the relationship between female religious activism and the boundaries of the public sphere, see Nancy Isenberg, "'Pillars in the Same Temple and Priests of the Same Worship': Woman's Rights and the Politics of Church and State in Antebellum America," *Journal of American History* 85, no. 1 (June 1998), 98–128.

117. Ryan, *Cradle of the Middle Class*, 105–144; Anne M. Boylan, "Women in Groups: An Analysis of Women's Benevolent Organizations in New York and Boston, 1797–1840," Journal of American History 71, no. 3 (Dec. 1984), 497–523, *Origins of Women's Activism*.

118. Hansen, *Strained Sisterhood*, 140–157; Lori Ginzberg, *Women in Antebellum Reform* (Wheeling, Ill., 2000), 74–81.

119. Ginzberg, *Women and the Work of Benevolence*, ch. 2. More generally, see Paula Baker, "The Domestication of Politics: Women and American Political Society, 1780–1920," *American Historical Review* 89, no. 3 (June 1984), 620–647; Boylan, "Timid Girls, Venerable Widows and Dignified Matrons."

120. Quoted in Hansen, *Strained Sisterhood*, 20.

121. Ibid., 23.

122. Theodore Dwight Weld to Angelina and Sarah Grimké, July 22, 1837, in *Letters of Theodore Dwight Weld, Angelina Grimké Weld and Sarah Grimké, 1822–1844*, ed. Gilbert H. Barnes and Dwight L. Dumond, 2 vols. (1943; reprint, Gloucester, Mass., 1965), 1:412; Angelina Grimké to Theodore Dwight Weld and John Greenleaf Whittier, August 20, 1837, in Ibid., 1:427–432, at 430.

123. Walters, *American Reformers*, 86–92, 106–109; Keith E. Melder, *Beginnings of Sisterhood: The American Woman's Rights Movement, 1800–1850* (New York, 1977), 113–128.

124. Richard J. Carwardine, *Evangelicals and Politics in Antebellum America* (Knoxville, Tenn., 1997), 16; Isenberg, "'Pillars in the Same Temple,'" addresses the issue of the relationship between the moral and the political in the public sphere for women.

125. Ginzberg, *Women and the Work of Benevolence*, ch. 4, describes the growing frustration of radical female reformers who concluded, ultimately, that "moral suasion is moral balderdash" in a society that defines political membership by the vote. John L. Thomas, "Romantic Reform," argues that the tendency of reformers to be uncompromising was their greatest flaw: they sought perfection and were willing to risk all to get it.

126. Hansen, *Strained Sisterhood*, 25–28.

127. On this topic, among others, see Susan Zaeske, *Signatures of Citizenship: Petitioning, Antislavery, and Women's Political Identity* (Chapel Hill, N.C., 2003).

128. For African American voluntarism, see McCarthy, *American Creed*, 98–120, 123–143, 151–159; Richard S. Newman, *The Transformation of American Abolitionism: Fighting Slavery in the Early Republic* (Chapel Hill, N.C., 2002), 86–130; Gary B. Nash, *Forging Freedom: The Formation of Philadelphia's Black Community, 1720–1840* (Cambridge, Mass., 1988); Theda Skocpol and Jennifer Lynn Oser, "Organization Despite Adversity: The Origins and Development of African American Fraternal Associations," *Social Science History* 28, no. 3 (Fall 2004), 367–437.

129. Cromwell, *The Other Brahmins*, 39–40; Hansen, *Strained Sisterhood*, 64–92.

130. Quoted in Ginzberg, *Women in Antebellum Reform*, 67–68.

131. George A. Levesque argues for the existence of a black "consciousness" caused by the growth of the black community and its residential segregation. Levesque, "Inherent Reformers." See also Lawrence J. Friedman, *Gregarious Saints: Self and Community in American Abolitionism, 1830–1870* (New York, 1982), 160–196.

132. Levesque, "Inherent Reformers."

133. For the importance of youth, see Joyce O. Appleby, *Inheriting the Revolution: The First Generation of Americans* (Cambridge, Mass., 2000), 11–14, 194–238; Banner, "The Protestant Crusade," 262–288, and "Religion and Reform in the Early Republic: The Role of Youth," *American Quarterly* 23, no. 5 (December 1971), 677–695; Boylan, "Timid Girls, Venerable Widows and Dignified Matrons"; Joseph F. Kett, *Rites of Passage: Adolescence in America 1790 to the Present* (New York, 1977), 62–108; Phillips, *Jedidiah Morse*, 122–124; Ryan, *Cradle of the Middle Class*, 127–132, 176–177; Wosh, *Spreading the Word*, 74–88. For the role of youth associations in fostering civic skills among adult citizens in the contemporary United States, see James Youniss, Jeffrey A. McLellan, and Miranda Yates,

"A Developmental Approach to Civil Society," in, *Beyond Tocqueville: Civil Society and the Social Capital Debate in Comparative Perspective*, ed. Bob Edwards, Michael W. Foley, and Mario Dani (Hanover, N.H., 2001), 243–253.

134. For the relationship between young men and the city, see Paul S. Boyer, *Urban Masses and Moral Order in America, 1820–1920* (Cambridge, Mass., 1978), 1–64; Kett, *Rites of Passage*, 86–108.

135. Banner, "The Protestant Crusade," 272.

136. Amy S. Greenberg, *Cause for Alarm: The Volunteer Fire Department in the Nineteenth Century* (Princeton, N.J., 1998); Paul G. Faler, *Mechanics and Manufacturers in the Early Industrial Revolution: Lynn, Massachusetts 1780–1860* (Albany, N.Y., 1981), 52–54.

137. Allmendinger, *Paupers and Scholars*; Wosh, *Spreading the Word*, 74–88.

138. Formisano, *Transformation of Political Culture*, 196–221.

139. Ronald P. Formisano and Kathleen Smith Kutolowski, "Antimasonry and Masonry: The Genesis of Protest, 1826–1827," *American Quarterly* 29, no. 2 (Summer 1977), 139–165; Steven C. Bullock, *Revolutionary Brotherhood: Freemasonry and the Transformation of the American Social Order, 1730–1840* (Chapel Hill, N.C., 1996), 277–279; Paul Goodman, *Towards a Christian Republic: Antimasonry and the Great Transition in New England, 1826–1836* (New York, 1988), 3–19; Wilentz, *Rise of American Democracy*, 272–279.

140. Formisano, *Transformation of Political Culture*, 203–204.

141. *An Abstract of the Proceedings of the Anti-Masonic State Convention of Massachusetts, Held in Faneuil Hall, Boston, Dec. 30 and 31, 1829, and Jan. 1, 1830* (Boston, 1830), 9–19. On the legal proceedings see Formisano and Kutolowski, "Antimasonry and Masonry."

142. Historians have recognized a link between Antimasonry and evangelical Christianity. In Genesee County, New York, where Antimasonry began, towns with a large number of churches and religious fervor generally supported the Antimasonic Party more enthusiastically than did other towns. In fact, religion serves as a better gauge of Antimasonic support than class. The same held true in Michigan, where Ronald P. Formisano argues that evangelical Christians from New England were more likely to subscribe to the antiparty attitudes of Antimasonry's political leaders. See Kathleen Smith Kutolowski, "Antimasonry Reexamined: Social Bases of the Grass-Roots Party," *Journal of American History* 71, no. 2 (September 1984), 269–293, esp. 279–282; Ronald P. Formisano, "Political Character, Antipartyism and the Second Party System," *American Quarterly* 21, no. 4 (Winter 1969), 683–709, esp. 690–695.

143. *Free Press*, January 16, 1831; February 9, 1831.

144. 1831 Antimasonic convention as quoted in Goodman, *Towards a Christian Republic*, 57. See also *Free Press*, November 12, 1832.

145. Emmons quoted in Goodman, *Towards a Christian Republic*, 57.

146. Ibid., 64.

147. Formisano, *Transformation of Political Culture*, 204–216; Goodman, *Towards a Christian Republic*, 148–150.

148. Formisano, *Transformation of Political Culture*, 213, 217–221; Goodman, *Towards a Christian Republic*, 54–79, 163–176. For an interpretation that emphasizes class over religion, see Brooke, *Heart of the Commonwealth*, 319–348.

149. *Boston Statesman*, October 13, 1832.

150. *Daily Advertiser*, October 3, 1831; Goodman, *Towards a Christian Republic*, 166.

151. Bullock, *Revolutionary Brotherhood*, 294–295.

152. *Free Press*, February 9, 1831.

153. "Address of the Antimasonic Convention, to the People of the United States," *Free Press*, October 19, 1831. See also the Antimasons' 1832 state convention address, reprinted in the *Free Press*, September 12, 1832; *Antimasonic Republican Convention, of Massachusetts, Held at Worcester, Sept. 5th & 6th, 1832* (Boston, 1832), 28–42, esp. 28–29.

154. Goodman, *Towards a Christian Republic*, 34–35; Formisano, *Transformation of Political Culture*, 207–208.

155. The letter is reprinted in the *Daily Advertiser*, December 31, 1831.

156. Formisano, *Transformation of Political Culture*, 211.

157. The debate is reprinted in the *Free Press*, March 20, 1833.

158. The memorial is reprinted in *Daily Advertiser*, January 3, 1834. The Grand Lodge's statement defending its freedom to associate echoes the petition that Amherst's proprietors presented when seeking a corporate charter for Amherst.

159. The trope of energy comes out of James Willard Hurst's famous essay, *Law and the Conditions of Freedom* (Madison, Wis., 1956). Hurst proclaimed that American law in the nineteenth century supported the release of dynamic energy. Law was a positive tool that sided with individuals who used property to promote economic growth. For Hurst, law articulated a consensus held by all Americans— that individuals are creative people that must be free to produce whatever is in their power. People had potential energy and law must establish contexts in which that energy could be unleashed. Hurst's focus was on economic life but the lessons that economic actors learned about the marketplace paralleled those learned about associated action in civil society.

160. There are many variations on the social control question. Examples include Griffin, *Their Brothers' Keepers*; Foster, *An Errand of Mercy*; Boyer, *Urban Masses and Moral Order in America, 1820–1920*; Johnson, *A Shopkeeper's Millennium*; Stansell, *City of Women*. See also R. J. Morris, "Voluntary Societies and British Urban Elites, 1780–1850: An Analysis," *Historical Journal* 26, no. 1 (March 1983), 95–118. For critiques of the "social control" thesis, see Lois W. Banner, "Religious Benevolence as Social Control: A Critique of an Interpretation," *Journal of American History* 60, no. 1 (June 1973), 23–41; Haskell, "Capitalism and the Origins of the Humanitarian Sensibility, Part One."

## 5. The Elite Public Sphere

1. [Beecher], *The Address of the General Union for Promoting the Observance of the Christian Sabbath, to the People of the United States, Accompanied by Minutes of the Proceedings and in its Formation* . . . (New York, 1828), as quoted in Richard R. John, "Taking Sabbatarianism Seriously: The Postal System, the Sabbath, and the Transformation of American Political Culture," *Journal of the Early Republic* 10, no. 4 (1990), 516–567, at 538–539. Petition numbers in Ibid., 542–543. My understanding of sabbatarianism relies on Bertram Wyatt-Brown, "Prelude to Abolitionism: Sabbatarian Politics and the Rise of the Second Party System," *Journal of American History* 58, no. 2 (September 1971), 316–341; James

R. Rohrer, "Sunday Mails and the Church-State Theme in Jacksonian America," *Journal of the Early Republic* 7, no. 1 (Spring 1987), 53–74; John, "Taking Sabbatarianism Seriously."

2. John, "Taking Sabbatarianism Seriously," 538. The 1 percent statistic is from Theda Skocpol, *Diminished Democracy: From Membership to Management in American Civic Life* (Norman, Okla., 2003), 26–28.

3. [William Ellery Channing], "Associations," *Christian Examiner* (September 1829), 105–140. Reprinted in William Ellery Channing, *The Works of William E. Channing*, ed. American Unitarian Association (Boston: American Unitarian Association, 1890), 138–158.

4. Richard P. McCormick, *The Second American Party System: Party Formation in the Jacksonian Era* (Chapel Hill, N.C., 1966), 37; Rogers Smith, *Civic Ideals: Conflicting Visions of Citizenship in U.S. History* (New Haven, Conn., 1997), 197–242.

5. Daniel Walker Howe has developed this thesis in several works. See: *The Unitarian Conscience: Harvard Moral Philosophy, 1806–1861* (Cambridge, Mass., 1970); *The Political Culture of the American Whigs* (Chicago, 1979); *Making the American Self: Jonathan Edwards to Abraham Lincoln* (Cambridge, Mass., 1997); and "Protestantism, Voluntarism, and Personal Identity in Antebellum America," in *New Directions in American Religious History*, ed. Harry S. Stout and D. G. Hart (New York, 1997), 206–238. See also Michael B. Katz, *The Irony of Early School Reform: Educational Innovation in Mid-Nineteenth Century Massachusetts* (Cambridge, Mass., 1968); David J. Rothman, *The Discovery of the Asylum: Social Order and Disorder in the New Republic* (1971; reprint, New York, 2002); D. H. Meyer, *The Instructed Conscience: The Shaping of the National Ethic* (Philadelphia, 1972); Joseph F. Kett, *Rites of Passage: Adolescence in America 1790 to the Present* (New York, 1977); J. B. Schneewind, *The Invention of Autonomy: A History of Modern Moral Philosophy* (New York, 1998).

6. Lemuel Shaw, "Address of Chief Justice Shaw," *The American Jurist* 9 (1831), 5–6, as quoted in Jeffrey Steven Kahana, "Regulating Labor: Tradition and Change in American Law, 1790–1850" (Ph.D. diss., Brandeis University, 2002), 112.

7. Howe, *Unitarian Conscience*, ch. 5, and *Political Culture of the American Whigs*. Robert F. Dalzell, *Enterprising Elite: The Boston Associates and the World They Made* (Cambridge, Mass., 1987), argues that many Whigs looked back to the small-town life of their youth, and sought to reconcile their own self-interested capitalist accumulation with the equally powerful motivation to do good and be virtuous and active members of a harmonious community. See also Paul Goodman, "Ethics and Enterprise: The Values of a Boston Elite, 1800–1860," *American Quarterly* 18, no. 3 (Fall 1966), 437–451; William F. Hartford, *Money, Morals, and Politics: Massachusetts in the Age of the Boston Associates* (Boston, 2001); Lawrence F. Kohl, *The Politics of Individualism: Parties and the American Character in the Jacksonian Era* (New York, 1989), 86–90. In *Inventing the Nonprofit Sector and Other Essays on Philanthropy, Voluntarism, and Nonprofit Organizations* (Baltimore, 1992), 170–187, Peter Dobkin Hall calls the Whig approach "civil privatism," in which private trustees of corporate institutions consider themselves better equipped to promote the common good than the state precisely because they are not beholden to public opinion. See also Peter Dobkin Hall,

*The Organization of American Culture, 1700–1900: Private Institutions, Elites, and the Origins of American Nationality* (New York, 1982), 109–111, 209–219. I have been greatly influenced by Hall's insight.

8. *Daily Advertiser,* April 7, 1821.

9. Quoted in Dalzell, *Enterprising Elite,* 154.

10. Hall, *Organization of American Culture;* Peter S. Field, *The Crisis of the Standing Order: Clerical Intellectuals and Cultural Authority in Massachusetts, 1780–1833* (Amherst, Mass., 1998), 30–46; James M. Banner Jr., *To the Hartford Convention: The Federalists and the Origins of Party Politics in Massachusetts, 1789–1815* (New York, 1970), 149–167; Goodman, "Ethics and Enterprise"; Ronald Story, *The Forging of an Aristocracy: Harvard and the Boston Upper Class, 1800–1870* (Middletown, Conn., 1980); Marshall Foletta, *Coming to Terms with Democracy: Federalist Intellectuals and the Shaping of an American Culture* (Charlottesville, Va., 2001).

In his groundbreaking work, historian Lawrence Levine observes that nineteenth-century America witnessed the "sacralization of culture" as such once-popular art forms as Shakespeare's plays and Italian operas were refined by elite institutions into something inaccessible to popular audiences. A new ideal of "high" art emerged in which artistic appreciation depended on a level of knowledge and cultivated taste beyond the reach of most ordinary people. Although Levine locates most of these changes in the latter half of the nineteenth century, historians of elite culture in Massachusetts argue that sacralization began in the decades preceding the Civil War. Peter S. Field, in particular, argues that Boston's Unitarian ministers created a secular intellectual culture as they lost popular influence to evangelicals. Unitarian ministers, who controlled or were members of Harvard and the Boston Athenaeum, and who wrote for journals such as the *Monthly Anthology* and the *North American Review,* made the disinterested examination of politics and culture the duty of a new intellectual class. See Lawrence W. Levine, *Highbrow Lowbrow: The Emergence of Cultural Hierarchy in America* (Cambridge, Mass., 1988); Field, *Crisis of the Standing Order.*

11. This argument has been made by Peter S. Field, Marshall Foletta, and Albrecht Koschnik. Koschnik notes that many of these changes began in the early 1800s as young Federalists in college relied on culture and art to carve out social roles for themselves in an increasingly democratic society. All three scholars deny the claim that Federalists "lost power" after the end of the War of 1812. Instead they point to the emergence of new cultural positions for success and influence. In Massachusetts, of course, Federalists also remained politically viable after 1815. Nonetheless, the larger point is true: as politics became less idealistic, those inclined to Federalism welcomed a place where they could use their knowledge to act for the common good without pandering to the interests of the electorate. See Field, *Crisis of the Standing Order;* Foletta, *Coming to Terms with Democracy;* Albrecht Koschnik, "Voluntary Associations, Political Culture, and the Public Sphere in Philadelphia, 1780–1830" (Ph.D. diss., University of Virginia, 2000), 194–359, and *"Let A Common Interest Bind Us Together": Associations, Partisanship, and Culture, 1775–1840* (Charlottesville, Va., 2007), ch. 5.

12. Hall, *Organization of American Culture,* 89; Field, *Crisis of the Standing Order,* 82–110.

13. Quoted in Ronald Story, "Class and Culture in Boston: The Athenaeum, 1807–1860," *American Quarterly* 27, no. 2 (May 1975), 178–199.

14. Story, "Class and Culture in Boston"; Josiah Quincy, *The History of the Boston Athenaeum, with biographical notices of its deceased founders* (Cambridge, Mass.: Metcalf and Company, 1851), 12–18.

15. Massachusetts General Court, *The Committee, Appointed to Make Inquiries into the Actual State of the Following Literary and Scientific Societies . . . Make the Following Statement . . .* (Boston, 1816).

16. Story, "Class and Culture in Boston."

17. *Daily Advertiser*, December 15, 1821.

18. *Daily Advertiser*, December 18, 1821; December 24, 1821; December 24, 1822; January 3, 1823; February 19, 1823; March 3, 1823; February 21, 1824; February 24, 1824; March 8, 1824.

19. The incorporation of the MGH is discussed in Chapter 3.

20. Dalzell, *Enterprising Elite*, 113–163; Story, *Forging of an Aristocracy*, 10–12; Peter Dobkin Hall, "What the Merchants Did with Their Money: Charitable and Testamentary Trusts in Massachusetts, 1780–1880," in *Entrepreneurs: The Boston Business Community, 1700–1850*, ed. Conrad Edick Wright and Katheryn P. Viens (Boston, 1997), 365–421, esp. 401–403; Foletta, *Coming to Terms with Democracy*, 142–144.

21. *Report of the Massachusetts General Hospital for the year 1823* (Boston, 1824) in Massachusetts General Hospital Manuscript Collections, Massachusetts Historical Society.

22. See the Massachusetts General Hospital's annual reports for 1829 and 1834 in Ibid.

23. Story, *Forging of an Aristocracy*, 135–159.

24. "Inaugural Address delivered in the Chapel of Harvard University, by the Hon. Isaac Parker, Chief Justice of Massachusetts, and Royall Professor of Law," *North American Review* 3, no. 7 (May 1816), 11–27.

25. *Daily Advertiser*, April 7, 1821.

26. Josiah Quincy, *The History of Harvard University*, 2 vols. (1840; reprint, New York, 1977), 2:442–443. For a discussion of Quincy's *History of Harvard*, see Robert McCaughey, *Josiah Quincy, 1772–1864: The Last Federalist* (Cambridge, Mass., 1974), 186–190.

27. Quincy, *History of Harvard*, 2:445–446, 450–451.

28. "Address of the Democratic State Central Committee to the Citizens of Massachusetts," *Boston Statesman*, October 24, 1846.

29. This paragraph and quotations taken from McCaughey, *Josiah Quincy*, 190–194.

30. "Senate Report on the Separation of College and State" (April 1854), as quoted in John S. Whitehead, *The Separation of College and State: Columbia, Dartmouth, Harvard, and Yale, 1776–1876* (New Haven, Conn., 1973), 151.

31. Story, *Forging of an Aristocracy*, 153.

32. Whitehead, *Separation of College and State*, 143–159, 199–208, 229–240. For the status of private nonprofit corporations following the Civil War, see Hall, *Inventing the Nonprofit Sector*, 36–41.

33. Thomas Jefferson to James Madison, September 6, 1789 in *Thomas Jefferson: Writings*, ed. Merrill Peterson, 959–964, at 959. On the Jeffersonians' and Democrats' fear of trusts, see Irvin G. Wyllie, "The Search for an American Law of Charity," *Mississippi Valley Historical Review* 44, no. 2 (September 1959),

203–221; Howard S. Miller, *The Legal Foundations of American Philanthropy, 1776–1844* (Madison, Wis., 1961); A. G. Roeber, "The Long Road to *Vidal:* Charity Law and State Formation in Early America," in *The Many Legalities of Early America,* ed. Christopher L. Tomlins and Bruce H. Mann (Chapel Hill, N.C., 2001), 414–441.

34. Hall, *Organization of American Culture,* 114–122; Hall, "Private Philanthropy and Public Policy: A Historical Appraisal," in *Philanthropy: Four Views,* ed. Robert Payton et al. (New Brunswick, N.J., 1988), 39–72, at 48–50; Hall, "What the Merchants Did with Their Money"; Story, *Forging of an Aristocracy.* See *The Trustees of Phillips Academy v. James King, Executor* (12 Tyng 545 [1815]); *William Bartlet & others v. James King, executor* (12 Tyng 537 [1815]); *Harvard College and Massachusetts General Hospital v. Francis Amory* (9 Pickering 446 [1830]); *The Inhabitants of Hadley v. The Trustees of Hopkins Academy* (14 Pickering 240 [1833]); *Chester Sanderson et al. v. Thomas White et al.* (18 Pickering 328 [1836]); *Roland Burbank v. David S. Whitney* (24 Pickering 146 [1839]); *Hubbard Bartlett & others v. Laura Nye & others* (4 Metcalf 378 [1842]); *William R. P. Washburn v. Samuel E. Sewall & others* (9 Metcalf 280 [1845]); *Elisha Tucker & others, Executors v. The Seaman's Aid Society & others* (7 Metcalf 188 [1843]); *Benjamin P. Winslow v. Daniel Cummings & others* (3 Cushing 358 [1849]); *Jerusha C. King v. David Parker & others* (9 Cushing 71 [1851]); *John W. Bliss & another v. The American Bible Society & others* (2 Allen 334 [1861]); *Caroline Saltonstall v. Charlotte Sanders* (11 Allen 446 [1865]); *Edmund Jackson v. Wendell Phillips & others* (14 Allen 539 [1867]).

35. Scott Gregory Lien, "Contested Solidarities: Philanthropy, Justice, and the Reconstitution of Public Authority in the United States, 1790–1860" (Ph.D. diss., University of Chicago, 2006), ch. 4; *Edmund Jackson v. Wendell Phillips & others* (14 Allen 539 [1867]).

36. *Thomas Barnes v. The Inhabitants of the First Parish in Falmouth* (6 Tyng 401 [1810]); *William Bartlet & others v. James King, executor* (12 Tyng 537 [1815]); *Hubbard Bartlett & others v. Laura Nye & others* (4 Metcalf 378 [1842]); *Elisha Tucker & others, Executors v. The Seaman's Aid Society & others* (7 Metcalf 188 [1843]); *Benjamin P. Winslow v. Daniel Cummings & others* (3 Cushing 358 [1849]); *Jerusha C. King v. David Parker & others* (9 Cushing 71 [1851]).

37. Wyllie, "The Search for an American Law of Charity"; Miller, *Legal Foundations of American Philanthropy;* Roeber, "The Long Road to *Vidal.*"

38. Field, *Crisis of the Standing Order,* 109.

39. Eliot quoted in Hall, *Organization of American Culture,* 217–218.

40. [Samuel A. Eliot], "Charities of Boston," *North American Review* 91, no. 188 (July 1860), 149–166. Also quoted in Hall, *Inventing the Nonprofit Sector,* 184. For the development of similar ideas in Philadelphia, see Koschnik, *"Let A Common Interest Bind Us Together",* ch. 5.

41. Nathan O. Hatch, "The Professions in a Democratic Culture," in *The Professions in American History,* ed. Nathan O. Hatch (Notre Dame, Ind., 1988), 1–13. See also Samuel Haber, *The Quest for Authority and Honor in the American Professions, 1750–1900* (Chicago, 1991); Haber, "The Professions," in *Encyclopedia of American Social History,* ed. Mary K. Cayton et al., 3 vols. (New York, 1993), 2:1573–1588; Thomas Haskell's introduction to *The Authority of Experts: Studies in History and Theory,* ed. Thomas Haskell (Bloomington, Ind., 1984), ix–xxxix. Historians have emphasized the rise of the modern professions during the late

nineteenth century as national professional societies identified the training and skills necessary for their members, while also creating barriers to prevent others from practicing. The roots of this professional culture lie in state-level societies during the antebellum era. The movement to professionalize grew out of many motives, some of which concerned the common good and others that were more selfish. For the late nineteenth century, see Robert H. Wiebe, *The Search for Order, 1877–1920* (New York, 1967), 111–132; Burton J. Bledstein, *The Culture of Professionalism: The Middle Class and the Development of Higher Education in America* (New York, 1976); Peter Novick, *That Noble Dream: The "Objectivity Question" and the American Historical Profession* (New York, 1988); Hall, *Organization of American Culture;* Dorothy Ross, *The Origins of American Social Science* (New York, 1991); Haber, *The Quest for Authority.* For the antebellum era, see Joseph F. Kett, *The Formation of the American Medical Profession: The Role of Institutions, 1780–1860* (New Haven, Conn., 1968); Ronald G. Walters, *American Reformers, 1815–1860* (New York, 1978), 203–206; Hall, *Organization of American Culture;* Donald Scott, *From Office to Profession: The New England Ministry, 1750–1850* (Philadelphia, 1978); Field, *Crisis of the Standing Order;* Foletta, *Coming to Terms with Democracy,* 135–181; Daniel Feller, *The Jacksonian Promise: America, 1815–1840* (Baltimore, 1995), 90–94.

42. For examples, see "Medical Societies. [A Review of] Medical Dissertations, read before the Massachusetts Medical Society . . . Boston. 1827. [and] Proceedings of a Convention of Medical Delegates at Northampton . . . Boston. 1827," *North American Review* 27, no. 60 (July 1828), 43–67; "Character and Abuses of the Medical Profession," *North American Review* 32, no. 71 (April 1831), 367–386; *Daily Advertiser,* October 15, 1836; May 21, 1839.

43. Story, *Forging of an Aristocracy,* 10–12; Hall, *Organization of American Culture,* 125–150.

44. This is Kett's argument in *Formation of the American Medical Profession.* See also Foletta, *Coming to Terms with Democracy,* 143–144. Similar debates took place in other states. See Feller, *Jacksonian Promise,* 90–94.

45. On the development of legal education and the legal profession in Massachusetts, along with the quotes of both Story and Parker, see Gerard W. Gawalt, "Massachusetts Legal Education in Transition, 1766–1840," *American Journal of Legal History* 17 (1973), 27–50; Lawrence M. Friedman, *A History of American Law* (New York, 1973), 303–333; Foletta, *Coming to Terms with Democracy,* 158–159, 162–163, 167–168.

46. Ibid. For Isaac Parker's address, see "Inaugural Address delivered in the Chapel of Harvard University, by the Hon. Isaac Parker, Chief Justice of Massachusetts, and Royall Professor of Law," *North American Review* 3, no. 7 (May 1816), 11–27.

47. Raymond B. Culver, *Horace Mann and Religion in the Massachusetts Public Schools* (New Haven, Conn., 1929), 112–113. Mann's memorial to the legislature is in his journal for March 13, 1838, *Life and Works of Horace Mann,* ed. Mary Mann and George Mann, 5 vols. (Boston: Lee and Sheperd, 1891), 1:101. For a discussion of Mann's life and ideas, see Jonathan Messerli, *Horace Mann: A Biography* (New York, 1972).

48. Horace Mann, "Means and Objects of Common-School Education" (1837), in *Lectures on Education* (1845), in *Life and Works of Horace Mann,* 2:77–78.

49. "Fourth Annual Report," in *Life and Works of Horace Mann*, 3:53–91.

50. *Life and Works of Horace Mann*, 5:212. For the relationship between Mann and science, see Christopher Grasso, "Skepticism and American Faith: Infidels, Converts, and Religious Doubt in the Early Nineteenth Century," *Journal of the Early Republic* 22, no. 3 (Fall 2002), 465–508, esp. 497–501.

51. Culver, *Horace Mann and Religion*, 127–148.

52. [Orestes Brownson], Review of "Second Annual Report of the Board of Education . . . ," *Boston Quarterly Review* (October 1839), 393–434.

53. Dodge's comments are reprinted in the *Daily Advertiser*, March 19, 1840. See Culver, *Horace Mann and Religion*, 136–148; Katz, *The Irony of Early School Reform*, 145–149; Carl F. Kaestle and Maris A. Vinovskis, *Education and Social Change in Nineteenth-Century Massachusetts* (Cambridge, Mass., 1980), 208–232.

54. *Daily Advertiser*, March 18, 1840.

55. See Kaestle and Vinovskis, *Education and Social Change*, 216.

56. *Resolves of the General Court of the Commonwealth of Massachusetts* (January 4, 1845).

57. *Resolves of the General Court of the Commonwealth of Massachusetts* (January 12, 1847).

58. Horace Mann, "Remarks at the Dedication of the Bridgewater State Normal Schoolhouse," August 10, 1846, in *Life and Works of Horace Mann*, 5:217–227.

59. A good discussion of Mann's pedagogical beliefs, and the controversies they raised, is Katz, *Irony of Early School Reform*, 115–160. The conflict is also discussed in Culver, *Horace Mann and Religion*, 189–204. For Mann's discussion of emulation, see his "Means and Objects of Common-School Education (1837)," in *Lectures on Education* (1845), in *Life and Works of Horace Mann*, 2:48–77. See also Carl F. Kaestle, *Pillars of the Republic: Common Schools and American Society, 1780–1860* (New York, 1983), 67, 89, 142–143.

60. Quotes and discussion from Katz, *Irony of Early School Reform*, 139–145.

61. Culver, *Horace Mann and Religion*, 193–195; Horace Mann to George Combe, July 30, 1844, in *Life and Works of Horace Mann*, 1:230–232.

62. Quotes and discussion from Culver, *Horace Mann and Religion*, 194–197.

63. Quotes and discussion from Katz, *Irony of Early School Reform*, 153–160. In the long term, teachers failed to achieve professional status comparable to lawyers and doctors. Because of their relatively low status, and because so many teachers were women, teachers never convinced the public that they were, or ought to be, trained professionals who shared a body of knowledge (the "science" of pedagogy) as advanced and complicated as those held by lawyers, doctors, engineers, or social scientists. Nonetheless, Mann's efforts, along with medical and legal reformers, demonstrate how Whigs deployed the concept of the professional to enhance their authority in a democratic society. See Wiebe, *The Search for Order*, 111–132.

64. Edward Bellamy, *Looking Backward* (New York: Signet Classic, 1960), 135.

65. Harry Watson, *Liberty and Power: The Politics of Jacksonian America* (New York, 1990), 101–104. Although most historians and political scientists emphasize the growth of the administrative state in the post–Civil War era, and in particular the centrality of civil service reform, the roots of these changes lie at the state level as Whigs struggled to reconcile their commitment to autonomy

with the realities of democratic politics. See Oscar Handlin and Mary Flug Handlin, *Commonwealth: A Study of the Role of Government in the American Economy: Massachusetts 1774–1861* (1947; reprint, Cambridge, 1969), 236–239; Foletta, *Coming to Terms with Democracy*, 135–181; Hall, *Organization of American Culture*; Martin J. Schiesl, *The Politics of Efficiency: Municipal Administration and Reform in America, 1800–1920* (Berkeley, Calif., 1977); William E. Nelson, *The Roots of American Bureaucracy, 1830–1900* (Cambridge, Mass., 1982); Stephen Skowronek, *Building a New American State: The Expansion of National Administrative Capacities, 1877–1920* (New York, 1982); Thomas K. McCraw, *Prophets of Regulation: Charles Francis Adams, Louis D. Brandeis, James M. Landis, Alfred E. Kahn* (Cambridge, Mass., 1984); James A. Morone, *The Democratic Wish: Popular Participation and the Limits of American Government* (New York, 1990), 87–128; Daniel P. Carpenter, *The Forging of Bureaucratic Autonomy: Reputations, Networks, and Policy Innovation in Executive Agencies, 1862–1928* (Princeton, N.J., 2001).

66. Edwin Merrick Dodd, *American Business Corporations until 1860, with Special Reference to Massachusetts* (Cambridge, Mass., 1954), 276–309; Handlin and Handlin, *Commonwealth*, 221; Arthur Darling, *Political Changes in Massachusetts, 1824–1848: A Study of Liberal Movements in Politics* (New Haven, Conn., 1925), 224–230.

67. *Resolves of the General Court of the Commonwealth of Massachusetts* (January 12, 1837); "An Act relating to Common Schools" (April 20, 1837), *Laws of the Commonwealth of Massachusetts, Passed by the General Court*, January 1837 session, ch. 241, p. 277.

68. Kaestle and Vinovskis, *Education and Social Change*, 210.

69. [Brownson], Review of "Second Annual Report . . . ," 393–434.

70. Journal, October 27, 1838, in *Life and Works of Horace Mann*, 1:107.

71. Journal, December 20, 1840, in *Life and Works of Horace Mann*, 1:141–142.

72. Horace Mann to George Combe, December 1, 1844, in *Life and Works of Horace Mann*, 1:230–232.

73. Hall, "Private Philanthropy and Public Policy," 50–58.

74. Harold M. Hyman and William M. Wieck, *Equal Justice under Law: Constitutional Development 1835–1875* (New York, 1982), 34–35; Dodd, *American Business Corporations*, 276–309; Handlin and Handlin, *Commonwealth*, 221; Darling, *Political Changes in Massachusetts*, 224–230. For the emergence of the Massachusetts Board of Railroad Commissioners, and its importance in the creation of future regulatory administrative agencies, see McCraw, *Prophets of Regulation*, 1–56.

75. *Resolves of the General Court of the Commonwealth of Massachusetts* (January 1841).

76. [Samuel A. Eliot], "Public and Private Charities of Boston," *North American Review* 61, no. 128 (July 1845), 135–159. For a discussion of Eliot, see Hall, "What the Merchants Did with Their Money," 408–416. See also [Samuel A. Eliot], "Charities of Boston," *North American Review* 91, no. 188 (July 1860), 149–166.

77. Even if we admit that many of their arguments were self-serving, the importance of Whig civic ideas should not be discounted. In *The Structural Transformation of the Public Sphere: An Inquiry into a Category of Bourgeois Society*, trans. Thomas Burger (Cambridge, Mass., 1989), Jürgen Habermas argues that the eighteenth-century public sphere of deliberation and consent had given way

by the twentieth century to one dominated by private commercial transactions. That is, the logic of the market had invaded the civic realm. Whigs tried to articulate a way to reconcile diversity and political conflict with their commitment to eighteenth-century ideas about civic virtue and the common good in large part to prevent civic life from being dominated by self-interest. The idea that civic activity in civil society requires specific virtues is made, among others, by William Galston, "Individualism, Liberalism, and Democratic Civil Society," in *The Essential Civil Society Reader: Classic Essays in the American Civil Society Debate*, ed. Don E. Eberly (Lanham, Md., 2000), 353–372.

78. Hall, *Inventing the Nonprofit Sector,* 37–38.

## 6. Democrats Strike Back

1. Sean Wilentz, *The Rise of American Democracy: Jefferson to Lincoln* (New York, 2005), 516–517; Marvin Myers, *The Jacksonian Persuasion: Politics and Beliefs* (Stanford, Calif., 1957).

2. George Bancroft, "An Oration Delivered before the Adelphi Society of Williamstown College in August, 1835" ("The Office of the People in Art, Government, and Religion"), as reprinted in *The American Intellectual Tradition: Volume I* (New York, 2001), ed. David A Hollinger and Charles Capper, 284–293.

3. John L. O'Sullivan, "The Democratic Principle," *The United States Magazine and Democratic Review* (October 1837), as excerpted in *Major Problems in American History*, Vol. 1: to 1877, ed. Elizabeth Cobbs Hoffman and Jon Gjerde (Boston, 2002), 238–239.

4. Matthew A. Crenson, *The Federal Machine: Beginnings of Bureaucracy in Jacksonian America* (Baltimore, 1975). For a critical assessment of Crenson's thesis, see Richard R. John, "Affairs of Office: The Executive Departments, the Election of 1828, and the Making of the Democratic Party," in *The Democratic Experiment: New Directions in American Political History*, ed. Meg Jacobs, William J. Novak, and Julian E. Zelizer (Princeton, N.J., 2003), 50–84. John argues that the Jacksonians' celebration of rotation in office emerged only after they were elected, suggesting that their true aim in removing federal officeholders and replacing them with Jackson men was to build the Democratic Party through patronage. John's thesis minimizes the ways in which Jacksonian ideas and interests coincided to make possible their actions.

5. "Daniel Webster's Reply [to Jackson's Bank Veto], July 11, 1832" as excerpted in *Major Problems in the Early Republic, 1787–1848*, ed. Sean Wilentz (Lexington, Mass., 1992), 389–391.

6. Discussion and quotes from Wilentz, *Rise of American Democracy*, 360–374.

7. On Democrats' ideas about majoritarianism and the dangers of powerful minorities, see Gerald Leonard, *The Invention of Party Politics: Federalism, Popular Sovereignty, and Constitutional Development in Jacksonian Illinois* (Chapel Hill, N.C., 2002); Wilentz, *Rise of American Democracy*; James L. Huston, *Securing the Fruits of Labor: The American Concept of Wealth Distribution 1765–1900* (Baton Rouge, La., 1998), 219–258; Daniel Feller, *The Jacksonian Promise: America, 1815–1840* (Baltimore, 1995), 160–184; Harry Watson, *Liberty and Power: The Politics of Jacksonian America* (New York, 1990); James A. Morone, *The Democratic Wish: Popular Participation and the Limits of American Government* (New York,

1990), 74–96; Myers, *The Jacksonian Persuasion*. Kathleen D. McCarthy, *American Creed: Philanthropy and the Rise of Civil Society* (Chicago, 2003), addresses the Jacksonian backlash against civil society but she attributes it to the Jacksonian commitment to white male democracy. While race and gender were vital to Jacksonian philosophy, the Democrats' opposition to civil society grew out of their Jeffersonian faith in direct democracy. In other words, McCarthy extracts the Jacksonian response to the new civil society from its Jeffersonian roots; in fact, the Jacksonians were torchbearers for the Jeffersonian fear of privately organized activity.

8. On the idea of competition, see Stanley I. Kutler, *Privilege and Creative Destruction: The Charles River Bridge Case* (Philadelphia, 1971); Richard R. John, "Private Enterprise, Public Good? Communications Deregulation as a National Political Issue, 1839–1851," in *Beyond the Founders: New Approaches to the Political History of the Early American Republic*, ed. Jeffrey L. Pasley, Andrew W. Robertson, and David Waldstreicher (Chapel Hill, N.C., 2004), 328–354; Joyce O. Appleby, *Capitalism and a New Social Order: The Republican Vision of the 1790s* (New York, 1984). According to Oscar Handlin and Mary Flug Handlin, *Commonwealth: A Study of the Role of Government in the American Economy: Massachusetts 1774–1861*, rev. ed. (Cambridge, Mass., 1969), 217, "those who despaired of abolishing the corporation hoped to render it innocuous by eliminating the last vestige of state favoritism. If this was primarily a business device, any token of governmental approval was unjust. If available at all, the capacity to act as a corporation should be available to any petitioner, with the state relegated to the minor role of registrar and deprived of any option."

9. My understanding of the Charles River Bridge controversy and the case relies on Kutler, *Privilege and Creative Destruction*. The political elements are also discussed in Ronald P. Formisano, *The Transformation of Political Culture: Massachusetts Parties, 1790s–1840s* (New York, 1983), 191–196.

10. *Boston Statesman*, February 13, 1830.

11. Lincoln's veto message is reprinted in *Boston Courier*, March 12, 1827.

12. Kutler, *Privilege and Creative Destruction*, 29–33.

13. Quoted in Kutler, *Privilege and Creative Destruction*, 43.

14. *The Proprietors of Charles River Bridge v. The Proprietors of Warren Bridge et al.* (7 Pickering 344 [1830]).

15. Kutler, *Privilege and Creative Destruction*, 54–61.

16. J. Willard Hurst, *Law and the Conditions of Freedom in the Nineteenth Century United States* (Madison, Wis., 1956).

17. Most recently on this topic, see Scott Gregory Lien, "Contested Solidarities: Philanthropy, Justice, and the Reconstitution of Public Authority in the United States, 1790–1860" (Ph.D. diss., University of Chicago, 2006), 81–83.

18. Martin Van Buren, "Thoughts on the approaching election in N. York" (March 1840), as discussed and cited in Leonard, *Invention of Party Politics*, 181–182.

19. *Boston Statesman*, January 22, 1831.

20. *Boston Statesman*, June 25, 1831.

21. *Boston Statesman*, March 21, 1835. The reference to secret societies is clearly intended for Antimasonic voters. Democrats hoped to capture as many Antimasonic voters as possible by emphasizing that Democrats, unlike Whigs, consistently fought against entrenched corporate power.

22. *Boston Statesman*, December 5, 1835. See also Ibid., January 26, 1833; October 12, 1839.

23. The divisions within the Democracy are outlined in Darling, *Political Changes in Massachusetts*.

24. Rantoul's speech is reprinted in Robert Rantoul Jr., *Memoirs, Speeches, and Writings by Robert Rantoul, Jr.*, ed. Luther Hamilton (Boston, 1854), 313–217; *Boston Statesman*, January 31, 1835; February 7, 1835.

25. *Boston Statesman*, November 6, 1835.

26. *Boston Statesman*, October 10, 1835.

27. *Boston Statesman*, May 5, 1838. See Lawrence M. Friedman, *A History of American Law* (New York, 1973), 316; Gerard W. Gawalt, "Massachusetts Legal Education in Transition, 1766–1840," *American Journal of Legal History* 17 (1973), 27–50.

28. Joseph F. Kett, *The Formation of the American Medical Profession: The Role of Institutions, 1780–1860* (New Haven, Conn., 1968), 132–80; Peter Dobkin Hall, *The Organization of American Culture, 1700–1900: Private Institutions, Elites and the Origins of American Nationality* (New York, 1982), 147–150.

29. *Boston Statesman*, April 13, 1839; April 27, 1839.

30. *Daily Advertiser*, May 21, 1839. The MMS may have known that the Medical Society of South Carolina won a similar case in 1823. See Bruce A. Campbell, "Social Federalism: The Constitutional Position of Nonprofit Corporations in Nineteenth-Century America," *Law and History Review* 8, no. 2 (Fall 1990), 149–188, at 161–162.

31. Kett, *Formation of the American Medical Profession*, 28–29; Handlin and Handlin, *Commonwealth*, 208–209. See also *Daily Advertiser*, October 15, 1836.

32. On the election, see Darling, *Political Changes in Massachusetts*, 251; Wilentz, *Rise of American Democracy*, 464.

33. Morton in *Resolves of the General Court of the Commonwealth of Massachusetts* (January 22, 1840).

34. Ibid. Similarly, David Henshaw condemned corporate monopolies, trusts, and mortmains, especially Harvard, which he described as "a seminary rich in mortmain funds, rich from the income thus wrung from the hand of labor, but musty from age and indolence, and loitering half a century behind the progress of the age." Henshaw is quoted in Darling, *Political Changes in Massachusetts*, 197–199. Peter Dobkin Hall and George E. Marcus argue that the Jacksonian attacks were unfair. Elite Bostonians certainly sought to sustain their family's position over generations, but they also feared the dead hand of the past. They hoped that by putting their wealth into philanthropic trusts overseen by competent managers, their wealth would always serve the present common good instead of simply being handed over to their own children. Nonetheless, Democrats were correct that philanthropic institutions in Massachusetts were building up large endowments beyond the public's reach. See Hall and Marcus, "Why Should Men Leave Great Fortunes to Their Children? Dynasty and Inheritance in America," in *Inheritance and Wealth in America*, ed. Robert K. Miller Jr. and Stephen J. McNamee (New York, 1998), 139–171.

35. *Resolves of the General Court of the Commonwealth of Massachusetts* (January 22, 1840).

36. Peter Dobkin Hall, "Private Philanthropy and Public Policy: A Historical Appraisal," in *Philanthropy: Four Views*, ed. Robert Payton et al. (New Brunswick,

N.J., 1988), 39–72, at 48; Stanley N. Katz, Burry Sullivan, and C. Paul Beach, "Legal Change and Legal Autonomy: Charitable Trusts in New York, 1777–1893," *Law and History Review* 51 (1985), 51–89; Ronald E. Seavoy, *The Origins of the American Business Corporation, 1784–1855: Broadening the Concept of Public Service during Industrialization* (Westport, Conn., 1982), ch. 6; Bruce A. Campbell, "Law and Experience in the Early Republic: The Evolution of the *Dartmouth College* Doctrine, 1780–1819" (Ph.D. diss., Michigan State University, 1973), 154. According to Katz et al., p. 82, the 1846 constitution did not outright prohibit special charters, and so special acts continued to be granted despite the Democrats' goals. On Charleston see McCarthy, *American Creed*, 179.

37. Louis Hartz, *Economic Policy and Democratic Thought: Pennsylvania, 1776–1860* (Cambridge, Mass., 1948).

38. Formisano, *Transformation of Political Culture*, 329–331; William F. Hartford, *Money, Morals, and Politics: Massachusetts in the Age of the Boston Associates* (Boston, 2001); Kevin Sweeney, "Rum, Romanism, Representation, and Reform: Coalition Politics in Massachusetts, 1847–1853," *Civil War History* 22 (1976), 116–137; Kinley J. Brauer, *Cotton versus Conscience: Massachusetts Whig Politics and Southwestern Expansion, 1843–1848* (Lexington, Ky., 1967); Samuel Shapiro, "The Conservative Dilemma: The Massachusetts Constitutional Convention of 1853," *New England Quarterly* 33, no. 2 (June 1960), 207–224, esp. 208–210.

39. "An Act relating to Joint Stock Companies" (May 15, 1851), *Acts and Resolves, Passed by the General Court of Massachusetts*, January 1851 session, ch. 133; "An Act to change the Organization of the Board of Overseers of the University at Cambridge" (May 22, 1851), *Acts and Resolves*, ch. 224, p. 691; John S. Whitehead, *The Separation of College and State: Columbia, Dartmouth, Harvard, and Yale, 1776–1876* (New Haven, Conn., 1973), 143–150.

40. *Official Report of the Debates and Proceedings in the State Convention, assembled May 4th, 1853, to Revise and Amend the Constitution of the Commonwealth of Massachusetts*, 3 vols. (Boston, 1853), 2:122–125.

41. Ibid., 3:75.

42. Ibid., 2:45–46. For a discussion of this process, see Ronald Story, *The Forging of an Aristocracy: Harvard and the Boston Upper Class, 1800–1870* (Middletown, Conn., 1980), 135–159.

43. *Official Report*, 2:254–256.

44. Sweeney, "Rum, Romanism, Representation, and Reform," 134–137.

45. *Resolves of the General Court of the Commonwealth of Massachusetts* (January 22, 1840); Carl F. Kaestle, *Pillars of the Republic: Common Schools and American Society, 1780–1860* (New York, 1983), 136–181, esp. 154–161. For Democratic critiques of centralization, see *Boston Statesman*, April 27, 1839. My understanding of this issue is greatly indebted to Carl F. Kaestle and Maris A. Vinovskis, *Education and Social Change in Nineteenth-Century Massachusetts* (Cambridge, Mass., 1980), 208–232.

46. Quoted in Kaestle and Vinovskis, *Education and Social Change*, 215–216.

47. Journal, February 2, 1840, in *Life and Works of Horace Mann*, ed. Mary Mann and George Mann, 5 vols. (Boston: Lee and Sheperd, 1891), 1:122.

48. Horace Mann to George Combe, February 22, 1840, in *Life and Works of Horace Mann*, 1:123–124.

49. Kaestle and Vinovskis, *Education and Social Change*, 216.

50. Quotes and discussion taken from Kaestle and Vinovskis, *Education and Social Change*, 208–232; Michael B. Katz, *The Irony of Early School Reform: Educational Innovation in Mid-Nineteenth Century Massachusetts* (Cambridge, Mass., 1968), 145–149.

51. Kaestle and Vinovskis, *Education and Social Change*, 218–230.

52. *Stebbins v. Jennings* (10 Pickering 172 [1830]); *Oakes v. Hill* (10 Pickering 333 [1830]). Quotation from "[Review of] Decision of the Supreme Judicial Court of Massachusetts, in a case relating to the Sacramental Furniture of a Church in Brookfield; with the entire Arguments of Hon. Samuel Hoar, Jr., for the Plaintiff, and of Hon. Lewis Strong, for the Defendant (Boston, 1832)," *Spirit of the Pilgrims* (July 1832), 402–424. For a discussion of Shaw's ruling and the orthodox response, see Leonard Levy, *The Law of the Commonwealth and Chief Justice Shaw* (Cambridge, Mass., 1957), 29–42.

53. "The Government and its Duties," *Boston Statesman*, August 20, 1831.

54. Everett's speeches are reprinted in the *Daily Advertiser*, April 25, 1833; April 26, 1833. See also *Independent Chronicle*, October 26, 1831, as quoted in William G. McLoughlin, *New England Dissent, 1630–1883: The Baptists and the Separation of Church and State*, 2 vols. (Cambridge, Mass., 1971), 2:1219; "Defence of Article Three," *Christian Examiner* (January 1833), 351–363.

55. McLoughlin, *New England Dissent*, 2:1217–1219.

56. *Boston Statesman*, February 19, 1831; "Third Article in the Declaration of Rights," *Spirit of the Pilgrims* (December 1831), 629–648; McLoughlin, *New England Dissent*, 2:1221–1223, 1245–1262.

57. "An Act relating to Parishes and Religious Freedom" (April 1, 1834), *Laws of the Commonwealth of Massachusetts, Passed at the Several Sessions of the General Court*, January 1834 session, ch. 183, p. 265.

58. Richard M. Johnson, *Report of the Committee on Post-Offices and Post-roads of the United States Senate* (January 1829), in *Social Theories of Jacksonian Democracy: Representative Writings of the Period, 1825–1850*, ed. Joseph L. Blau (New York, 1947), 274–281. For discussions of the report, see Bertram Wyatt-Brown, "Prelude to Abolitionism: Sabbatarian Politics and the Rise of the Second Party System," *Journal of American History* 58, no. 2 (September 1971), 316–341, at 335; James R. Rohrer, "Sunday Mails and the Church-State Them in Jacksonian America," *Journal of the Early Republic* 7, no. 1 (Spring 1987), 53–74, at 68–69; Richard R. John, "Taking Sabbatarianism Seriously: The Postal System, the Sabbath, and the Transformation of American Political Culture," *Journal of the Early Republic* 10, no. 4 (1990), 517–567, at 558–560.

59. Rohrer, "Sunday Mails and the Church-State Theme," 69–71. The report is reprinted in the *Daily Advertiser*, February 10, 1829.

60. McCarthy, *American Creed*, 126–133.

61. On this point, see John, "Taking Sabbatarianism Seriously," 560.

62. Forty percent of its founders were Unitarian ministers. On the founding of the MSSI, see Robert L. Hampel, *Temperance and Prohibition in Massachusetts, 1813–1852* (Ann Arbor, Mich., 1982), 13–24.

63. Robert H. Abzug, *Cosmos Crumbling: American Reform and the Religious Imagination* (New York, 1994), 86–90; Ronald G. Walters, *American Reformers, 1815–1860* (New York, 1978), 126–127.

64. *Boston Statesman*, January 22, 1831.

65. "An Act for the due regulation of Licensed Houses" (March 24, 1832), *Laws of the Commonwealth of Massachusetts, Passed by the General Court*, ch. 156, p. 473; Hampel, *Temperance and Prohibition*, 56.

66. "An Act to regulate the sale of Spirituous Liquors" (April 20, 1838), *Laws of the Commonwealth of Massachusetts, Passed by the General Court*, January 1838 session, ch. 157, p. 442; Hampel, *Temperance and Prohibition*, 56–78.The law was less restrictive than many regulations passed in the counties because it continued to permit the manufacture and sale of liquor.

67. *Boston Statesman*, April 18, 1835. See also *Boston Statesman*, June 16, 1838.

68. *Boston Statesman*, November 23, 1839.

69. Darling, *Political Changes in Massachusetts;* Formisano, *Transformation of Political Culture*, 298–299; Hampel, *Temperance and Prohibition*, 86–87.

70. *Resolves of the General Court of the Commonwealth of Massachusetts* (January 22, 1840).

71. *Columbian Centinel*, November 16, 1839, as quoted in Hampel, *Temperance and Prohibition*, 87. Boston *Atlas*, December 24, 1839. See also *Atlas*, March 16, 1839; August 5, 1839; November 16, 1839.

72. *Daily Advertiser*, September 14, 1831. See also *Daily Advertiser*, October 10, 1838; *Resolves of the General Court of the Commonwealth of Massachusetts* (January 10, 1839). On police power, see Levy, *Law of the Commonwealth*, 229–265; William J. Novak, *The People's Welfare: Law and Regulation in Nineteenth-Century America* (Chapel Hill, N.C., 1996), 19–50; Christopher L. Tomlins, *Law, Labor, and Ideology in the Early American Republic* (Cambridge, Mass., 1993), 35–59. On Whig responses to temperance, see Hampel, *Temperance and Prohibition*, 81–83; Jonathan D. Sassi, *A Republic of Righteousness: The Public Christianity of the Postrevolutionary New England Clergy* (New York, 2001), 154–163, 190–192.

73. Discussion and quotes taken from Levy, *Law of the Commonwealth*, 232–237.

74. *Democratic Review* (March 1839), as quoted in Lawrence F. Kohl, *The Politics of Individualism: Parties and the American Character in the Jacksonian Era* (New York, 1989), 29.

75. [Orestes Brownson], "Ultraism," *Boston Quarterly Review* 1 (July 1838), 377–384.

76. "Tendency to Moral Intemperance," *Free Press*, October 3, 1838.

77. Wilentz, *Rise of American Democracy*, makes a strong case for an alliance between laborers and Democrats.

78. My understanding of the labor question in Massachusetts is indebted to Christopher L. Tomlins, "Criminal Conspiracy and Early Labor Combinations: Massachusetts, 1824–1840," *Labor History* 28, no. 3 (Summer 1987), 370–385, and *Law, Labor, and Ideology*. See also Carl Siracusa, *A Mechanical People: Perceptions of the Industrial Order in Massachusetts, 1815–1880* (Middletown, Conn., 1979); Gary John Kornblith, "From Artisans to Businessmen: Master Mechanics in New England, 1789–1850" (Ph.D. diss., Princeton University, 1983); Sean Wilentz, *Chants Democratic: New York City and the Rise of the American Working Class, 1788–1850* (New York, 1984); Lisa Beth Lubow, "Artisans in Transition: Early Capitalist Development and the Carpenters of Boston, 1787–1837" (Ph.D. diss., University of California, Los Angeles, 1987), 310–391; Ronald Schultz, *The Republic of Labor: Philadelphia Artisans and the Politics of Class, 1720–1830* (New York, 1993).

79. "Resolution of Master Carpenters," in *A Documentary History of American Industrial Society*, ed. John R. Commons et al. (Cleveland, Ohio, 1910–1911), 6:76–77. "Resolutions of 'Capitalists,'" in Commons, *Documentary History*, 6:79–81. On the strike, see Tomlins, *Law, Labor, and Ideology*, 183–184.

80. Arthur B. Darling, "The Workingmen's Party in Massachusetts, 1833–1834," *American Historical Review* 29, no. 1 (October 1923), 81–86; Formisano, *Transformation of Political Culture*, 222–244.

81. Tomlins, *Law, Labor, and Ideology*, 185–199.

82. On the 1832 strike, see Formisano, *Transformation of Political Culture*, 228–231; Tomlins, *Law, Labor, and Ideology*, 186–187.

83. "Statement of the Journeymen, from the *Independent Chronicle and Boston Patriot*, May 23, 1832," in *Documentary History*, ed. Commons, 6:83–86.

84. "Meeting of Merchants and Ship-owners, from the *Independent Chronicle and Boston Patriot*, May 19, 1832," in *Documentary History*, ed. Commons, 6:81–82.

85. Lemuel Shaw quoted in Tomlins, "Criminal Conspiracy and Early Labor Combinations," 375; Levy, *Law of the Commonwealth*, 203.

86. This paragraph draws from Tomlins, "Criminal Conspiracy and Early Labor Combinations." Thacher's 1832 charge is reprinted in Ibid., 379–380, 383–385.

87. Seth Luther (1833) quoted in Tomlins, *Law, Labor, and Ideology*, 190.

88. Frederick Robinson, "An Oration delivered before the Trades' Union of Boston and Vicinity, July 4, 1834," as excerpted in *Social Theories of Jacksonian Democracy*, ed. Blau, 320–342. Also quoted in Tomlins, "Criminal Conspiracies and Early Labor Combinations," 378–379.

89. Quoted in Siracusa, *A Mechanical People*, 133.

90. Formisano, *Transformation of Political Culture*, 237, 243; Tomlins, *Law, Labor, and Ideology*, 180, 195–196.

91. *Boston Statesman*, September 19, 1840. Also quoted in Siracusa, *A Mechanical People*, 134.

92. *Commonwealth v. Hunt* (4 Metcalf 111 [1842]). See Levy, *Law of the Commonwealth*, 183–206; Tomlins, *Law, Labor, and Ideology*, 180–219. The charges raised against the journeymen all rested on the common law crime of conspiracy. Conspiracies covered collective crimes. A conspiracy was whenever any two or more persons conspired to do an illegal action or to undertake a legal action by illegal means. Groups could be charged with conspiracy even when the actions they took were legal for individuals. In theory, the crime of conspiracy was applicable to any group. In the Massachusetts case of *Commonwealth v. Judd* (2 Tyng 329 [1807]), Chief Justice Parsons applied it to a cabal of two persons who sought to sell impure indigo as the real thing. For the most part, the conspiracy doctrine was applied to laborers' associations that sought to use their collective power to raise wages by refusing to work for employers that either did not meet their demands or that hired nonmember laborers.

93. The municipal court decision is published in *Reports of Criminal Cases, tried in the Municipal Court of Boston, before Peter Oxenbridge Thacher, judge of that Court from 1823 to 1843*, ed. Horatio Woodman (Boston, 1845). See also Levy, *Law of the Commonwealth*, 186–187; Tomlins, *Law, Labor, and Ideology*, 203–205.

94. Marjorie S. Turner, *The Early American Labor Conspiracy Cases: Their Place in Law: A Reinterpretation*, Social Science Monograph Series 1, no. 3 (San Diego,

1967), 68–72. For a discussion of how the freedom of association limited traditional forms of collective action in the Whiskey Rebellion and in the cordwainers' cases, see Johann N. Neem, "Freedom of Association in the Early Republic: The Republican Party, the Whiskey Rebellion, and the Philadelphia and New York Cordwainers' Cases," *Pennsylvania Magazine of History and Biography* 127, no. 3 (July 2003), 259–290.

95. Christopher L. Tomlins, *The State and the Unions: Labor Relations, Law, and the Organized Labor Movement in America, 1880–1960* (New York, 1985).

96. James Brewer Stewart, *Holy Warriors: The Abolitionists and American Slavery* (New York, 1976), 29–31; Ronald G. Walters, *The Antislavery Appeal: American Abolitionism after 1830* (Baltimore, 1976), 22–23; Richard S. Newman, *The Transformation of American Abolitionism: Fighting Slavery in the Early Republic* (Chapel Hill, N.C., 2003), 110–112.

97. Stewart, *Holy Warriors*, 50–73; Newman, *Transformation*, 107–130.

98. Donald Scott, *From Office to Profession: The New England Ministry, 1750–1850* (Philadelphia, 1978), 76–94; Newman, *Transformation*, 131–151. On the Unitarians, see Daniel Walker Howe, *The Unitarian Conscience: Harvard Moral Philosophy, 1806–1861* (Cambridge, Mass., 1970), esp. 207–305.

99. Newman, *Transformation*, 6. See also Anne M. Boylan, *The Origins of Women's Activism: New York and Boston, 1797–1840* (Chapel Hill, N.C., 2002), 158–166.

100. Walters, *American Reformers*, 80.

101. *Fifth Annual Report of the Massachusetts Anti-Slavery Society* (1837), as quoted in Newman, *Transformation*, 131.

102. For the relationship between abolitionists and older, more genteel evangelical ministers, see Scott, *From Office to Profession*, 95–111; Walters, *Antislavery Appeal*, 37–53; Stewart, *Holy Warriors*, 56–59.

103. *Daily Advertiser*, July 4, 1834.

104. Harrison Gray Otis quoted in Leonard L. Richards, *"Gentlemen of Property and Standing": Anti-Abolition Mobs in Jacksonian America* (New York, 1970), 58–59. See also Hartford, *Money, Morals, and Politics*, 95–96.

105. *Boston Statesman*, January 19, 1839; January 26, 1839. On Marcus Morton and antislavery, see Jonathan Earle, "Marcus Morton and the Dilemma of Jacksonian Antislavery in Massachusetts, 1817–1849," *Massachusetts Historical Review* 4 (2002), 61–88.

106. *Daily Advertiser*, August 20, 1835.

107. Walters, *Antislavery Appeal*, 3–18.

108. *Daily Advertiser*, August 22, 1835. See Brauer, *Cotton versus Conscience*, 23–26.

109. Stewart, *Holy Warriors*, 69–71; McCarthy, *American Creed*, 145–147; Richards, *Gentlemen of Property and Standing*, 51–75; Wilentz, *Rise of American Democracy*, 408–409.

110. *Boston Courier*, September 1835, as quoted in Hartford, *Money, Morals, and Politics*, 95–96.

111. Hartford, *Money, Morals, and Politics*, 97–98; Russel B. Nye, *Fettered Freedom: Civil Liberties and the Slavery Controversy, 1830–1860* (1963; reprint, Urbana, Ill., 1972), 143–144.

112. Susan Zaeske, *Signatures of Citizenship: Petitioning, Antislavery, and Women's Political Identity* (Chapel Hill, N.C., 2003), 11–28; Don L. Smith, "The

Right to Petition for Redress of Grievances: Constitutional Development and Interpretations" (Ph.D. diss., Texas Tech University, 1971); Edmund S. Morgan, *Inventing the People: The Rise of Popular Sovereignty in England and America* (New York, 1988).

113. See Stewart, *Holy Warriors*, 81–83; Newman, *Transformation*, 132–140; Zaeske, *Signatures of Citizenship*, 38, 53–59, 105–125; Nancy A. Hewitt, *Women's Activism and Social Change: Rochester, New York, 1822–1872* (Ithaca, N.Y., 1984), 91–93.

114. Keith E. Melder, *Beginnings of Sisterhood: The American Woman's Rights Movement, 1800–1850* (New York, 1977), 72–75; Zaeske, *Signatures of Citizenship*, 105–144.

115. *Daily Advertiser*, February 13, 1836.

116. *Atlas*, March 26, 1842; see also *Atlas*, January 29, 1842; January 31, 1842.

117. *Boston Statesman*, February 9, 1839. See also *Boston Statesman*, March 13, 1847, concerning the right of the Massachusetts General Court to pass resolutions on issues involving slavery.

118. Andrew Jackson, "Farewell Address" (March 4, 1837), as reprinted in *Social Theories of Jacksonian Democracy*, ed. Blau, 1–20, quotation at 7–8.

119. Calhoun quoted in Nye, *Fettered Freedom*, 58.

120. Richard R. John, *Spreading the News: The American Postal Service and Disorder in American History* (Cambridge, Mass., 1995), 257–283; Michael Schudson, *The Good Citizen: A History of American Civic Life* (New York, 1998), 105–108.

121. Earle, "Marcus Morton and the Dilemma of Jacksonian Antislavery"; Wilentz, *Rise of American Democracy*; Eric Foner, *Free Soil, Free Labor, Free Men: The Ideology of the Republican Party before the Civil War* (New York, 1970).

122. Newman, *Transformation*, 140–144. See also Zaeske, *Signatures of Citizenship*, 73–104.

123. Nye, *Fettered Freedom*, 201–202. For a discussion of the legality of mobs, see Richard B. Kielbowicz, "The Law and Mob Law in Attacks on Antislavery Newspapers, 1833–1860," *Law and History Review* 24, no. 3 (Fall 2006), 559–600.

124. *Boston Statesman*, October 24, 1835. On mobs, see Richards, *Gentleman of Property and Standing*. On changing ideas about mobs, see Paul Gilje, *The Road to Mobocracy: Popular Disorder in New York City, 1763–1834* (Chapel Hill, N.C., 1987), esp. 100–119; Charles W. McCurdy, *The Anti-Rent Era in New York Law and Politics, 1839–1865* (Chapel Hill, N.C., 2001).

125. Garrison quoted in John L. Thomas, *The Liberator: William Lloyd Garrison* (Boston, 1963), 3, 7.

## Conclusion

1. As many historians have noted, *Democracy in America* shares some of the biases of Tocqueville's Whig informants. Most recently see Garry Wills, "Did Tocqueville Get America?," *New York Review of Books* 51, no. 7 (April 29, 2004); Sean Wilentz, "Many Democracies: On Tocqueville and Jacksonian America," in *Reconsidering Tocqueville's* Democracy in America, ed. Abraham Eisenstadt (New Brunswick, N.J., 1988), 207–228.

2. Alexis de Tocqueville, *Democracy in America*, trans. Arthur Goldhammer (New York, 2004), 491, 219–220. In his notebook Tocqueville recorded Sparks

making the following comment: "The political dogma of this country is that the majority is always right. By and large we are well satisfied to have adopted it, but one cannot deny that experience often gives the lie to the principle . . . Sometimes the majority has wished to oppress the minority." See "Conversation with Jared Sparks, on the Tyranny of the Majority," in *The Tocqueville Reader: A Life in Letters and Politics*, ed. Olivier Zunz and Alan S. Kahan (Oxford, 2002), 180–184. For a discussion of Tocqueville and his relations with New England Whigs, including Sparks, see George Wilson Pierson, *Tocqueville in America* (1938, reprint, Baltimore, 1996), 367–368, 390–425. Tocqueville also discussed these issues in Philadelphia with Charles Jared Ingersoll, a former Federalist of New England descent. Ibid., 474–475, 480–482.

    3. Tocqueville, *Democracy in America*, 598–599.

    4. Ibid., 589. See also Ibid., 10, 489, 585–609, 787–813. On this reading of Tocqueville, see James T. Kloppenberg, "Life Everlasting: Tocqueville in America," in *The Virtues of Liberalism* (New York, 1998), 71–81; Stefan-Ludwig Hoffmann, "Democracy and Associations in the Long Nineteenth Century: Toward a Transnational Perspective," *Journal of Modern History* 75, no. 2 (June 2003), 269–299.

    5. For one example of an American discovering that the proliferation of voluntary associations in an independent civil society could promote solidarity, see [Samuel A. Eliot], "Public and Private Charities of Boston," *North American Review* 61, no. 128 (July 1845), 135–159. For a discussion of Eliot, see Peter Dobkin Hall, "What the Merchants Did with Their Money: Charitable and Testamentary Trusts in Massachusetts, 1780–1880," in *Entrepreneurs: The Boston Business Community, 1700–1850*, ed. Conrad Edick Wright and Katheryn P. Viens (Boston, 1997), 365–342, at 408–416. See also [Samuel A. Eliot] "Charities of Boston," *North American Review* 91, no. 188 (July 1860), 149–166. The focus on solidarity guides much recent work on civil society, including Robert Putnam, *Bowling Alone: The Collapse and Revival of American Community* (New York, 2000); Robert Wuthnow, *Loose Connections: Joining Together in America's Fragmented Communities* (Cambridge, Mass., 1998); and Robert N. Bellah et al., *Habits of the Heart: Individualism and Commitment in American Life* (Berkeley, Calif., 1985). For a historical critique of this Tocquevillian assumption, see Jason Kaufman, *For the Common Good? American Civic Life and the Golden Age of Fraternity* (New York, 2003). For a discussion of Tocqueville's argument in relation to contemporary debates over civil society, see Johann N. Neem, "Squaring the Circle: The Multiple Purposes of Civil Society in Tocqueville's Democracy in America," *The Tocqueville Review/ La Revue Tocqueville* 27, no. 1 (2006), 99–121.

    6. Tocqueville, *Democracy in America*, 215–223.

    7. Peter Dobkin Hall, "A Historical Overview of Philanthropy, Voluntary Associations, and Nonprofit Organizations in the United States, 1600–2000," in *The Nonprofit Sector: A Research Handbook*, ed. Walter W. Powell and Richard Steinberg, 2nd ed. (New Haven, Conn., 2006), 32–65, at 41–42; Peter Dobkin Hall, *The Organization of American Culture, 1700–1900: Private Institutions, Elites and the Origins of American Nationality* (New York, 1982), 220–239; Kathleen D. McCarthy, *American Creed: Philanthropy and the Rise of Civil Society* (Chicago, 2003), 192–200.

    8. On Eliot, see Peter Dobkin Hall, *Inventing the Nonprofit Sector and Other Essays on Philanthropy, Voluntarism, and Nonprofit Organizations* (Baltimore, 1992), 37–38.

9. Nathan O. Hatch, ed., *The Professions in American History* (Notre Dame, Ind., 1988); Dorothy Ross, *The Origins of American Social Science* (New York, 1991); Samuel Haber, *The Quest for Authority and Honor in the American Professions, 1750–1900* (Chicago, 1991), and "The Professions," in *Encyclopedia of American Social History*, ed. Mary K. Cayton et al., 3 vols. (New York, 1993), 2:1573–1588; James A. Morone, *The Democratic Wish: Popular Participation and the Limits of American Government* (New York, 1990), 97–128; Thomas Haskell's introduction to *The Authority of Experts: Studies in History and Theory*, ed. Thomas Haskell (Bloomington, Ind., 1984), ix–xxxix.

10. Hall, "Historical Overview," 47. See also Hall, *Organization of American Culture*, esp. 261–281, and "Private Philanthropy and Public Policy: A Historical Appraisal," in *Philanthropy: Four Views*, ed. Robert Payton et al. (New Brunswick, N.J., 1988), 39–72, esp. 50–66; Barry D. Karl and Stanley N. Katz, "The American Private Philanthropic Foundation and the Public Sphere, 1890–1930," *Minerva* 19, no. 2 (Summer 1981), 236–270; David C. Hammack, "Foundations in the American Polity, 1900–1950," in *Philanthropic Foundations: New Scholarship, New Possibilities*, ed. Ellen Condliffe Lagemann (Bloomington, Ind., 1999), 43–68; Michael Schudson, *The Good Citizen: A History of American Civic Life* (New York, 1998), 144–187, 211–219; Judith Sealander, "Curing Evils at Their Source: The Arrival of Scientific Giving," in *Charity, Philanthropy, and Civility in American History*, ed. Lawrence J. Friedman and Mark D. McGarvie (Cambridge, 2003), 217–239; William E. Nelson, *The Roots of American Bureaucracy, 1830–1900* (Cambridge, Mass., 1982); Stephen Skowronek, *Building a New American State: The Expansion of National Administrative Capacities, 1877–1920* (New York, 1982). For a nuanced appraisal of the influence of foundation-based experts in making public policy in the first three decades of the twentieth century, see Judith Sealander, *Private Wealth and Public Life: Foundation Philanthropy and the Reshaping of American Social Policy from the Progressive Era to the New Deal* (Baltimore, 1997). The elite public sphere that connected experts in private institutions to independent agencies and bureaus within government was never complete; the Jeffersonian commitment to direct popular control always exerted a countervailing pressure, leading to what William E. Nelson, *Roots of American Bureaucracy*, 113–114, has called an "amalgam" combining and holding in tension divergent governing philosophies.

11. Charles Francis Adams, "Railroad Inflation," *North American Review* (1869), as quoted in Thomas K. McCraw, *The Prophets of Regulation: Charles Francis Adams, Louis D. Brandeis, James M. Landis, Alfred E. Kahn* (Cambridge, Mass., 1984), 15. McCraw's biography of Adams in *Prophets of Regulation*, 1–79, helps us connect the Whigs' world to the nineteenth-century/early twentieth-century world of professional experts.

12. Elisabeth S. Clemens, *The People's Lobby: Organizational Innovation and the Rise of Interest Group Politics in the United States, 1880–1925* (Chicago, 1997); Michael Kazin, *The Populist Persuasion: An American History* (New York, 1995), 79–106.

13. Kazin, *Populist Persuasion*, 27–46; Chester McArthur Destler, *American Radicalism, 1865–1901: Essays and Documents* (New York, 1963).

14. Thomas Goebel, *A Government by the People: Direct Democracy in America, 1890–1940* (Chapel Hill, N.C., 2006); Clemens, *The People's Lobby*.

15. Kazin, *Populist Persuasion*, 49–77; Clemens, *The People's Lobby*, 100–144.

16. *Final Report of the Commission on Industrial Relations, including the Report of Basil M. Manly* (Washington, D.C., 1916), 80–86. For a discussion of the commission, see Joseph C. Kiger, *Philanthropic Foundations in the Twentieth Century* (Westport, Conn., 2000), 22–25; Karl and Katz, "American Private Philanthropic Foundations," 783; Sealander, *Private Wealth and Public Life*, 224–234; Robert H. Bremmer, *American Philanthropy*, 2nd ed. (Chicago, 1988), 112–115, 152–154, 164–167.

17. On the 1969 tax reform act, see Hall, *Inventing the Nonprofit Sector*, 72–75; Andrew Rich, *Think Tanks, Public Policy, and the Politics of Expertise* (New York, 1004), 57–61; Bremmer, *American Philanthropy*, 181–183, 190–195; Eleanor L. Brilliant, *Private Charity and Public Inquiry: A History of the Filer and Peterson Commissions* (Bloomington, Ind., 2001); John G. Simon, "The Regulation of American Foundations: Looking Backward at the Tax Reform Act of 1969," *Voluntas* 6, no. 3 (October 1995), 243–254. The rise of conservative foundations in the past few decades has proven this effort to be a failure. See Alice O'Connor, "Bringing the Market Back In: Philanthropic Activism and Conservative Reform," in *Politics and Partnerships: Associations and Nonprofit Organizations in American Governance*, ed. Elisabeth S. Clemens and Doug Guthrie (forthcoming, University of Chicago).

18. Arthur F. Bentley, *The Process of Government* (1908, reprint, Cambridge, Mass., 1967), 222.

19. See David B. Truman, *The Governmental Process: Political Interests and Public Opinion* (1951, reprint, New York, 1971); Robert Dahl, *Pluralist Democracy in the United States: Conflict and Consent* (Chicago, 1967). For a discussion of the development of interest group theory in political science, see Frank R. Baumgartner and Beth L. Leech, *Basic Interests: The Importance of Groups in Politics and Political Science* (Princeton, N.J., 1998).

20. Mancur Olson Jr., *The Logic of Collective Action: Public Goods and the Theory of Groups* (Cambridge, Mass., 1965).

21. Theda Skocpol, *Diminished Democracy: From Membership to Management in American Civic Life* (Norman, Okla., 2003); Putnam, *Bowling Alone*, 48–64. For changing organizational strategies in response to changing state structures, in addition to the above, see Brian Balogh, "'Mirrors of Desires': Interest Groups, Elections, and the Targeted Style in Twentieth-Century America," in *The Democratic Experiment: New Directions in American Political History*, ed. Megan Jacobs et al. (Princeton, N.J., 2003), 222–249; Lizabeth Cohen, *A Consumers' Republic: The Politics of Mass Consumption in Postwar America* (New York, 2003), 345–397; Clemens, *The People's Lobby*; Joel H. Silbey, *The American Political Nation, 1838–1893* (Stanford, Calif., 1991), 215–254; Schudson, *The Good Citizen*, 274–281.

22. On the civil rights movement's grassroots elements, see Harvard Sitkoff, *The Struggle for Black Equality 1954–1980* (New York, 1981). On the grassroots aspects of popular conservatism, see Lisa McGirr, *Suburban Warriors: The Origins of the New American Right* (Princeton, N.J., 2001); J. Anthony Lukas, *Common Ground: A Turbulent Decade in the Lives of Three American Families* (New York, 1985).

# Acknowledgments

This book began under the guidance of Peter S. Onuf at the University of Virginia. No one has done more to help me think through the subject than Peter. Peter is also my model of what it means to be a good citizen of the historical profession. His generosity sets high standards. At Virginia I also benefited from the advice of the other members of my dissertation committee. Charles W. McCurdy and Allan Megill spent several years discussing, reading, and commenting on aspects of this study, and it is much better for their efforts. Krishan Kumar reminded me of the importance of thinking across academic disciplines. I would also like to thank my other Virginia teachers Paul Halliday, Michael Holt, Stephen Innes, Joseph Kett, David Mattern, Erik Midelfort, John Stagg, Heather Warren, and Olivier Zunz, as well as my fellow graduate students Charles Irons, Ted Kilsdonk, Albrecht Koschnik, Sarah Meacham, Maire Murphy, Sharon Murphy, Rob Parkinson, Leonard Sadosky, Richard Samuelson, Brian Schoen, Aaron Sheehan-Dean, Eric Vettel, Aaron Wunsch, and the participants in Peter Onuf's Early American Seminar.

My interest in democracy and citizenship originated during my undergraduate years at Brown University. Professor Ted Sizer and Don Ernst first taught me that democracy is an ongoing moral project. I dedicate this work to them for taking me under their wing and for teaching me why ideas matter. Professor Gordon S. Wood inspired me to study the development of American democracy from an historical perspective. His course on the early republic opened up a new world in which all people—from the bottom to the top—sought to make sense of what it means to live in a free society. At Brown I was also fortunate to have the opportunity to learn from Professors Tim Harris, James T. Patterson, and John L. Thomas. Professor Thomas's recent passing is a loss to the profession. He remains an inspiration for all teachers—challenging, provocative, passionate, and caring.

John L. Brooke has read and commented on almost every draft of this study, and his critical pen was invaluable. Anne M. Boylan, Elisabeth S. Clemens, Richard R. John, Albrecht Koschnik, and Gordon S. Wood each read the entire manuscript and provided useful feedback at crucial moments. T. H. Breen, Peter S. Field, Peter Dobkin Hall, David Hammack, Daniel Walker Howe, Jack Rakove, and Conrad Edick Wright commented on sections of this work. I appreciate their willingness to help a student seeking their expertise.

At my new home in the history department at Western Washington University, Chris Friday, who was chair when I was hired, has worked consistently to make Western a welcoming place for me to continue my intellectual development. I also benefited much from conversations with my new colleagues Kathleen Kennedy and Mart Stewart. I thank Western for granting me leave during my first year to take a postdoctoral fellowship.

Kathleen McDermott at Harvard University Press and Professor Patrice Higonnet, editor of the Harvard Historical Studies series, supported my work and helped see it through completion. Institutional support was provided by the University of Virginia, the Social Science Research Council's Program on Philanthropy and the Nonprofit Sector, the Aspen Institute Nonprofit Sector Research Fund, and the John Nicholas Brown Center for the Study of American Civilization at Brown University. I spent a wonderful year on a postdoctoral fellowship at the interdisciplinary Center on Religion and Democracy at the University of Virginia. Slavica Jakelić made the Center a welcoming and intellectually stimulating environment.

Parts of this argument were published in different form as "The Elusive Common Good: Religion and Civil Society in Massachusetts, 1780–1833," *Journal of the Early Republic* 24, no. 3 (Fall 2004), 381–417, and "Politics and the Origins of the Nonprofit Corporation in Massachusetts and New Hampshire, 1780–1820," *Nonprofit and Voluntary Sector Quarterly* 32, no. 3 (September 2003), 344–365.

My parents, Nuru and Ruxana Neemuchwalla, and my sister Sabina Neem sacrificed much to send me to college, and for that I can never repay them. They continue to be important sources of support. My parents-in-law Mac and Harriett Destler offered constant encouragement. My partner Kate Destler not only provided love and support but was also an important critic. It is possible that she read as many drafts of this work as Peter Onuf. I thank her for too many things to list here. Kate's and my son Rylan was born in October 2006, after most of this work was completed. I thank him for waiting to let me finish my book, and for bringing so much joy into the world.

# Index